Teresa Hayter is the author of *Aid as Imperialism* and *The Creation of World Poverty*. Her research for this book was financed by a grant from the Social Science Research Council.

Catharine Watson worked as a researcher in the Office of Environmental Affairs at the World Bank in Washington DC from May 1979 to June 1980.

Unless otherwise stated, the $ sign refers throughout to United States dollars.

Teresa Hayter
Catharine Watson

Aid

Rhetoric and Reality

Pluto Press

London and Sydney

First published in 1985 by Pluto Press Limited,
The Works, 105a Torriano Avenue, London NW5 2RX
and Pluto Press Australia Limited, PO Box 199, Leichhardt,
New South Wales 2040, Australia

Cover designed by Clive Challis A.Gr.R.
Set by Photobooks (Bristol) Limited

Printed in Great Britain by Guernsey Press, Guernsey, C.I.

British Library Cataloguing in Publication Data
Hayter, Teresa
    Aid : rhetoric and reality.
    1. Economic assistance   2. Banks and banking,
    International
    I. Title   II. Watson, Catharine
    338.91'09172'4   HC60

ISBN 0 86104 626 9

Contents

Preface

This book, or my part of it, was financed by a three-year grant from the Social Science Research Council (now the Economic and Social Research Council). The grant paid my salary and expenses, including travel to India, Algeria, Peru and Washington (twice) over the period January 1981 to January 1984. I owe the idea of applying to the SSRC entirely to Tom Woolley, who is a lecturer in sociology at the Oxford Polytechnic.

I am also very grateful for the support of the Oxford Polytechnic, which administered the grant, and especially to Dr. Renata Barber, head of the Social Studies department.

I continue to be surprised that the SSRC financed the research. One of their conditions was that I should have the backing of a 'Review Panel', in order to 'provide balance' and assist my access to the Bank. I am very grateful to the people who agreed to be on this panel. I hope I have not made too many calls on their advice; they certainly have no responsibility for what I have written.

The title of the research project was 'The World Bank and the conditionality of aid'. In my application I undertook to 're-examine the conclusions reached in *Aid as Imperialism*' in the light of 'the considerable changes that have taken place in World Bank policies in the last 10 years, in particular the much greater importance now attached to the alleviation of extreme poverty'. I have re-examined these conclusions. But what I have seen has not caused me to change them to any great extent.

The biggest concern of the SSRC seems to have been that I would not have access to the World Bank. This concern is potentially a bar to the financing of any critical research on the institutions of capitalism, which are unlikely to welcome such investigation. And in fact my access to the Bank has been limited. This has meant that, as before, the bulk of my information has come from the officials, politicians and economists whom I interviewed in the Third

World. I owe them a great debt. I wish I had used their information more adequately; but that would have meant a book even longer than this one.

I hope that those Bank officials who did talk to me, sometimes at length and quite openly, will not feel let down, or that their case for more openness is weakened by my persistence in criticising the Bank. I think some of them felt genuinely that their work was contributing to the alleviation of poverty in the Third World, that they had nothing to hide, and that talking to me might convince me to change my view of the Bank. The fact that, in spite of their efforts, I have not become a supporter of the Bank, does not mean that they were wrong in their belief that Bank officials should be more open and willing to talk to their critics. On the contrary the continued hostility of their colleagues provided further proof that the Bank had not significantly changed. As it was, I had to tell myself that my sample of Bank officials was a biased one and that the officials who saw me, with a few maverick exceptions, were the most sympathetic and progressive to be found in the Bank. They also tended to be concentrated in the research departments of the Bank and therefore to be somewhat remote from the Bank's actual operations. I had to make assumptions about the officials who refused to see me. Occasionally they had genuine excuses or were simply too busy. Sometimes they were nervous; this applied to one of the officials involved in the Bank's lending to Nicaragua in the early years after the Sandinistas' victory. Mostly they were just the inveterate reactionaries who know quite well that they have nothing to gain by talking to me.

In 1981 I had several appointments in the Information Department of the Bank to discuss my request for official interviews with senior management in the Bank. Eventually the reply came: the Bank 'had been burnt once and did not see why it should be burnt again'. I was told I was allowed to request interviews on an individual basis. I gathered that a memorandum had been circulated through the Bank instructing officials to talk to me only in general terms, and not to give me any details of operations.

By 1983 the situation seemed to have changed. I was told that Mr. Clausen, who had by then become president of the Bank, had a policy of greater openness towards the press and outsiders. His director for Information and Public Affairs, Frank Vogl, was a former journalist of the London *Times* and was said to be sympathetic towards the need to divulge information to the public. The Bank is, after all, a public institution, partly financed from public funds; there are no very valid grounds on which to justify its secretiveness (see pp. 75–76). I was directed to Tom Blinckhorn, also a former journalist, for whose goodwill I should like to express my appreciation. The Bank agreed that I could have press accreditation, through the *Guardian*, to attend its annual meetings. But in practice the attitude of Bank officials had changed little, if at all. In 1981 I was able to interview only one senior official in the Latin American and Caribbean department of the Bank; he had specified that the interview was on a personal basis and had not allowed me to take notes. In 1983 I saw none of them. One official, reputedly quite progressive, telephoned to cancel an appointment. He said he had talked to his colleagues and their position was that documents they had given me in the past (which ones?) had not been fairly used. Mason, Asher and Ayres, members of the liberal establishment who have written books on the Bank, were 'acceptable'; I was not.[1] In reply to my statement that the unwillingness of Bank officials to talk created the suspicion that they were not sincerely committed to the Bank's stated goals, the official said that although this was now the official position in the Bank, he and his colleagues were not prepared to take the risk of greater openness.

Their attitude was of course based partly on their experience with my previous book and some inevitable embroidery of that experience. They seemed to think that I had had a thesis in 1967 to which I had bent the facts, and that I had betrayed confidences. Neither of these beliefs was strictly correct. My ideas in the 1960s about aid had been changed by observation of the facts, and I received hardly any confidences in 1967 from Bank officials and no access to unpublished documents. The Bank attempted first to stop the research and then to stop its publication. It did succeed in stopping my then employers, the Overseas Development Institution, from publishing the draft, even as amended in response to the Bank's criticisms. But it was unable to stop its publication by Penguin Books as *Aid as Imperialism*. This did admittedly have an Appendix which published the communications of Bank officials attempting to stop the book's publication. But these were hardly 'confidences'.

I have written this book in collaboration with Cathy Watson

who has, unlike me, worked inside the Bank and had access to its documents. Cathy has written most of the chapter on agriculture, including all of the sections on livestock projects and Colombia, and nearly all of the material on Nicaragua. She has provided not only some hard information on agricultural projects, but also much enthusiasm and support for the book as a whole – especially at times when mine faltered.

Richard Kuper has done an enormous amount of very valuable editing work, for which we are very grateful. William Pike kindly wrote a paper for us on Tanzania, from which most of the material on Tanzania in chapter 9 is extracted. I also owe a great debt to Gavin Williams, Betsy Hartman and Jim Boyce, in Oxford, who have supported and advised me and commented on the draft, especially, in Gavin's case, on the general section on agriculture (for the inadequacies of which he is not responsible). I am also very grateful to Stephany Griffith-Jones for comments on the chapter on the IMF, and for being on the SSRC's panel, and to Sue Cunninghame for comments on the private banks chapter. And to Helen Miller for typing most of the first draft. And to my children for putting up with the last few months' slightly frantic work.

Teresa Hayter, June 1984

Preface

When I left the World Bank in June 1980, having worked there as a researcher in the Office of Environmental Affairs from May 1979, I knew that I must make public three things: the poor supervision of Bank projects, the impact of Bank projects on land distribution, and the ecological damage caused by Bank projects, particularly in the tropical forest areas. I am grateful to Teresa Hayter for agreeing to write this book together and for working my material into hers.

My one reservation about my role in this book is that it might have repercussions for the Bank officials with whom I worked. I stress, therefore, that none of my colleagues and friends at the World Bank were aware that I was writing about the Bank; the first time that they will know of this book's existence will be when they see it in print.

I would like to thank two people for helping to make my contribution to this book possible: Michael Simmons of the *Guardian*, who, by accepting the first article I ever had published, encouraged me to write more, and William Pike, who was my companion throughout the writing.

I hope that my contribution to this book will, by giving hard facts, add fuel to criticisms of aid. I also hope that it will help to convince people that destruction of the environment is a political issue.

Catharine Watson, May 1984

List of Abbreviations

AID	Agency for International Development (the US government aid agency)
Afr DB, Asian DB	African Development Bank, Asian Development Bank (regional multilateral banks modelled on the World Bank)
Caribbean DB	Caribbean Development Bank (a regional multilateral bank modelled on the World Bank)
CPP	Country Program Paper (confidential documents of the World Bank discussing lending policies for particular countries)
DAC	Development Assistance Committee (organisation attached to the OECD which produces statistics on aid)
EDF	European Development Fund (multilateral aid fund financed by EEC members)
EEC	European Economic Community
EFF	Extended Fund Facility (a three-year drawing arrangement from the IMF)
EIB	European Investment Bank (development bank financed by the EEC)
FAO	Food and Agricultural Organisation (specialised agency of the United Nations)
IBRD	International Bank for Reconstruction and Development (the formal name for the World Bank; usually refers to the institution making loans at near commercial rates of interest)
IDA	International Development Association (the World Bank's soft-loan affiliate)
IDB (or IADB)	Inter-American Development Bank (a

	regional multilateral bank modelled on the World Bank)
IFAD	International Fund for Agriculture and Development (a United Nations organisation)
IFC	International Financial Corporation (a World Bank affiliate lending to the private sector)
IMF	International Monetary Fund
LIBOR	London Interbank Offered Rate (the rate at which banks borrow)
MDB	Multilateral Development Bank (usually refers to the World Bank and regional development banks)
NICs	Newly Industrialising Countries (usually refers to Argentina, Brazil, Greece, Hong Kong, South Korea, Mexico, Portugal, Singapore, Spain, Taiwan and Yugoslavia)
OECD	Organisation for Economic Co-operation and Development (set up to co-ordinate the economic policies of European countries and to do research; now also includes the US, Australia, New Zealand and Japan)
OED	Operations Evaluation Department (part of the World Bank)
OPEC	Organisation of Petroleum Exporting Countries (the oil producers' cartel)
PPAR	Project Performance Audit Results (the products of the OED)
SDR	Special Drawing Rights (the international currency issued by the IMF)
SUNFED	Special United Nations Fund for Economic Development (the UN financial agency proposed by Third World countries but not supported by the developed countries)
UN	United Nations
UNCTAD	United Nations Conference on Trade and Development (the organisation through which Third World countries have put forward demands for better treatment by the

	developed countries, especially in trade matters)
UNDP	United Nations Development Programme (a UN body which finances mainly pre-investment studies)
UNIDO	United Nations Industrial Development Organisation (specialised agency of the United Nations)
WHO	World Health Organisation (specialised agency of the United Nations)

Introduction

Over the last four centuries a situation of massive world inequality has become established. A few countries, mainly in Europe and North America, appropriate a proportion of the world's wealth which is totally unrelated to the size of their population. They have achieved this situation not just by using their own resources, productive skills and efforts, but by appropriating those of the rest of the world on a massive and unprecedented scale, and by methods which have had little to do with fair exchange and more to do with plunder, loot and military might.

Once the situation has been established, the appropriation of wealth can be continued by less obviously violent and unjust means. The free play of market forces, the so-called principle of comparative advantage, and so on, ensures that wealth continues to flow from the poor to the rich, and that the hardship associated with capitalist recession is borne disproportionately by the poor. When these fail to work, the rich can and do use their financial and military power to preserve their economic advantages, by methods which range from the 'voluntary' restraint on textile exports from the Third World under the Multi-Fibre Arrangement, to outright military intervention, as in Vietnam and now Central America.

Meanwhile, the governments of the rich countries of the West and their ruling class claim, with considerable hypocrisy, that they are providing 'aid' to help the Third World to escape from the underdevelopment and poverty which they and their predecessors created and continue to create. But much of this aid fails to alleviate poverty even in the immediate context in which it is provided; and its overall purpose is the preservation of a system which damages the interests of the poor in the Third World. To the extent that it is effective in this underlying purpose, aid from the major Western powers therefore probably does more harm than good to the mass of the population of the Third World.

Socialists believe in the need to end inequality and exploitation. The existence of aid, like charity, presupposes the continued existence of these evils. But it obviously makes no sense to oppose any conceivable transfers of resources from rich to poor during the necessarily long period of transition to socialism on a world scale. Attempts to end exploitation under capitalism can be accompanied by more direct forms of financial solidarity in the form of transfers of money to governments or groups in the Third World. This will be discussed in the concluding chapter.

The book as a whole, however, is concerned with aid as it is now, not as it conceivably might become. It would be preferable to abandon the use of the word 'aid' altogether because it is such an obvious misnomer. It might instead be called export subsidy, public subsidy for private profit, debt insurance, funds for counter-insurgency, or whatever. But there is no adequate short substitute for the word. So we propose, again, to use it, without the inverted commas with which it ought always to be surrounded, and in the expectation that it will one day lose its original meaning and become established, as it ought to be, as a dirty word, remote from its original charitable connotations.

The first part of the book attempts to describe, in general, the various forms of capital flows to the Third World which come under the heading of 'aid' and also the activities of two types of institution which generally do not: the private commercial banks and the IMF. The private commercial banks have become central to all discussions about the international financial system; no book that attempts to deal with the financial relationships between the developed and developing countries can ignore them. The IMF, particularly now, affects the economic situation of Third World countries in ways which few of them can escape. Both the private banks and the IMF claim to be 'helping' the Third World. With friends like these . . .

Part II deals with an institution whose rhetoric departs more than usually from its reality, and still apparently deceives some: the World Bank. The IMF and the World Bank have been described as the 'joint police' of the international financial order. The Bank, no doubt because its rhetoric deludes and development is not a fashionable subject, has also been described as the 'forgotten sister' of the IMF, to be used to soften the impact of the IMF, thus peddling more illusions.[1] For the Brandt commissioners, the Bank is 'the leading development institution', which has recently 'given assistance over a broader front and expanded and liberalised its operations'. 'It has placed great emphasis on anti-poverty programmes', says the Brandt report. 'Its policy statements and the analyses of its staff have had great influence, particularly among donors of aid. Its successive Presidents have given valuable leadership to the world development effort, often ahead of opinion in the major shareholding countries.'[2]

The concluding chapter is mainly about alternatives.

Part I

Capital flows to the Third World

1. Definitions

In its current usage, the word aid generally refers to transfers of resources from governments or public institutions of the richer countries to governments in the Third World. It is, generally speaking, a post-Second World War phenomenon. Imperialist governments did not describe any expenditures they made on colonial administration and conquest, on railway systems to transport minerals and raw materials to the ports for transhipment to Europe, as aid. After the Second World War, such expenditures came to be known as foreign assistance or 'aid'. When the colonies became independent, they began to receive loans and grants from other governments as well as their former colonial rulers, usually to finance projects in the economic and social infrastructure and in agriculture. The colonial powers gave or lent money to assist in the mechanics of de-colonisation. For example, the British government made loans to the Kenyan government with which to compensate the white settlers who abandoned the land they had stolen, and to the Tanzanian government to pay the pensions of colonial civil servants who decided not to stay on; this too was called 'aid'. Aid was used to assist commercial exporters to penetrate new markets or retain old ones, to help to assure adequate supplies of raw materials, and to counter subversion.

Since the 1960s such expenditures have been recorded in statistics by the Development Assistance Committee (DAC) of the OECD (Organisation for Economic Co-operation and Development, formerly the OEEC; DAC membership includes the United States, Canada, Australia, New Zealand, Japan and 12 West European countries). The DAC also records, but in less detail, statistics on aid provided by the Soviet Union and East European countries, a few other non-OECD countries such as India, and, since the oil-price rises of the 1970s, the OPEC countries. It has no figures on aid from China or Cuba.

In the early days of the aid phenomenon, the term often included private transactions with the Third World. The campaigners for the famous, but now abandoned, 1 per cent target were actually campaigning for the rich countries to spend 1 per cent of their GNP on both official *and* private grants, loans and investments in the Third World. The private component included direct investment by private companies based in the 'donor' country, portfolio investments, export credits, and bank lending. The British regularly exceeded this 'aid' target by a large amount simply because their economy was historically dependent on private investment and banking in the Third World, mainly their former Empire; they were never very high in the DAC league table as far as government aid was concerned and by the 1980s were about halfway down it.

The DAC now includes in what it calls Official Development Assistance only grants and loans with high 'concessionality', or reduction in interest rates below current commercial levels and lengthening of repayment periods beyond current commercial norms: it describes these as loans with a 'grant element' of at least 25 per cent, which means the face value of the loan 'less the discounted cost to the recipient of the flow of future service payments', at a discount rate of 10 per cent. The DAC records other lending and investment, including lending on near-commercial terms from official international agencies such as the World Bank, in what it calls 'non-concessional flows'. The omission of World Bank loans, apart from loans from the IDA (International Development Association), from statistics on Official Development Assistance is an anomaly, since the World Bank is explicitly recognised by the DAC to be the leading aid organisation, whose verdicts on policy and desirable geographical allocation have a major influence on Western governments and aid agencies.

In reality of course the distinction between what is called aid and what are merely commercial and banking transactions remains rather unclear. Export credits often include a 'soft' or aid component as an added inducement to the borrowing country to obtain its supplies from that particular source. For example the *Financial Times*, reporting that expenditure cuts in Indonesia might lead to a loss of contracts for the British companies Balfour Beatty and Goving, commented:

There seems little likelihood that the British and Swedish governments will be able to grant soft loans big enough to allow the project to go ahead as scheduled. Most of the British finance for the project was arranged by Barclays International with backing from the Export Credits Guarantee Department and the Overseas Development Authority [the government department in charge of 'aid'].[1]

Another *Financial Times* article, describing what sounds like a modern version of the Scramble for Africa, reports Lord Carrington's woe at the inroads being made into Britain's traditional markets in Kenya by the French, armed with 'a mixture of aid and trade credit' tied to the purchase of French goods, with the 'soft terms' at around 4 per cent interest rates over 25–35 years. ' "We have the ashes of Joan of Arc between us" ', said a French diplomat with a smile; and a Kenyan official noted that: ' "Soft credit facilities are very tempting . . . even though there could be long-term costs – such as compatibility of existing and new equipment . . ." ' Britain, the *Financial Times* notes, 'of course offers incentives of its own . . . the three contracts under consideration . . . would qualify for as much as £5 million from the Aid for Trade Provision [ATP], a government fund which helps UK exporters compete with subsidised competition'.[2] The ATP was set up by the Tory government under their policy of giving even greater weight to 'political, industrial and commercial considerations' in the British 'aid' programme and by 1982 absorbed nearly a tenth of it. As the *Financial Times* commented:

It has helped British companies build a steel mill in Mexico and a power station in India, but it is an abuse of the principle of aiding the poor. Instead it is usually helping the more successful British companies with projects in the richer countries in the developing world.[3]

Perhaps one day the DAC will carry the process of tightening up its definitions to its logical conclusion and drop the notion of assistance altogether from the statistics it compiles. Meanwhile the DAC gives a break-down of what it calls 'total net resource receipts of developing countries' between 'Official Development Assistance' and 'Non-concessional flows'; the latter include official and private components. (See Table 1). In addition,

Table 1   DAC Statistics on capital flows in 1981

	$ Billion	%
Official Development Assistance	35.51	34.1
Non-concessional flows	68.49	65.9
of which:		
official multilateral agencies	5.00	4.8
official loans	9.00	7.7
private bank loans	25.00	24.0
bond lending	2.50	2.4
export credits	13.35	12.9
private direct investment	14.64	14.1
Total	**104.00**	**100.00**

Source: OECD, Development Co-operation, Efforts and Policies of
   the Members of the Development Assistance Committee, 1982
   Review, November 1982, Table V-2, p. 51 *and* Table V-4, p. 53.

the DAC records that in 1981 developing countries received $2.02
billion in grants from voluntary agencies and $6.18 billion from
the IMF (International Monetary Fund).

Historically, the major form of investment in the colonial and
semi-colonial countries was bond lending: investors in the
metropolitan countries bought shares in railways, mines and port
authorities in Latin America, India or Africa. During the 1930s
there were widespread defaults on this type of lending; 70 per cent
of all Latin American bonds defaulted. It is now a small component
of total flows, amounting to $2.5 billion from DAC members in
1981, and it is limited to very few countries considered 'creditworthy', including Algeria, Brazil, Israel, Mexico, Spain and
Venezuela.

In addition, companies in the metropolitan countries invest
directly in the Third World. This is what is called 'private direct
investment' in the DAC's terminology; it amounted to $14.64
billion in 1981. The DAC claims for it the following virtues: it
'provides a unique combination of long-term finance, technology,
training, know-how, managerial expertise and market experience'.[4]

Direct foreign private lending is necessarily tied to projects which the investors control, at least partly; there can be no defaults, only loss of profits; thus many people in the advanced capitalist countries look to it with longing as a substitute for the reckless excesses of unconditional bank lending (see below). Companies based in the metropolitan countries have traditionally invested in the Third World to secure their sources of raw materials; more recently to get around import restrictions on finished products such as motor cars; and more recently still in order to take advantage of very low wages in the Third World, for example by having the more labour-intensive parts of their manufacturing processes carried out there.

They may set up wholly-owned subsidiaries in the Third World, or joint ventures with local private entrepreneurs and sometimes the state; some governments only allow minority participation by foreign investors. What is classified as foreign investment does not however always involve the bringing in of new capital from abroad or investment in new productive or other facilities. It might better be described as foreign *control* of investment. At times nearly half of the recorded foreign investment has merely been the buying up of local concerns already producing for a given market. Some 80 per cent of the capital used in 'foreign private investment' is likely to have been raised locally, supplied often by the local subsidiaries of New York or London-based banks which take deposits from local elites. The figures given by the DAC include reinvested earnings, the proportion of the profits made by a factory, mine or other business which is not remitted abroad. They are described as 'net' investment but they are net only in the sense that they are net of disinvestment or repatriation of capital: repatriated profits, which appear in the current account rather than the capital account of balance of payments statistics, are not deducted. These profits are moreover notoriously high, and understated in official statistics.[5]

Export credits from DAC members, which are a method of financing direct exports to the Third World, amounted, according to the DAC's figures, to $13.35 billion in 1981. They are used to finance about 10 per cent of DAC members' exports of all goods to developing countries and about 20 per cent of their exports of capital goods.[6] They include loans from official export credit agencies such as the US Export-Import Bank and the British ECGD

(Export Credit Guarantees Department), supplier credits from private exporters or 'buyer credits' from the exporter's bank. They are the least expensive type of external borrowing, after aid, available to developing countries; interest rates are well below those charged by the banks and often below those of the World Bank. They might be lower still if there were no restrictive agreements among OECD members intended to limit the competition involved in the scramble for markets among developed countries' exporters. Which is why the developed countries often offer, as a means of getting round the agreed minimum interest rates on export credits, a combination of export credits and 'aid', on which soft terms are considered a virtue.

Lending by private commercial banks to the Third World fell off after the defaults of the 1930s, since banks as well as individuals had put their money into the defaulted bonds; many of them collapsed with the combined effects of depression and defaults. Bank lending to the Third World resumed in the 1960s, usually to governments or with government guarantees. But it only took off in the 1970s. And in the early 1980s the question of the Third World's debt to the banks became central to discussions on international financial questions; it is discussed at greater length below (pp. 22–36).

After the Second World War, official flows of capital to the underdeveloped countries seemed set to replace private flows. Indeed the creation of the International Monetary Fund and the World Bank at Bretton Woods in 1944 was seen by the then US Secretary of the Treasury, Henry Morgenthau, as the achievement of his lifelong ambition to 'drive the usurious moneylenders from the temple of international finance', a sentiment which has considerable relevance today, considering the extortionate rates of interest currently charged by the banks.[7] 'Aid', which in 1970 amounted to almost half of capital flows, was down to about a third of total flows by 1981.

Official aid to the Third World from DAC members rose relatively slowly during the 1970s. In nominal terms, i.e., before allowing for inflation, it increased from $7 billion in 1970 to $35.6 billion; but the increase in real terms was, according to DAC statistics, only from $14.7 billion in 1970 to $21.2 billion in 1981, in terms of 1978 dollars. Recently, aid has been static or declining. For example, British aid was $2.7 billion in 1979, the last year of the Labour government, $1.8 billion in 1980 and $2.2 billion in 1981. This decline is explained mainly by general budgetary constraints, but also by the declining interest and belief in the value of official intervention in development in the Third World, especially among Reaganites and Thatcherites. US aid is now equalled by aid from Saudi Arabia, and is of course much lower as a percentage of national income (see Table 2).

Table 2 Sources of Official Development Assistance in 1981

	$ billion	as % of GNP
DAC countries	25.6	0.35
of which:		
United States	5.8	0.20
France	4.2	0.73
West Germany	3.2	0.47
Britain	2.2	0.44
Netherlands	1.5	1.08
Sweden	0.9	0.83
OPEC countries	7.8	1.46
of which:		
Saudi Arabia	5.8	4.77
USSR and Eastern Europe	2.1	0.14
Total	**35.9**	**0.37**

Source: OECD, *op. cit.,* Table 1.7, p. 183.

Nearly a quarter of Official Development Assistance, or $8 billion (and around a third in the two years before 1981) and another $5 billion of 'non-concessional flows' came from institutions with an international membership, or the so-called multilateral agencies. In 1980–81, for example, 34.4 per cent of British aid was channelled through multilateral agencies, principally the World Bank and the European Development Fund. By far the most important of these multilateral 'aid' institutions, both in the size of its lending and, perhaps more important, in the extent of its influence over the lending decisions of other governments and institutions, is the World Bank. The World Bank and the IMF together often dominate the external financial relationships of Third World governments. In addition there are a number of regional banks, including the Inter-American Development Bank, the African Development Bank, and the Asian Development Bank, which are more or less closely modelled on the World Bank; and the Common Market and the OPEC countries have set up a range of multilateral institutions to channel funds to the Third World, no fewer than six in the case of the OPEC countries, whose operations are ultimately controlled by the countries providing the money.

Money is also channelled through the specialised agencies of the United Nations, nearly all of it in the form of 'technical assistance', or money to pay for studies, 'experts' and training. The UN agencies operate on the principle of one country, one vote; their membership includes the Soviet Union, East European countries and Cuba; and their staff is recruited on a strict national quota basis. But their resources are relatively small, and in practice many of them work in close collaboration with the World Bank. They include, for example, the FAO (Food and Agricultural Organisation), the WHO (World Health Organisation), UNDP (United Nations Development Programme). (See Table 3.)

In spite of the increasingly dominant role of the World Bank in particular in the aid-giving process, what is known as 'bilateral' aid, or aid directly from one government to another, now represents, in simple volume terms, a little over three-quarters of the total. A little over half of this bilateral aid (55 per cent in 1981), and about a third of US aid, is provided for particular projects, which are determined in negotiations between the governments providing and receiving the money. The aid usually finances part of the total cost of the project, often only the direct foreign exchange expenditures required in its initial phases. Thus it may finance the machinery, materials and skills which it is considered need to be imported from abroad for the construction of, for example, a dam, a railway, a power station, harbour, hospital or school; but it will not finance the foreign exchange expenditures required to keep it running, including expenditures on spare parts for imported machinery.

The other 45 per cent of bilateral aid was divided into: sector aid

Table 3 Net disbursements of loans and grants by multilateral agencies, 1980

| | $ million | |
	Concessional	Non-concessional
IBRD	107	3,166
IDA	1,543	–
IFC	–	295
IDB	326	567
African DB and Fund	96	97
Asian DB	149	328
Caribbean DB	43	13
EEC/EIB	1,013	257
IMF Trust Fund	1,636	–
IFAD	45	–
United Nations Specialised Agencies	2,487	–
Arab OPEC Funds	294	128
Total	**7,759**	**4,849**

Source: OECD, *op. cit.*, Table II.C.2, p. 233. See also glossary of initials.

(12 per cent); food aid (10 per cent); disaster relief (2 per cent); debt relief (3 per cent); general non-project assistance (15 per cent); and other (3 per cent).[8]

'Sector aid' is defined as money for local development banks, or for a number of small projects in a particular sector or area, for example. 'Food aid' consists mostly of agricultural commodities supplied by the United States from its surplus production under programmes such as Food for Peace. Usually the government which receives the aid must pay for the food supplied in its own currency; the US government then uses the money for its diplomatic and other expenses in the country concerned or lends it back to the government for agreed projects. 'General non-project assistance' includes loans and grants to pay for the import of specified goods and services, and general finance for balance of payments and budget support, which is sometimes referred to as 'programme aid'. The dividing line between 'project' and 'non-project' assistance is blurred. Donors tend to prefer identifiable projects, visible signs of their supposed generosity; bags of food labelled 'A Gift from the United States', serving to obscure the massive flow of involuntary gifts in the other direction. The governments at the receiving end of these gifts would naturally prefer to receive money to be used as they thought fit. The snag, from their point of view, is that donors tend to view programme, or non-project, aid as a vehicle for imposing conditions of a more general nature at central government levels, such as cuts in government expenditure or devaluation.

A little over half of all DAC members' aid is 'tied', which means it must be spent on importing goods and services from the country providing it. In 1981 78.3 per cent of grants and 72.4 per cent of loans from Britain were tied, and a further 1.4 per cent and 2.8 per cent 'partially tied'. For the United States the corresponding percentages were 54.7 per cent, 72.4 per cent, 17 per cent and 13.2 per cent. France was near to the DAC average on tying and Sweden and Norway were much better than the average.[9] The worst effect of tying aid is that the money is not available to finance goods produced locally and local skills; the aid therefore provides, partly intentionally, an inducement to governments to commit their resources to projects which have a high import content and moreover to increase the proportion of the necessary materials and skills that are imported from abroad. When the aid is in the form of a loan, this must eventually be repaid in foreign currency. Even when it is provided as a grant, its effect may still be that continuing dependence is created on supplies of skills, materials, and spare parts from abroad; this, again, is partly the intention. In addition, tying the aid to procurement from particular countries, and sometimes to particular sources within that country, limits or eliminates choice between different technologies and can enable firms to dispose of outdated or otherwise uncompetitive goods. It also tends to result in goods and services being provided at prices well above world market prices; calculations have shown that on average the prices of goods financed by aid exceed world market prices by 25 to 30 per cent. Such price disadvantages may cancel out the advantages of concessional terms, when the 'aid' is in the form of a loan or a grant associated with export credits, so that it would have been cheaper for the borrowing government to buy on the open market and borrow entirely at commercial rates of interest.

Of the amounts now classified as Official Development Assistance by the DAC, around three-quarters are grants. For Britain the percentage of aid committed as grants in 1981 was 93.9 per cent; for Norway, New Zealand and Australia it was 100 per cent; for the US it was 82.2 per cent; for West Germany it was 61.6 per cent; and for Japan it was 43.6 per cent. Average interest rates on the remaining 25 per cent of total aid were 2.6 per cent; maturities were 29.1 years; and grace periods were 10.1 years.[10] This represents a considerable 'softening' of terms compared to previous years, as a result, partly, of DAC pressures on its member governments.

There is no doubt that some governments in the Third World have become heavily dependent on aid, 'hooked', as Rehman Sobhan puts it, 'on the narcotic of aid'.[11] Without it, they would possibly not survive, and certainly there would have to be drastic changes in their countries' economies. The DAC gives some figures on the extent of dependence in the group of 'low income countries', or the 30 countries with annual incomes per head of less than $600, mainly in Sub-Saharan Africa and the Indian subcontinent. In 1979 aid represented an average of 4 per cent of their GNP, 30 per cent of their imports, and 23 per cent of their investment. The average of course conceals wide variations: 15 per cent, 63 per cent and 136 per cent for Bangladesh; 5 per cent, 34 per cent and 66 per cent for Ethiopia; 2 per cent, 18 per cent and 24 per cent for Ghana; 1 per cent, 18 per cent and 7 per cent for India, a country with a relatively low dependence on imports and aid.[12] Although there is supposed to have been a shift in the distribution of aid towards lower income countries, some better-off countries are also heavily dependent on aid. Aid to Israel, for example, which is almost entirely from the USA and West Germany, was equal to 43.9 per cent of its GNP in 1980. (The figure does not include military aid, of course.) Aid to Egypt was 5.5 per cent of its GNP; to Morocco, 3.7 per cent; to El Salvador, 2.9 per cent; to the Dominican Republic, 1.9 per cent; to Turkey, 1.7 per cent; these percentages, but not the figures for low income countries, would increase considerably if loans at higher rates of interest from multilateral agencies such as the World Bank were included.[13]

The United Nations, in its Statistical Yearbooks, publishes figures on what it calls 'disbursements to individual developing countries of bilateral official development assistance from developed market economies and from multilateral institutions'.[14] The figures again exclude 'non-concessional', especially World Bank, loans; the richer countries would appear to get more if they did not. It shows the average amount of aid per head of 1977 population for the years 1976–8 (see Table 4).

As those who deny the importance of political considerations in the determination of aid like to point out, the most obvious determinant of relative eligibility for aid is size. Small countries get a lot more per head than large countries. India, often thought of as the archetypal aid-dependent country, gets $1.8 per head; even Bangladesh gets only $8.24 per head; St. Pierre-et-Miquelon gets $3,614; the Falklands/Malvinas currently get close on a million. It also helps to be a small dependency of France.

But of course the hostility of Western donors, especially major Western donors, to left-wing policies in the Third World has a powerful effect on the geographical allocation of aid. Commonly aid is stopped or virtually stopped when governments adopt left-wing policies, nationalise foreign assets or otherwise displease the West; it is resumed if these governments are overthrown in coups and replaced, as they often are, by viciously right-wing military regimes. Chile, Indonesia and Brazil are perhaps the clearest examples of this phenomenon; other countries, such as Algeria, Peru, Jamaica and many others, have experienced interruptions and resumptions of aid according to the political nature of their governments.

It is difficult to give an overall quantified picture of the phenomenon, partly because governments vary over time in the countries providing aid as well as in those receiving it. But, for example, aid from DAC members to Vietnam went down from $702 million in 1974 to $151.9 million in 1980, which reflects mainly the decline in Western aid after the liberation of Saigon; the decline would have been much greater if Vietnam had not received $91.9 million in 1980 from Social-Democratic Sweden; $2.6 million of the 1980 total was from Britain, which had however spent $15.9 million on aid to Vietnam in 1979, the last year of the Labour government. Aid to Kampuchea from DAC members went from $305.5 million in 1974 to $0.2 million in 1978, but up again to $48.6

Table 4 Aid per head based on 1977 population

	$		$
Algeria	7.59	Jamaica	28.57
Angola	6.30	Martinique	658.44
Botswana	75.35	Nicaragua	16.99
Central African		Panama	19.93
Republic	90.65	Peru	6.33
Djibouti	300.55	St. Pierre and	
Egypt	36.69	Micquelon	3,614.00
Ethiopia	4.42	West Indies	
Ghana	7.86	(plus Malvinas)	69.44
Guinea-Bissau	63.46	Afghanistan	4.17
Mozambique	8.46	Bangladesh	8.24
Réunion	682.86	Kampuchea	0.05
St. Helena	934.00	India	1.80
Somalia	23.54	Indonesia	4.12
Tunisia	36.08	Israel	216.12
Tanzania	21.20	Jordan	49.34
Zimbabwe	1.10	S. Korea	5.42
Barbados	32.40	Laos	11.45
Belize	87.60	Lebanon	15.63
Bolivia	17.10	Malaysia	5.12
Colombia	2.65	Pakistan	6.85
Costa Rica	16.16	Philippines	4.56
Cuba	4.17	Saudi Arabia	1.80
El Salvador	10.23	Singapore	4.59
French Guiana	1,265.00	Sri Lanka	15.60
Guadeloupe	521.70	Syria	9.41
Guatemala	1.30	Vietnam	5.17
Guyana	21.32		
		Average	7.44

Source: United Nations, *Statistical Yearbook 1979/80*, pp. 401–3

million in 1980. Several post-revolutionary governments which got virtually nothing from, for example, the United States, Britain, West Germany or the World Bank, nevertheless got some aid from two countries in particular: Sweden and the Netherlands, which both had relatively progressive aid policies for most of the 1970s. Angola, for example, out of total aid receipts from DAC members in 1980 of $35.8 million, received $8 million from the Netherlands and $17 million from Sweden; it got nothing from Britain in 1980 and only $0.1 million in 1979, from the Labour government. Mozambique got a little more: a DAC total of $114.8 million, with $35.8 million from Sweden, $18.3 million from the Netherlands, $11.4 million from Denmark, $10.8 million from Britain, $10.5 million from Norway, and $9.0 million from the US. Neither country was a member of the World Bank. Their total bilateral and multilateral receipts, of $52.6 million for Angola and $159.2 million for Mozambique, compare with the $396.2 million total aid, plus $29.7 million from the World Bank, for Kenya, a country with a somewhat larger population but also a higher income per head. Cuba received a total of $11.1 million from DAC countries, of which $3.8 million was from the Netherlands and another $3.8 million from Sweden; it got $0.1 million from West Germany and nothing from Britain and the United States or, of course, the World Bank, of which it is no longer a member.[15] (See also pp. 222–6 on Nicaragua and pp. 214–22 on Grenada.) Donors' preferences can also be seen in the figures on the percentage distribution of individual donors' aid. They show, not surprisingly, that donors' bilateral aid is concentrated in countries with which they have political alliances and past colonial connections (see Table 5).

Table 5 Distribution of aid, 1979–80 annual averages

USA	%	Britain	%
Multilateral	32.4	Multilateral	40.7
Israel	18.6	India	10.9
Egypt	14.0	Bangladesh	4.7
Turkey	3.4	Tanzania	3.3
Bangladesh	3.2	Zambia	2.9
Indonesia	2.9	Sri Lanka	2.8
Pacific Islands	2.1	Pakistan	2.6
India	1.7	Kenya	2.4
Portugal	1.3	Sudan	2.1
Nicaragua	1.0	Egypt	1.8
Philippines	1.0	Malawi	1.6
Peru	0.9	Zimbabwe	1.6
		Ghana	1.6
	82.8	Nepal	1.1
		Solomon Islands (Br)	1.1
		Indonesia	1.0
		Botswana	1.0
			83.2

IDA	%		%
India	36.6	Sudan	2.2
Bangladesh	11.3	Burma	2.2
Pakistan	5.1	Zaire	1.6
Egypt	3.4	Nepal	1.6
Kenya	3.3	Mali	1.4
Ethiopia	2.6	Cameroon	1.4
Tanzania	2.6	Madagascar	1.3
Indonesia	2.5	Yemen	1.3
			80.1

Total DAC	%		%
Multilateral	34.2	Papua New Guinea	1.2
Egypt	4.8	Sri Lanka	1.2
Israel	4.5	Burma	1.1
Bangladesh	3.6	Zambia	1.0
Indonesia	3.2	Sudan	0.9
India	3.1	Vietnam	0.8
Turkey	2.6	Philippines	0.8
Tanzania	2.2	Morocco	0.8
Réunion	1.9	Cameroon	0.8
Martinique	1.9	Peru	0.8
Pakistan	1.7	New Caledonia	0.8
Zaire	1.3	Senegal	0.7
Thailand	1.3	Guadeloupe	0.7
Kenya	1.2	Tunisia	0.7
		Polynesia (Fr)	0.7
		Ivory Coast	0.6
		Upper Volta	0.6
			81.4

Source: OECD., *Development Co-operation, 1982 Review, op. cit.*, Table 1.12, pp. 188–9.

2. Private banks

Increasingly during the 1970s, Third World governments had another source of finance to turn to: the private commercial banks. Although their lending was highly concentrated among relatively few better-off countries, it appeared to be unaffected by political considerations, or any other considerations except that of getting rid of the money. Most of the bank loans to developing countries have been made through the so-called Euro-markets, originally fed with dollars from US balance of payments deficits, and which are not subject to US or other national banking regulations on the degree of exposure permitted to individual banks. After the oil price rises of the early 1970s there was a massive influx of so-called 'petrodollars' into these markets, which came from the surpluses of OPEC countries which were unwilling or unable to invest them in their own economies. These surpluses could not be profitably invested in the advanced capitalist countries either, engulfed as they were in their recession. So the banks found what their publications described as a 'sink-hole' for their money in the Third World and Eastern Europe, in the shape of governments eager and willing to invest it or at least take it, in Mexico, Brazil, Argentina, Poland, Romania, the Philippines, South Korea. At the Annual Meetings of the World Bank and the IMF, Finance Ministers were pursued by bankers offering them money with no strings attached. 'Just sign on this napkin', they were reputed to have said amid the extravagant abundance of their parties. The process came to be known as the 'recycling' of OPEC surpluses or petrodollars.

In 1970, the banks lent $7.73 billion to developing countries. By 1981, they were lending $25 billion. In 1980, net private bank lending to all developing countries was $22 billion. Of that, nine so-called NICS (Newly Industrialising Countries) got $16 billion, of which $9 billion went to Brazil and Mexico alone. A further $5 billion went to 'middle income countries'. The 'low income countries' got $0.6 billion. The corresponding figures for total debt at the end of 1981 were $180 billion, $114 billion, $73 billion, $37 billion, and $5 billion, plus $24 billion for some OPEC countries which not only used all their receipts from oil, but borrowed additional amounts from the banks.[1]

During much of the 1970s, real interest rates on this debt were very low or even negative (below the rate of inflation), and debt levels were not considered to be a problem. But at the end of the 1970s interest rates rose dramatically. Average interest rates were 7 per cent in 1975 and 18 per cent in 1981, and maturities shortened. The effect was similar to the much protested about oil price shocks. Because of rising interest rates at the end of 1979, Third World debt service charges rose by $7.5 billion.[2] Because the increases were the result of the actions of the economic authorities in the advanced capitalist countries, and, after 1980, Reaganomics in particular, they have been described as the 'Reagan interest shock'. A further effect of recession, deflationary policies and protectionism in these countries is that both the volume and the prices of the main exports of developing countries have been declining, for reasons outside the latter's control. Furthermore, when in the summer of 1982 Mexico declared that it could not meet payments on its debts, the banks responded with a sudden and drastic slow-down in new lending throughout the indebted countries. Even more disruptively, they withdrew short-term trade financing facilities, which are normally rolled over in much the same way as a company's overdraft facilities. And they have bumped up interest rate spreads and rescheduling fees to unprecedented heights.

There is, therefore, a debt crisis. Although the burden of high interest payments affects very large numbers of countries, it is only the very largest borrowers that are considered a threat to the banking system. Most of these, apart from the Philippines and Poland, are in Latin America. In 1982, the debt service of all developing countries, including interest payments and capital repayments, was estimated by the DAC to amount to 19 per cent of their export earnings; the rule of thumb 'danger level' for a particular country is considered to be 20 per cent. Interest payments alone absorbed 9 per cent. About half of these payments were to private banks. The corresponding figures for Low Income

Countries were 23 per cent and 9 per cent, for Middle Income Countries 16 per cent and 8 per cent, for NICs 24 per cent and 13 per cent.[3] For some individual countries the situation is of course much worse. Zambia, which has been dramatically affected by the decline in the price and markets for copper, had a debt service ratio of 7 per cent in 1974 and 24 per cent in 1981; by 1983 this had risen to nearly 50 per cent.[4] The corresponding ratios for Brazil and Mexico in 1981 were 13 per cent and 32 per cent, and 19 per cent and 28 per cent.[5]

These figures include only public, and not private, debt to the banks. They also exclude debts with maturities of less than a year, since it has been usual, until recently, for these debts to be rolled over more or less automatically. If such short-term debt is included, the debt crisis looks much worse, since it amounts to nearly a third of total debt. Thus Morgan Guaranty Trust, in its publication *World Financial Markets*, published figures on debt service ratios including short-term debt in 1982 which showed Argentina's as 179 per cent of its exports, Mexico's 129 per cent, Ecuador's 122 per cent, Brazil's 122 per cent, Chile's 116 per cent, the Philippines' 92 per cent, and South Korea's 54 per cent. The corresponding figures for interest payments alone as a percentage of exports were 44, 37, 30, 45, 40, 18 and 11 per cent respectively. By 1983 they were still higher (see estimates in Table 6).

An article in the *Financial Times*, 'The dangers of short-term debt', points out that 'On a traditional yardstick [the developing countries'] debt service ratio rose only slightly to 19 per cent from 16 per cent in the five years 1977–1981'. But:

> after inclusion of short-term debt and invisible export earnings . . .debt service payments actually took about half their current account balance of payments receipts last year compared with less than one third in 1977, Amex says in its latest Bank review.[6]

The result was that the Annual Meetings of the IMF and the World Bank, in Toronto in 1982 and Washington in 1983, were almost entirely devoted to the subject of debt. Both were massively attended by bankers; 9,000 or so of them in Washington, lavishly entertaining delegates, guests and press; one bank spent $2 million on one party.[7] The first Brandt report on the North-South divide devoted much space and many of its more concrete proposals to

Table 6 Projected ratios of interest payments to exports in
1983

	%
Argentina	50
Brazil	46
Chile	50
Mexico	46
Venezuela	29
Total Latin America including Caribbean	**42**
Algeria	14
Indonesia	21
Korea (South)	18
Philippines	48
Nigeria	11
Total other ldcs	**12**

Source: Pedro-Pablo Kuczynski, 'Latin American Debt: Act Two',
Foreign Affairs, Fall 1982.

the problems of the banks, but preceded these with chapters on
poverty and development. In its second report, published in 1983,
the banks came unashamedly top in its list of concerns and the
need to ensure their survival became the prime justification for
increases in official transfers of resources to the Third World.[8]

Many of the biggest banks have loans amounting to multiples of
their capital base which may never be repaid. For example,
according to estimates made in 1982 by Bankers Trust, the nine
largest us banks have lent almost twice their capital and reserves to
six countries: Brazil, Mexico, Korea, Argentina, the Philippines
and Taiwan. Some of the biggest have lent the equivalent of half or
more of their capital to one country: Mexico. The largest British
clearing banks, Barclays, Lloyds, the Midland and National
Westminster, are in similar positions; Lloyds Bank and Midland
Bank are each said to have loans to Latin America which represent
180 per cent of their total equity base; Barclays' and Natwest's

Latin American loans also exceed their capital base, though by a smaller amount.[9] They also have doubtful loans to potentially bankrupt corporations in their own countries.

If the loans were written off, their depositors might panic and attempt to withdraw their money, the banks would not have the cash, and they would in theory have to shut down.[10] In the 1930s the US banking system contracted by a third as banks collapsed; the result was an intensification of the depression. Some commentators forecast a return to barter trade; Latin American countries have already been forced, by the non-co-operation of the banks, to conduct their trade on a cash basis, and this tends to cut it down further. The 'lender of last resort' functions of central banks mean that in a crisis of mass withdrawals of deposits the banks are supposed to be bailed out, and their depositors protected, by central banks creating enough cash to satisfy all comers. In May 1984, this is what happened: to prevent a run on Chicago Illinois, the eighth largest US bank, the US Federal Reserve Board (central bank) and other banks 'put together a $7.5bn rescue package . . . and the Fed allowed [Continental Illinois] to borrow an estimated $4bn . . .'[11] The Fed, to calm the ensuing fears, promised to 'lend boldly' to help any other banks in difficulties.[12] But clearly the sums involved are very large, and in theory the big US banks could be wiped out if a few of the big Latin American debtors defaulted.

The bankers flocked to the Third World partly because the profits were, and are, very high. In partial recognition of the risks involved, they charge interest at various mark-ups above LIBOR (the London Inter-bank Offered Rate, the rate at which they borrow). Their reaction to the crisis has been to charge ever higher rates of interest; in 1983 Mexico was being charged interest at 4 per cent above LIBOR, thus more than cancelling out the slight dip in general interest rates in that year. In addition, the banks charge massive fees for rescheduling. They are, therefore, raking it in. In spite of occasional admonitions from their central banks, and some demands that their accounts should reflect reality by making greater provision for bad debts, they continue to publish record profits and to hand out record dividends to their share-holders. Even though, in some cases, they are having to make new loans merely to get their exorbitant interest payments, on paper they look better than ever: more profits and more assets (i.e. loans). As incomes per head in developing countries fall, so the profits of the banks go up. 'No-one ever became a banker to become popular,' says Anthony Harris in the *Financial Times*; 'but I would hate to change places with one now; it must be like a bad case of halitosis . . . there would indeed be something deeply offensive about the current spectacle of bankers boasting about the profits they make out of rescheduling, if one seriously believed that the debts would ever be repaid in full.'[13]

The banks' claims to be doing a brilliant job in recycling the OPEC surpluses to governments in need, always hollow considering the limited number of governments thus favoured, now ring more hollow than ever. There was a time, in the 1970s, when their activities were widely proclaimed as a triumph for the virtues of the free market.

> Now [the banks] have been accused of irresponsibility, and the borrowers of profligacy. We would not be so harsh . . . Before the criticism became widespread, the banking system had been congratulated – not least by itself – for having satisfactorily managed the 'recycling' of OPEC surpluses. The weaknesses of leaving so much to the market were apparent, especially in its 'herd behaviour' . . . But for the most part borrowers, lenders and the world economy in general benefitted from the high levels of activity which the flows permitted . . .

Thus the second Brandt report.[14] And for a bit of the self-congratulation:

> the commercial banks have transferred excess savings of the OPEC countries to the non-oil producing developing countries in the form of loans. They have thereby taken risks, especially as to credit-worthiness, which their OPEC depositors were not willing to take themselves, and have helped the developing countries to finance their balance of payments deficits arising from the increased cost of oil imports . . . In my opinion this transfer of funds represents a triumph for the largely private sector commercial banks of the industrialised countries. As Walter Wriston, Chairman of Citicorp, told Anthony Sampson in 1980: '"It was the greatest transfer of wealth in the shortest time frame and with the least casualties in the history of the world."'[15]

The 1982 Mexican debt crisis put an end to all that. In the summer of 1982, Mexico declared that it could not meet payments on its $83 billion debt. Mexico had been exceptionally sought-after as a borrower because of the apparent security of its massive oil revenues and reserves (so much for financing oil-induced deficits). When the oil market collapsed, its situation rapidly changed. At that point the banks, rather than cutting their profits and writing off their bad debts, came running to governments and the IMF (so much for taking risks). They also, by their actions, succeeded in generalising the crisis. Thus, says Carlos Langoni, former Governor of the Central Bank of Brazil,

> The concept of country risk usually applied by commercial banks quickly turned into regional risk, covering whole continents, in an irrational attempt to correct in a few months the overlending of many years . . . The Brazilian case dramatically illustrates the devastating consequences. In the first six months of 1982, Brazil was able to borrow normally in the market at an average of $1.5 billion a month. Just after the Mexican default, Brazil's access to the market was cut by half. Automatic borrowing virtually disappeared in the last quarter of the year. Market borrowing was replaced by negotiated borrowing and market forces by bureaucratic meetings. The increasing number of jet hours involved symbolize the higher transaction costs.
>
> There is no logical reason why the bankers' view of the Brazilian economy changed so radically from one month to another . . . the country lost about $4 billion of inter-bank deposits and about $2 billion of trade-related lines of credit.[16]

It has even been suggested that the banks deliberately made the situation worse than it need have been, not only by reducing their net lending almost to zero and cutting off short-term credit, but also by bumping up their profits, in order to get governments to bail them out.[17] This is perhaps the only explanation for their behaviour – other than plain stupidity. If the bankers were acting in the long-term interests of most of us, they would be doing in the Third World what they have in fact been doing for some potentially bankrupt corporations in the First World: charging interest rates at or below the rates at which they borrow and even letting them off their debt service for a period altogether, in the expectation that by doing so they are investing in the long-term recovery, and thus capacity to repay, of their clients. In that case there might be some justification for their asking governments, especially the US government, which are largely responsible for the high rates at which they borrow, for some relief. As it is their actions are almost totally destructive of the prospects for growth in the indebted Third World countries and thus of the banks' prospects of getting their money back from them in the long run. They are effectively killing the goose that lays the golden eggs. But of course they have another goose to turn to: tax-payers in the North, who will no doubt have to fork out in the end.

Meanwhile the banks are in fact getting assistance from governments in the North. This takes the form, to a great extent, of IMF exactions from the Third World countries. During the 1970s governments had been able to avoid going to the IMF and, with the help of the banks, had carried out expansionary policies which the IMF would not have agreed to. Now governments attempting to reschedule their debts to the banks, which means postponing repayments on the basis of new agreements with the banks, must go to the IMF and accept the conditions attached to the receipt of IMF money. Governments, including some governments which had previously been praised for their efficient use of resources, are told to 'put their houses in order': cut their budget deficits in order to pay extortionate rates of interest which in turn are largely caused by – US budget deficits. This means that the government concerned must agree to cut imports, investment, food subsidies, wages, whatever else can be done to divert resources to the banks. In Mexico, for example, it was thought likely that four million people would lose their jobs; bread and tortilla prices were doubled; public expenditure was slashed; and wages declined. In Brazil, the IMF demanded an annual reduction of 20 per cent in wages; between 1981 and 1982, the number of Brazilians earning less than half the official minimum wage had already increased by a third to over 10 million and many people resorted to raiding supermarkets for basic foodstuffs.[18] The government assistance so far thus mainly takes the form of speeding up the killing of the golden goose (see p. 47). This is in effect a means of shifting the burden of bailing out the banks, for the time being, from tax-payers in the North to the poor in the Third World, who, up to now, have borne an overwhelming proportion of the burden of adjustment. It is probably as short-sighted as the actions of the banks themselves.

Thus the main government response to the debt crisis has been to agree, early in 1983, to an increase of 47½ per cent in IMF quotas. Even this was whittled down, later in the year, by US insistence that countries' access to IMF money should be correspondingly reduced, from 150 per cent of their quota to 102½ per cent, except in exceptional circumstances (see p. 40). In addition, governments have provided bridging loans, directly and through the BIS (Bank for International Settlements, the central bankers' bank). World Bank loans have sometimes been part of the package; for example the Bank offered to lend $1.5 billion to Brazil, double the previous year's lending; and the banks themselves have been expected to make some contribution, in the form of new loans. Thus, in an *ad hoc* response to rescheduling necessities, 'rescue packages' have been assembled (see Table 7). But the amounts involved are derisory compared to the needs.

'Why should Mexico turn to the IMF?' a senior Government official asked rhetorically in Mexico City. 'Our IMF quota is SDR 800m ($900m). So what could we borrow? $2bn or $3bn spread out over three years? $2bn is what we need to borrow *each month* this year to meet our gross borrowing needs of $25bn. Politically the IMF remains taboo in this country and it is not worth the political pain of explaining an approach to it for one month's money.'[19]

Table 7 Rescue packages begun since 1982 Mexican crisis

	IMF	BIS	New bank loans	Bank rescheduling	Government loans
Mexico	3.8	1.85	5	19.7	4
Argentina	2.2	0.5	2.6	5.5	
Brazil	6	1.2	4.4	4	1.23
Yugoslavia	0.65	0.5	0.75	1	1.3

Source: *Financial Times*, January 31 1983

Nevertheless Mexico had to go to the IMF a month or so later. Venezuela, secure in the possession of its massive oil reserves, held out a lot longer. Cuba, which is not a member of the IMF, had to sign an agreement with its Western creditors acting as 'a proxy' for the IMF and imposing IMF-type conditions.[20] Brazil's coming to terms with the IMF was initially postponed, with the help of a bridging loan from the US government, until after its elections, and the difficulty of getting the IMF's wage cut through the Brazilian Congress caused talk of the government abandoning its newly-adopted semi-democratic constitution.

Nobody genuinely supposes that the 'rescue' attempts are in the interests of the borrowers: 'the attempts so far made to address the crisis are widely understood, even at the highest levels in business and the international agencies, as attempts to rescue the banks rather than the borrowers, however much our own Governor and others may protest to the contrary'.[21]

Margaret Thatcher was hardly persuaded to allow the British banks to enter into rescheduling negotiations with the Argentinian government, before any official ending of hostilities, out of goodwill towards Argentina. In Parliament she said that if they did not, Argentina would have more cash with which to buy weapons; i.e., it would stop servicing its debt. Similarly Douglas Hurd, junior minister at the Foreign Office, admitted that the refusal to negotiate on Poland's debts, supposedly in retaliation against the declaration of martial law, had had the 'slightly absurd' consequence of granting Poland a *de facto* moratorium. As *Euromoney* (Fall 1983) put it:

The economic recovery has ended. An economic boom has taken its place. But do not expect that boom to help the developing debtor countries much. It will not, because interest rates will be used to control it, and it is interest rates that now matter most to the Third World.

LIBOR is now the single most important economic factor for the debtor LDCs. They are unable to participate in the resurgence of growth that sweeps outwards from America because interest payments swallow export earnings and kill growth. The market economies of the developing world, the future of capitalism outside its traditional bastions, are under more external pressure than they have been for a generation.

America led the recovery and exported it through its trade deficit, financing both its trade and budget deficits by keeping interest rates high and attracting foreigners into Treasury bills . . . growth got out of hand . . . the policymakers lifted interest rates again . . . Do not expect that policy to change. It will not, because it works . . .

Meanwhile the pleas of Third World governments for more money, for example through a new and unconditional issue of SDRs (see below, p. 38), are ignored, imports are cut by as much as a third, growth is choked off, and the suffering of the poor is intensified. Many countries have already suffered a more prolonged decline in income per head than they did in the last big capitalist crisis, in the 1930s. The extent to which their populations can be squeezed through IMF austerity programmes is apparently limited only by basically political calculations: how far can the considerable capability of Third World governments, in Latin America in particular, to repress discontent be stretched before there is an explosion? The Fund, as adjudicator between tax-payers in the North and the poor in the South, has to strike a balance between appearing too soft and provoking any recurrences of the by now notorious 'IMF riots'. The Brazilian people made their point rather strongly in demonstrations in Sao Paolo in April 1983. Newspaper photographs of Brazilian riot police are captioned: 'Are the fears of blood on the streets just a negotiating tactic?'[22]

A further political calculation in this game is: What is it that prevents these governments from openly repudiating their debts in such a way that the big banks would be forced to declare defaults and, in consequence, would either collapse or have to be bailed out in earnest? Walter Wriston of Citibank, the banks' most prominent ideologue and publicist, proclaimed that 'countries don't go bust'. In the nineteenth century, individuals and companies in the United States borrowed on a big scale from numerous investors and banks and regularly defaulted. Similarly in the 1930s, both borrowers and lenders were relatively dispersed and there were of course many defaults. Nowadays, governments deal directly with the united ranks of their creditors. They may fail to pay for months at a time; for example in August 1983, Brazil, according to its Finance Minister, was $2 billion in arrears;[23] Venezuela had $600 million of arrears in interest payments and a five-month standstill on repayment of $13 billion of debt due in 1983, and its tardiness in payment caused an open display of hostility by bankers in London;[24] their ability to pay even interest depends on further loans and reschedulings. But defaults are not declared and governments remain tied into the pretence that they will one day repay their debts. They continue to negotiate with the IMF and they continue to extract whatever sacrifices they can from their people in the cause of servicing their mountainous debts.

It is hard to understand why they do not simply repudiate these debts. By 1981 the net outflow of private, mainly bank, funds from developing countries was $21 billion.[25] The big Latin American debtors are running trade surpluses. Any painfully achieved increases in their exports go straight into debt servicing, rather than into imports. Since the IMF's method of cutting imports is severe overall deflation (see below), sectors of industry are, according to some commentators, in danger of becoming irreversibly damaged. This is turn damages the debtor countries' prospects of growing, exporting and repaying debts in the future. Brazil is said to have contingency plans for default: to be stockpiling oil and essential imports and arranging barter deals with Mexico. Brazil is widely acknowledged to be capable of surviving a default without major disruption; Brazilian economists have done calculations which show that, even taking into account various increased costs resulting from a credit boycott by the West, Brazil would be financially better off if it repudiated its debt; and most sections of business favour at least a moratorium. Argentina is also tipped as a likely defaulter, since it is self-sufficient in oil and food. After President Alfonsín took office at the end of 1983, his refusal to accept IMF-imposed stagnation as the price of an agreement with the banks contributed greatly to the nervousness of the creditors. The major debtors in Latin America have already been denied the most useful facility offered by the banks, which is short-term trade credit. It would be possible, in theory, for them to find alternative financial channels for making the cash payments for their imports and exports which are currently made through the big New York banks. Cuba's trade, for example, has been financed by Canadian and Belgian banks.

The banks undoubtedly have immense power to disrupt the trade of governments of which they do not approve. Shortly after the Sandinistas won power in Nicaragua, officials in the Nicaraguan central bank were visited by an irate private cotton exporter, responsible for a large percentage of Nicaragua's exports. He had made a large shipment of cotton to a client in Germany, who had notified him that the amount due had been paid into his account in Manufacturers Hanover Trust. He had received a statement from the bank to the effect that the balance in his account was nil. His assumption, not surprisingly, was that the Sandinistas had stolen the money. When the matter was investigated by the Nicaraguan authorities, they found that it was the bank itself which had looted the account of a private individual in order to satisfy some of the creditors of Somoza, the Nicaraguan dictator overthrown by the Sandinistas. When the Sandinistas, having decided to assume responsibility for all of Somoza's debts, came to renegotiate the debt, it was only with the greatest difficulty that they succeeded in getting an equivalent sum deducted from the amount they were expected to pay. Any legal redress against the action of 'Manny Hanny' was apparently impossibly difficult. The government has naturally transferred its account from Manufacturers Hanover – into Citibank. Citibank is the most notoriously political of all the big New York banks. But Citibank is thought to find it impossible to take any unilateral illegal action against Nicaragua's trade for fear of losing other profitable Caribbean central bank accounts.

Clearly the effects of any unilateral repudiation of debt would be complicated and unpredictable – but not necessarily insuperable. The theory of one investment banker was that the only plausible explanation for the failure of Latin American ruling elites to take the obvious step of defaulting was that, knowing their political tenure was not assured, they did not wish to close off their well-established escape route into jobs in Wall Street. More generally, it is clear that most existing governments in Latin America do not wish to put themselves outside the pale of the international financial community with whom they consort, in the Washington Sheraton IMF/Bank meetings and elsewhere, and with whom they share interests of class. The absence of open defaults is in a sense merely an illustration of the pre-eminence of class over national interests. But, in addition, the immediate effects of debt repudiation would cause problems, at least in the short term, for the local banks and businesses which are the main allies and supporters of these governments. Better, therefore, if they can transfer the burden of debt servicing to the poor, in the form of cuts in government social expenditures, subsidies and wages, rather than embarking on any real restructuring of their economies and their financial and trading links, which might diminish their dependence on Northern capital.

More surprising perhaps is the lack of any progress towards the formation of a debtors' cartel. The lenders, while proclaiming their opposition to the interference in the sanctity of the market implied in the formation of a debtors' cartel, have undoubtedly succeeded in forming a powerful lenders' cartel. Not so the debtors. Their potential power to destroy the Western banking system seems not to have been used, as, in theory, it could be, to extract better terms from official lenders and the banks. Nevertheless the possibility of a cartel is repeatedly raised. In 1982, before Mexico finally gave in and went to the IMF, according to Mexican Cabinet documents leaked to the British television programme *Panorama*, secret meetings were held between Mexico, Brazil and Argentina at which the Mexicans tried to persuade Brazil to join in a debtors' cartel with the objective, presumably, of avoiding having to accept an IMF austerity programme.[26] The attempt was unsuccessful, no doubt because the Brazilians hoped at that time to avoid the sort of debt crisis and harsh impositions then occurring in Mexico. Subsequently a meeting of the Organisation of American States in Caracas was again expected by many to result in the formation of some sort of debtors' organisation, but in fact produced no more than joint requests for better treatment and more official lending.

In April 1984 there was the astonishing spectacle of a debtors' cartel in reverse. Argentina refused to come to an agreement with the IMF in time to release a loan from the banks which would have enabled Argentina to pay interest arrears and thus saved the banks from having to record their loans to Argentina as non-performing in their April accounts. To rescue them from this occurrence, the governments of Brazil, Mexico, Colombia and Venezuela actually lent Argentina money with which to pay up. The idea was that they would get their money back when Argentina came to terms with the IMF.

But time and further IMF exactions can change all this. In the spring of 1984 successive rises in US interest rates caused the Latin American debtor countries to make further attempts to organise some opposition to the $3.3 billion that would be added to their interest payments in a year. Bankers in New York and London are scornful:

> The cocktail party theory of a debtor's cartel is not the real world. There are too many different trade patterns among debtors, different political systems and different stages of negotiations with the IMF. [27]

But the same could have been said of the members of OPEC. The threat remains, and may limit the degree of harshness with which the West can impose its conditions on the suffering debtors.

Meanwhile all kinds of proposals are made in the creditor countries: by bankers that governments or official agencies, the IMF or the World Bank, should take over the banks' debts; by economists that the debts should be sold off at a discount, supposing anyone would buy them; occasionally, by the right, that the forces of the market should take their toll of the banks; recently, as a result of the obduracy of the Argentinians and the continuing rise in interest rates, and with somewhat more urgency, by Europeans and even by the US monetary authorities, including Paul Volcker, and by Martin Feldstein, retiring economic adviser to the Reagan administration, that a more 'long-term' solution should be sought, including the 'capping' of interest rates or the capitalisation of interest payments. But the US administration remains obdurate that the debt should be dealt with on a 'case by case' basis. And in the main the authorities wait, Micawber-like, for the never-never land of a spontaneous capitalist recovery.

3. The International Monetary Fund

Most prominent of all the official institutions lending money to Third World governments is, of course, the International Monetary Fund (IMF). Its transactions are not usually recorded in statistics on aid; the IMF is sometimes thought of as merely a 'rolling fund', receiving as much in repayments as it lends out at any one time. But it has become a major source of short-term finance for governments with balance of payments problems, and in most recent years has been a net lender to the Third World. The DAC records as a 'memo item' that drawings from the Fund were $6.18 billion in 1981, which is a little less than disbursements from the World Bank (IBRD and IDA, see below) in that year.

Both the IMF and the World Bank were set up at the Bretton Woods Conference in 1944. The IMF was intended to finance short-term balance of payments adjustment, with the particular purpose of avoiding exchange rate instability and competitive devaluations of the type that existed in the 1930s. The British, represented by Lord Keynes, who together with other European countries expected to need the IMF after the war, argued that its resources should be made available unconditionally. The US government disagreed and the principle of conditionality became, in the early years of the Fund's operations, firmly established at the heart of the Fund.

Although the Soviet Union was represented at the Bretton Woods negotiations, it did not become a member of the IMF or the World Bank. Some East European countries joined but later withdrew; some later rejoined; China joined in 1980; Angola and Mozambique are not members and Cuba withdrew after its revolution in 1959. The IMF's membership includes all of the major Western powers except Switzerland and nearly all of the Third World countries which became independent after the Second World War.

The IMF's managing director, unlike the World Bank's presidents, has traditionally been a West European. But its deputy, and the head of the Western Hemisphere department, have been North Americans. Its day-to-day activities are quite closely controlled by its executive directors, five of whom are appointed by the United States, Britain, France, West Germany and Japan, and one by Saudi Arabia; the rest are elected by groups of the remaining members. Although the IMF, like the World Bank, has a Board of Governors, each representing one member, it meets only once a year and has no effective power. Voting power on the executive board is weighted according to the size of members' quotas or financial contributions, which means in practice that a limited number of major powers have a majority in ordinary decision-making and that the United States can veto any attempt to change the IMF's Articles of Agreement. Especially in the earlier period of unchallengeable United States financial hegemony the US executive director in the IMF had overwhelming power.

Unlike the World Bank, the IMF has not up to now raised money by borrowing in commercial markets. The IMF has not therefore, until recently, had the close connections with the banking community and Wall Street which have characterised the World Bank. Its resources have been derived from its members' subscriptions, supplemented since 1962 by borrowing from central banks under the General Arrangement to Borrow (GAB). Its accounts are now denominated in SDRs, or Special Drawing Rights. These were established in 1970 and are intended as a new reserve asset, which according to some views, should replace gold and the dollar. The SDRs created by the Fund are allocated periodically to members of the Fund free of conditions; allocations are in proportion to quotas, in spite of some hopes that they might be allocated only or predominantly to Third World members as a form of aid. The value of SDRs is set in relation to a basket of currencies; at April 30 1981 1 SDR was worth $1.20.

The size of members' quotas is related to the size of their national income, reserves and trade and to some extent to political considerations; thus the size of Saudi Arabia's quota does not fully reflect the size of its contributions to the Fund. The IMF's initial subscriptions amounted to $8.8 billion. By 1982, after a succession of quota increases and the addition of new members, they amounted to $65 billion; and as a result of the current debt crisis a further quota increase of 47½ per cent was agreed at the beginning of 1983. Before this increase, the size of Fund quotas in relation to world trade had been declining drastically: from 12 per cent of world imports in 1965 to about four per cent in 1980, and the 1983 increase in quotas will not of course restore it to anything like its 1965 level.[1] Only part of these quotas is in currencies freely usable by the Fund, since around three-quarters of quotas is provided in members' own currencies, most of which are non-convertible. In addition, under the GAB, the IMF was able to borrow SDR 5 billion a year in 1981 and 1982 from Saudi Arabia and a far smaller amount from the industialised countries, which nevertheless controlled its use.

The Fund's financing arrangements are extraordinarily complicated and unconducive to brief explanation.[2] The IMF does not, strictly speaking, make 'loans'; it sells hard, or usable, currencies to its member governments up to a certain percentage of their quotas, in return for their own currencies. Governments must 'repurchase' their currencies after a period of time, usually three to five years, but up to 10 years in the case of the Extended Fund Facility established in 1974; countries whose needs are large in relation to their quotas can also make drawings from the Supplementary Financing Facility, set up in 1979. Since 1981 the Fund has charged a uniform rate of interest of 6.5 per cent on its ordinary resources.

Drawings from the Fund are made in *tranches*: drawings under the first tranche (25 per cent of a member's quota) can be made free of conditions; under subsequent tranches and under the EFF and SFF, conditions for drawing become progressively more strict (see below). Since 1953 the Fund has made Standby Arrangements, under which it is agreed that a government can make drawings from the Fund, when and if it needs to, up to a stated amount over a stated period, one year under ordinary credit tranche facilities and three years under the Extended Fund Facility, provided that it complies with agreed conditions. These conditions are embodied in a Letter of Intent, which is usually drafted by IMF officials but signed by the country's Minister of Finance. Letters of Intent are not intended to be published, although they are frequently leaked. Governments could draw up to 150 per cent of their quotas under ordinary Credit Tranche Purchases and up to 165 per cent under the Extended Fund Facility in the early 1980s,[3] but this limit was reduced to $102\frac{1}{2}$ per cent of the new quotas in September 1983, at US insistence.

Since 1963, the Fund has also provided money under its Compensatory Financing Facility. This is supposed to compensate countries for shortfalls in their export earnings which result from falling commodity prices. Conditions imposed under this facility were liberalised a little in the 1970s. But the amounts available cover only about half of the requirements for compensation, conservatively estimated, and less than one-twelfth of African countries' terms of trade deterioration from 1978 to 1981.[4] Two other sources of finance, the Oil Facility and the Trust Fund, were set up in the 1970s; the Trust Fund has since been exhausted; the Oil Facility has lapsed and was not renewed when the price of oil increased again in 1979.

The IMF was not set up to lend to the Third World. As late as the 1970s over half of the drawings from the Fund were made by industrialised countries, including Britain and Italy, and 60 per cent of drawings between 1974 and 1976 from the low-conditionality Oil Facility, most of whose funds were contributed by Third World OPEC countries, were attributable to industrialised countries. But, except in the early period and in part of the 1970s, the main users of the Fund's resources have been developing countries and its pressures have become increasingly familiar, and unpopular, in the Third World. At first Third World countries having recourse to the IMF were mainly in Latin America, where balance of payments problems became acute as a result of their attempts to grow rapidly. But by now practically every independent country in the world has made drawings from the Fund at one time or another, and nearly all of them have also been subject to Fund conditionality.

The principle of conditionality is embodied in the statutes of the Fund, which have been used as the legal basis for its subsequent great expansion. Thus, the IMF's Articles of Agreement state, among other things, that it should promote exchange stability; assist in the elimination of foreign exchange restrictions; and make its resources available under adequate safeguards, so that balance of payments disequilibria could be corrected. Keynes's original idea of a clearing union, providing automatic access to resources in effect three or four times the size of those agreed for the IMF at Bretton Woods, and with supervisory powers of a technical nature only in the field of exchange rates, was abandoned. Access to the Fund's resources were made conditional, under Article V, on members complying with the views of the Fund. These were to be set forth in reports made by it on members which, in its view, were using the resources of the Fund 'in a manner contrary to the purposes of the Fund'. Under Article VIII, members are supposed to avoid restrictions on current payments, discriminatory currency arrangements or multiple currency practices and to maintain convertibility on current account. It was accepted that most countries would be unable to comply immediately with these provisions, so under Article XIV countries were permitted 'for a transitional period' to maintain currency restrictions. But such countries, which include nearly all of the Third World countries which became members of the Fund, are expected to 'consult' annually with the Fund and are subject to Fund reports which may recommend the abandonment of certain restrictions and declare the government ineligible to receive Fund assistance if it fails to comply.

In practice the operations of Fund conditionality soon went beyond even what was implied in its Articles of Agreement. The United States view was that the IMF should not, as its Articles state, merely provide more or less automatic access to its resources to help them to deal with their balance of payments problems without resorting to severe deflation, but that it should exercise control and scrutiny over all drawings and should have discretion to promote what it considered to be appropriate domestic policies in its member countries. The Fund, clearly reflecting the interests of the United States as the dominant industrial power, began to see one of its major objectives as the promotion of the multi-lateralisation of trade, in other words the achievement of free trade and free access to the markets of Europe and the Third World, including protected colonial markets.[5] Thus agreements with the IMF now invariably conclude with the standard under-taking that the government will not introduce new, or intensify existing, exchange or import controls. Some go further and specify measures of liberalisation; thus, for example, 'liberalisation of the exchange system' was included in more than a fifth of the upper tranche programmes agreed in 1963–72 and nearly half of the 1973–5 programmes.[6]

IMF conditionality takes three forms: 'preconditions', or the actions a government must take before the IMF will consider lending to it; performance criteria, which are quantified targets at the end of Letters of Intent and which the government must meet, or renegotiate, if it is to remain eligible for IMF money; and other measures which are embodied in the programme set out in the Letter of Intent but which are not specified as conditions which must be adhered to on pain of cancellation of the IMF stand-by. IMF programmes are negotiated by missions which travel out to the country concerned often two or three times over a period of months. The negotiations are of course not publicly conducted and it is normally difficult to determine to what extent the measures to be taken would have been taken in any case, and to what extent they are the result of the ideas and pressures of the IMF officials concerned.

Fund programmes are primarily designed to deal with balance of payments problems. Increasingly, the management of the Fund has argued that it contributes to the resolution of payments problems in two ways: first by providing money, and secondly by making its provision conditional on governments carrying out programmes which will improve their balance of payments situation.[7]

Thus the performance criteria set by the IMF and the other measures included in its programmes are not ends in themselves; they are supposed to contribute to resolving balance of payments crises. Its chosen means for achieving this is the classic instrument of monetary policy: the control of credit, or ceilings on the amounts that may be borrowed by the public and private sectors, often with a sub-ceiling for the public sector. Credit ceilings are the central performance criterion in practically every IMF programme. The IMF has been credited with some responsibility for the current revival in the fortunes of monetarism: 'it is an accepted part of the history of economic thought that the writings of IMF economists played a large role in the post-war renewal of interest in monetary approaches to the BOP.'[8] Like the monetarists, the IMF believes that money controls more or less everything. For example the official Fund history states that:

> Ceilings on domestic credit expansion were emphasised
> because performance criteria in stand-by arrangements were
> based on the view . . . that changes in the supply of money

and credit in an economy had a strong impact on aggregate domestic demand and a related effect on the balance of payments.[9]

The specified changes are, of course, downwards, and it is from restrictions in credit expansion that most of the well-known deflationary effects of Fund programmes derive.

There are other performance criteria as well. Especially recently, there are often restrictions on the amount a government may borrow from abroad. There are sometimes quantified balance of payments targets, an admission presumably that not all Fund heads of missions believe in the efficacy of their monetary instruments. Devaluation is frequently part of an IMF package; it has been suggested that in the period 1973 to 1981 devaluation was either a performance criterion or linked to IMF programmes in half the cases of IMF upper tranche or EFF credits.[10] All agreements, as has been said, conclude with an undertaking that the government will not intensify restrictions on trade and payments abroad.

Apart from the specific, quantified performance criteria, the programmes themselves have become increasingly comprehensive. Excessive demand appears generally to be considered the main problem and practically always a problem of a sort. This is the case even in recent programmes where the Fund has acknowledged the existence of factors outside governments' control, such as increases in the price of oil and interest rates and declines in export markets and prices. The IMF's remedies for balance of payments problems are almost wholly market-orientated and almost invariably require an overall reduction in levels of demand, combined, if necessary, with devaluation, in order to increase the profitability of exports and reduce the attractiveness of imports. When the Fund is said to be making 'concessions', this usually means concessions to the desire of governments to pursue more expansionary policies or to retain controls on imports and capital outflows. Thus negotiations may centre on the size of the government budgetary deficit that the Fund is willing to allow. Although officials maintain that it is up to the government to determine how it will bring about a reduction in its deficit, the Fund in practice is more likely to insist on cuts in expenditure than on increases in taxation; the former are said to be 'easier'. The inclusion of sub-ceilings for the public sector in the IMF's credit ceilings also involves a decision on the allocation of expenditure between the public and private sectors, and usually a more severe restriction of the former. Since its early days in Latin America, the IMF has had an interest in the effect of government spending on inflation and a particular hostility towards government spending for 'social' purposes, said to be inflationary.

It has also, especially since the mid-seventies, discovered another 'principal cause' of balance of payments problems which is said to be 'cost and price distortions', not only 'related to the exchange rate', but also 'related to other prices and wages'.[11] As a result, its agreements frequently contain undertakings by governments to remove subsidies on food and other items of mass consumption and to keep down wages. This activity has proved to be a potent source of the now notorious 'IMF riots', for example in the street protests against food price rises in Egypt in 1977. The IMF programme for the elimination of the rice subsidies in Sri Lanka may have exacerbated already existing national problems and led indirectly to the outbreak of violence in Sri Lanka in 1983. Venezuela's refusal to go to the IMF during 1983 was said to be caused by its unwillingness to accept IMF demands to reduce wages.

In Brazil negotiations with the IMF broke down in the summer of 1983 over the Fund's demand that wage indexation should be abandoned and that wage increases should be held 20 per cent below the rate of inflation. The demand threatened to provoke a constitutional crisis, with the Brazilian congress refusing to endorse the measure; and Carlos Langoni, billed a few months earlier as needing no IMF arm-twisting since he was 'by training an orthodox monetarist of the Chicago School' for whom 'keeping the money supply under control and reducing government expenditure, especially through the cutting of subsidies, are articles of faith',[12] resigned as governor of the Central Bank rather than sign an agreement with the IMF on those terms. He castigated the IMF's inflation targets as 'unrealistic' and even talked of excessive sacrifices being imposed on the people. He said later in an article in *Euromoney* (October 1983):

> It is completely unfair that developing countries should bear the full burden of the adjustment process through declining real income per head. There are some indications that the average rate of profit of the commercial banks may not fall, but even increase as a result of rescheduling . . . The social

costs involved, even taking into account real economic constraints, are higher than they need be . . . [the IMF] has not yet been able to find a reasonable balance between the structural nature of the economic problems, which require time for correction, and the rigidity imposed by its internal theology.[13]

The IMF was not set up with the Third World in mind, let alone to promote development or the redistribution of wealth. It is practically unheard of for its programmes to contain any measures designed to protect the poor against the effects of austerity and most of its programmes do clearly have immediate harsh effects for them: reduction in government expenditures for social purposes, removals of price subsidies, increases in the price of imported goods, reductions in real wages, increases in unemployment, and so on. They have frequently also led to cut-backs in investment and in the rate of growth or even to decline. Fund officials maintain not only that their stabilisation measures are necessary to re-establish balance of payments equilibrium but also, in response to widespread criticism, that they are an essential prerequisite to growth.[14] But the reality is that the IMF is basically concerned with balance, at whatever level.

In Turkey, 'one of the IMF's pet successes',[15] balance had indeed been achieved in 1983, at a massive cost in economic hardship, with wages cut by 44 per cent over the previous 3 years, and in political repression. But unemployment had increased to around 18 per cent and investment had either been stagnant or falling for the preceding five years since Turkey embarked on IMF austerity:

> With Turkey needing to modernise its antiquated capital
> structure, many businessmen agree with Mr. Halit Narin,
> President of the Turkish Employers' Confederation, Tisk,
> when he says 'You cannot say we are on the right track. We
> have not been investing and a country which does not invest
> has no future.'[16]

Thus local industrialists, hit both by deflation and by import liberalisation, are often among the most vociferous critics of the Fund.

Possibly the most widespread criticism of the Fund is that it demands adjustment which is too abrupt and too damaging to long-term growth prospects. Even two economists in the research department of the Fund, engaging in some self-criticism, admit that 'programs designed to achieve quick results on the balance of payments via sharp deflation are likely to have significant and undesirable effects on output, employment and factor incomes, particularly in the short run.'[17] In a book based on considerable access to Fund sources, Tony Killick comments that this 'calls into question the standard Fund assertion that stabilisation promotes long-run development. This makes it all the more regrettable that the EFF concept has not in practice marked much change from standard short-term programmes.' The programmes of the Fund, says Killick, can have serious effects on countries' long term growth prospects, and: 'In our view the Fund has neglected the cost-minimisation task . . .'[18]

Another orthodox critic, Carlos Langoni, (see above p. 44) says:

> The Fund asks too much of the developing countries in too short a time. So far, about half of the countries in the EFF programme have had to ask for a waiver. Since the need for an adjustment programme arises so suddenly, there is often a dangerous conflict between the Fund's requests and what is politically and socially viable within the country.
>
> The problem is not simply availability of resources. There is also a problem of attitudes. The adjustment programme of the Fund is labelled 'structural', but in practice it applies mechanically the same system of performance evaluation used under the traditional stand-by arrangements . . . theological, rather than mathematical, reasoning is used to arrive at the figures.
>
> A longer period of adjustment appears to be needed . . .[19]

These are criticisms within neo-classical orthodoxy. They reject the Fund's contention that there is no alternative, within that orthodoxy, to its policies. Fund officials tend to respond to questions about hardship for the poor by saying 'there is no alternative', as if their questioners were merely naive. And yet even De Larosière, managing director of the Fund, at a press conference at the 1983 Annual Meetings in Washington, let the cat out of the bag by giving contradictory answers to two questions. In response to a Canadian journalist's question about the effect of IMF programmes on the suffering of the poor, he said that, on the contrary, the Fund was easing the burden of adjustment by providing money and that there was no alternative due to lack of money. Two questions later he was accused, by a presumably right-wing Chilean, of 'retarding' the process of adjustment; on the contrary, he said, we are accelerating it. (By which he presumably meant that the IMF was causing governments to adopt harsher adjustment programmes than they otherwise would do.)

It is in fact open to the Fund to provide more money itself in individual cases and also to demand, for example, a less rapid reduction of the public sector deficit and more realistic inflation targets. It might then arrive at a wider estimated 'financing gap' to be filled by foreign banks, in reduced receipts or increased lending, or perhaps by the US and other governments. By making rigid and often unattainable demands, the Fund is making a judgement about how much can be extracted from the Third World for the sake of the commercial banks and ultimately tax-payers in the North. Different judgements could be made.

That this is so is implied by the fact that the degree of harshness with which IMF conditionality is applied, though not its general direction, is affected by the political importance attached to the survival of the government concerned by the major powers. Thus Killick writes:

What, now, of the principle of uniformity of treatment, defined by the Fund as meaning that 'for any given degree of need the effort of economic adjustment sought in programs be broadly equivalent among members'? However seriously the management may seek to achieve this outcome, it is unable to do so. Executive Directors, civil servants and members of the Fund's staff all agree that in practice there are considerable inequalities of treatment, affecting perhaps a quarter to a third of all agreements. The stringency of policy conditions will in practice often depend upon whether the government which has applied for a credit has powerful allies within the Executive Board. If a country is thought to be of key political or strategic importance the Executive Directors of the more powerful countries may lobby the Managing Director, the result often being a softening of terms. Vietnam has been prevented from obtaining a credit altogether because of a *de facto* US veto. Among countries widely regarded as having benefited from influential patronage are Pakistan, Yugoslavia, Turkey, Liberia and Zaire.[20]

The list could be extended. For example Egypt arguably has received lenient treatment from the Fund both because of its importance to United States' Middle Eastern policy and because of its people's riotous reaction to earlier IMF exactions. Similarly, it is clear from leaked minutes of the discussions on the IMF's Executive Board on the 1982 loan to South Africa, which was publicised in South Africa as a vindication of the government's policies, that many directors believed that the decision to lend to South Africa was a political one, not justified on the basis of genuine balance of payments need and involving less stringent conditionality than elsewhere.[21]

El Salvador probably provides the most blatant example of US political favouritism, overriding technical considerations; in 1981 a loan to El Salvador was accepted by the Board lacking even the endorsement of the Fund's staff.[22]

Discrimination works of course in the other direction. The Reagan administration, according to a report published by the House Foreign Affairs Sub-Committee, has a 'hit list' of countries with left-wing governments which former Secretary of State Haig said should not 'get a penny of indirect aid' from the IMF and other multilateral institutions. One of the best documented cases of discrimination is that of Jamaica. The Manley government in Jamaica adopted a strongly anti-imperialist rhetoric; it had friendly relations with Cuba; its internal policies, defined by Manley as 'democratic socialism', were intended to shift resources to the poor. The government was subjected both to violent CIA-orchestrated destabilisation and to harsh exactions by the IMF. In 1978 the IMF succeeded in imposing a complete turn-around in the economic policies of the Jamaican government, including devaluation, a 25 per cent reduction in real wages, tight restrictions on government spending and measures supposed to encourage the private sector. The IMF made this possible by failing the government on what in other countries would have been regarded as a technicality:

> [In] the December 15 (1977) performance test . . . the net
> domestic assets of the Bank of Jamaica failed to be under
> the required ceilings of J$355 million by the ridiculously
> small amount of J$9 million, or 2.6 per cent. This was
> because certain foreign loans on which the Jamaicans had
> counted failed to materialise, at least in time. But the Fund
> seized immediately on Jamaica's delinquency as grounds for
> suspending the agreement, refusing payment of US$15
> million due on the second tranche . . ., preventing
> disbursement of a US$30 million World Bank loan . . . and
> holding up a US$32 million package from a commercial
> banking consortium.[23]

The Fund then demanded, and got, 'shock treatment', so that its
mission chief, Finch, was able to send a congratulatory cable to the
government:

> Happy to report that . . . IMF Board gave its warm approval
> to the EFF programme with Jamaica . . . All who spoke
> praised Jamaican government for its courageous decisions
> and commended it for the appropriateness of the shifts in
> economic policy . . . Most Eds [executive directors]
> accepted inevitable uncertainties in speed of response of
> private sector and several warned that restoration of
> confidence by investors inside and outside Jamaica could be
> slow . . .[24]

Although 'The Jamaican government proceeded to carry out
every single aspect of the new agreement both in letter and spirit',[25]
Jamaica failed to meet the foreign reserves test in the programme
mainly because of external factors beyond its control: the increase
in oil prices and interest rates on its foreign debt. The IMF used the
failure as an opportunity for further tightening of the screw.
Although the government formulated an alternative plan and
broke with the IMF, the IMF austerity had by then taken its toll of
the government's popularity. Destabilisation intensified, prominent Jamaican businessmen made public threats to kill Manley,
and Manley's PNP lost the elections to the right-wing pro-imperial-
ist JLP under Edward Seaga.

Seaga's government got immediate substantial commitments of
aid and an agreement with the IMF on terms probably easier than

those imposed on Manley. But by August 1982, according to the *Financial Times*, Seaga himself had become

> the focus of unrelenting criticism from the island's business community, just under two years after gaining its support with a strongly pro-business platform. Businessmen have been angered by the effects of the Government's policy of progressively dismantling import controls on manufactured goods . . . [According to the president of the Jamaica Manufacturers Association, 33 factories had been closed because of the effects of the Government's policies.] The Government is also facing continued difficulties in obtaining adequate foreign currency to allow local businessmen to import raw materials and machinery.[26]

Another country which is well known for its problems with the IMF is Tanzania. As Nyerere asserted in a 1980 new year message to diplomats, entitled 'No to IMF Meddling',

> We expected [the IMF's] conditions to be non-ideological, and related to ensuring that money lent to us is not wasted, pocketed by political leaders or bureaucrats, used to build private villas at home or abroad, or deposited in private Swiss bank accounts . . . Tanzania is not prepared to devalue its currency just because this is a traditional free market solution to everything . . . It is not prepared to surrender its right to restrict imports by measures designed to ensure that we import quinine rather than cosmetics, or buses rather than cars for the elite.
>
> My government is not prepared to give up our national endeavour to provide primary education for every child, basic medicines and some clean water for all our people. Cuts may have to be made in our national expenditure, but we will decide whether they fall on public services or private expenditures. Nor are we prepared to deal with inflation and shortages by relying only on monetary policy regardless of its relative effect on the poorest and less poor . . .
>
> [The IMF] has an ideology of political and social development which it is trying to impose on poor countries irrespective of their own clearly stated policies. And when

we reject IMF conditions we hear the threatening whisper: 'Without accepting our conditions you will not get any money, and you will get no other money.'[27]

Others make similar points. For example, I.S. Gulati, in the Indian newspaper *Business Standard*, wrote as follows:

First, the structural adjustment a borrowing country seeks to make to correct its external imbalance need not be on the lines considered appropriate by the external financing agency; indeed hardly any of the developing countries, including India, could have had in mind the structural adjustment of the type that Fund-designed market-oriented programmes are now seeking to impose on them . . .

It is one thing, I believe, to follow one's own self-designed programme of structural adjustment reflecting the country's socio-economic priorities, and quite another for a country to be asked to follow a programme that is designed for it by someone else with an entirely different set of priorities and then to be put on a leash with respect to its implementation.[28]

After the Indian government committed itself to an EFF of over $5 billion (5 billion SDRs) in 1981, containing the standard credit ceilings and commitments to import liberalisation, the Communist Party-Marxist Government of West Bengal published a pamphlet written by seven economists and others denouncing it, and including a chapter on alternative proposals to meet India's balance of payments difficulties. One of the basic arguments in the pamphlet was that India did not in fact need the IMF's money, let alone its prescriptions, even though the conditionality, in India's case, was relatively mild.[29]

Nyerere's reference to Swiss bank accounts is given added point by the fact that the IMF made a loan to Nicaragua a few days before Somoza was overthrown by the Sandinistas. The money, as usual, was paid into Nicaragua's account in the US Federal Reserve Board. It was then paid, as usual, into Nicaragua's account in the Manufacturers Hanover Trust. Then it vanished. It was recorded only as having gone into a numbered account, i.e., a Swiss bank account. It could not be traced, or recovered by the Sandinistas for the use of Nicaragua. Not surprisingly, the Sandinista government has so far refused to enter into any relationship with the Fund or to make any attempt to obtain its 'seal of approval' in negotiations with its private bank creditors.

One model of the type of policies which are approved by the Fund is provided by the Pinochet government in Chile. The IMF has in fact been deeply involved in Chile since the murderous coup against Popular Unity in 1973, and Chile was one of only five governments which made stand-by arrangements with the IMF in the upper credit tranches between 1974 and 1976. The Brazilian government, for example, took an explicit policy decision not to draw on upper credit tranches because of its desire to pursue more expansionist and heterodox policies. But the Chilean authorities under Pinochet were actually eager to enter into agreements with the IMF in the upper credit tranches in order to gain international approval for their policies.[30] During most of the period since 1973, the IMF not only strongly supported the extreme monetarist policies of Pinochet's economic team, but at times took positions to the right of this team, notably on the question of wage cuts, or intervened to support the position of the more right-wing elements among potential economic policy makers. Thus the first Chilean team that negotiated with the IMF in November 1973 contained both members of the armed forces and some civilians, including right-wing Christian Democrats. The IMF reportedly criticised some of the civilian members of the team for offering '"easy solutions (though not the best for the country)"', thus strengthening the position of 'the advocates of orthodoxy'.[31] There were at first some disagreements. The Chilean authorities wanted to maintain real wages at the very low level to which they had declined during 1973, partly as a result of massive price increases after the coup. The Fund wanted them to be reduced even further; it also wanted an immediate devaluation. The programme that was adopted incorporated further declines in real wage levels: 'So as to ensure that real wages would correspond to those suggested by the Fund mission, the fiscal and credit ceilings agreed upon in the stand-by arrangement assumed the wage policy recommended by the Fund'.[32] Chile also agreed to an immediate devaluation, further exchange rate adjustment at frequent intervals, an increase in taxation and large cuts in subsidies on items of mass consumption.

In 1975 the Chilean economic authorities embarked on a further brutal turning of the screw, the now notorious 'shock treatment'. The IMF was fully behind it, indeed partly responsible for it. Chile did not yet have access to much private bank lending, so it was dependent on official support and therefore the IMF. The 1975 IMF mission was very critical of the Chilean authorities' failure to curb demand sufficiently in 1974 and particularly of 'excessive' nominal wage increases, by which it meant that the cuts in real wages were not big enough. The system of wage and salary indexation was considered, to use a favoured Fund euphemism, too 'inflexible', even though it implied a further decline in real wages; a new 'more flexible' formula was accordingly adopted, and workers plunged further into penury. Adhering without wavering to the increasingly doubtful diagnosis that inflation was caused exclusively by excessive demand, the agreement eventually reached for an upper tranche drawing from the Fund demanded its further brutal contraction.

The Chilean team which negotiated this agreement became known as the 'Chicago boys'. Pinochet described them thus:

> We, the members of the Armed Forces, understand that in the government we require technical experts. I am not referring to politicians. We only want technical experts, not belonging to parties or having political commitments. We want people who will come only to collaborate with the government.[33]

But their 'technical expertise' was of a particular variety. Jorge Cauas, given the rank of a 'super-minister' in overall charge of economic policy, was a former senior official in the World Bank. The new minister of economics and the president and vice-president of the Central Bank had been trained at Chicago University and had close personal links with it. And so on. Their position was reinforced by a visit from the two arch-priests of monetarism, Milton Friedman and Arnold Harberger.[34] Their influence almost totally displaced that of traditionally powerful groups such as the owners of Chilean national industry and the managers of state enterprises who had depended on protectionist policies and government intervention.

These advocates of ultra-orthodoxy not only carried out the savage austerity measures of the 'shock treatment', under which industries unable to survive increased competition combined with plummeting demand could go to the wall. They also had a religious belief in the virtues of free trade and the doctrine of comparative advantage. In these beliefs they actually appear to have gone further than the IMF; the massive reduction in tariffs and other protective measures carried out in August 1975 appear not to have been at the behest of the IMF. But in its 1976 Report the IMF praised these policies and expressed the hope that they would continue to be pursued in 1976; and its 1977 Report commended the 'opening up' of the Chilean economy as one of the 'major achievements of Chilean economic policy'. National income fell during 1975 by 18.2 per cent and industrial output by more than 27 per cent. Unemployment increased to 16.2 per cent in 1975 and 20 per cent in March 1976, having averaged 5 per cent in the 1960s. Chile became effectively a de-industrialising country.[35]

From 1976, Chile began to have difficulties in getting money from official sources. The human rights lobby in the US under Carter, and pressures from some European governments such as the British Labour government and the Swedish government, made access to the IMF and the World Bank more difficult. There was no stand-by agreement with the IMF in 1976. Staggeringly, the main divergence with the Fund continued to be on the question of wages, which the Fund wanted reduced yet further to levels which even the Chilean government thought would have political consequences too difficult to repress. But relations with the IMF remained cordial, its praise in its reports fulsome, and Chile drew substantial amounts under the low-conditionality Oil Facility and Compensatory Financing Facility. Moreover, Chile no longer needed the IMF's seal of approval; its financing needs were taken over by the private banks. As *Euromoney* commented: 'Chile has arguably staged an economic turnaround which appears to have impressed the international banking fraternity. Due to the function of this country as a much needed sink-hole for excess banking liquidity, it is plain that doubts over lending to countries that contravene Human Rights are fast being dismissed'.[36]

Since then, doubts of another kind have taken over. The effects of the monetarist medicine on the Chilean economy have clearly been so disastrous that by the early 1980s, and even before the main onset of the international banking crisis, Chile was giving serious cause for concern.

By February 1983, it was possible for a *Financial Times* leader to comment that: 'Foreign banks must be holding their own post mortem on how they came to commit so much money to such a frail vessel'; and in August: 'Chile's economic health is today very delicate indeed'. In 1982, Chile's gross domestic product fell by 14 per cent. During 1981, partly as a result of a flood of liberalised imports, 431 Chilean companies went bust, including the largest fruit-exporting firm, Safco, and the Crav sugar company, one of Chile's biggest food conglomerates. Eight banks and finance companies, including the two biggest, would no doubt have collapsed as well if the government had not taken them over and closed three of them. Workers of course continued to suffer. The minimum wage of $180 a month was abolished for those under 21 and over 65. More than a third of the workforce was either unemployed or getting $35 a month for full-time menial work, in the government's 'minimum employment programme'.[37] At the beginning of 1983, foreign banks agreed to a three month moratorium on repayment of Chile's debt (two-thirds of which was private) and the government was being subjected to pressures by its foreign creditors to agree to bail out a dozen Chilean companies with large foreign debts. It appeared that a combination of these pressures and opposition from Chilean business might cause Chile to embark on a programme of public works and even import and exchange controls.

Meanwhile, the government had gone back to the IMF. It made an agreement in December 1982 and two months later had so totally failed to meet its conditions that a complete renegotiation was required. The agreement had stipulated that Chile's loss of foreign exchange reserves must be not more than $600 million in 1983 as a whole; but the reserves fell by $625 million in January alone. 'Bankers still look to a new agreement with the IMF as a major source of guidance on the Government's future economic policy. But there are serious doubts, after the past two months' hysteria, about the Pinochet government's ability to implement successfully any agreement that may be reached'.[38] And popular protests and demonstrations have resumed on a large scale, at last threatening the survival of the Pinochet government.

Chile may be regarded as an extreme case. But in the mid-1970s, the economic policies followed by the Pinochet government were clearly close to the IMF's ideal. The IMF has, it is true, supported governments elsewhere whose policies are very different. But in each case the measures demanded by the Fund arguably represent moves towards a Chilean-type 'ideal'. IMF prescriptions do not vary in fundamental ways. They vary mainly in the degree of rigour with which they can be applied, not in the nature of the measures sought. Governments with access to private bank lending, such as the Brazilian, Mexican and Peruvian governments in the 1970s, could largely evade them. In countries with political structures and economic policies different from those favoured by the IMF, mutual 'concessions' are made; IMF drawings by Yugoslavia in the 1960s and early 1970s, for example, were conditional on measures of liberalisation and moves towards opening up to the world market; it is clear that in this case the IMF got what it could but that there was no realistic possibility of a sudden conversion on the part of the Yugoslav authorities to the magic of the market.[39]

The governments that succeeded in avoiding IMF conditionality in the 1970s, especially in Latin America, often did so in order to have the freedom to pursue more expansionist policies and to intervene actively on behalf of national industry, private as well as public. Nearly all of them are now in crisis. But so are the governments which went to the IMF. The 'rate of recidivism' among IMF borrowers is very great: 'of the 54 countries which have accepted austerity programs during the past 10 years, 43 have required subsequent programs. Approximately 13 of these countries have found it necessary to apply for additional assistance over the course of from four to ten consecutive years.'[40] The solutions, if any, provided by the IMF are short-term, as well as painful.

Whether or not the Fund is 'successful' in the context of one country, in the sense of re-establishing balance at however low a level, it has been argued by quite orthodox critics that it makes no sense to apply these policies worldwide. Thus Anthony Harris of the *Financial Times* says: 'The IMF is seeking to apply British policies to the whole world; again it is not clear that the solution can be generalised in this way . . .' And on the IMF's insistence on keeping down real wages everywhere: 'As a senior British official sourly remarked: "The IMF's answer is that everyone must become more competitive with everyone else." '[41] Furthermore: 'Insisting on fiscal and monetary austerity throughout the world cannot eliminate all countries' current account deficits, but only redistribute them – as well as ensure that the IMF contributes to the very world recession that it most fears. The IMF [annual] report fails to tackle this issue.'[42] This theme is naturally echoed by the Brandt commissioners who, in their second report, say the IMF 'should avoid advocating policies for a number of countries which, when carried out by all of them together, will reduce world income at a time when expansion is needed'.[43]

Leaving aside the question of the speed and extent of adjustment required, even the second Brandt report notes that 'there is typically more than one way of achieving external equilibrium; but the Fund generally assumes a very limited range of possibilities'. Killick states, 'There is also much homogeneity of view among [the IMF's] professional staff, which is partly self-selected because of the Fund's fairly well-known approach to stabilisation; peer pressures, informal selection and promotion norms reinforce this homogeneity'.[44] The Brandt report does not specify what other possibilities might be. But one obvious one is the use of import controls. Even the Brandt report does hint that, in spite of its 'strong commitment to an open trading environment', it might consider the Fund to be 'excessively' anxious to do away with import controls.[45] Import and exchange controls are of course anathema to the Fund; but it can be argued that 'when a country's imports contain a large proportion of essentials, as so often happens in developing countries, payments imbalances will respond only to very large changes in total spending. Thus, while aggregate monetary tools may improve a country's payments situation, they often do so only at very great cost to the economy, both in short-term lower employment and production, and in a long-term decline in investment, which limits future growth . . . the Fund's strong position, developed within the context of an international commitment to trade liberalisation, has even less justification within the framework of the new wave of protectionism . . . in the developed countries.'[46] And the Fund's aversion to the use of direct controls to achieve external balance is of course reflected in its prescriptions for internal policies, which are clearly and overwhelmingly biased towards reliance on market forces for the regulation of the economy.

There is one way in which governments could adjust. They could default on their debts (see above, p. 33). They could at the same time reduce their dependence on trade with and borrowing from the industrialised West, and in fact might have to do so if they openly defaulted on their debts. This option, like socialism, is clearly not among those on the agenda of the Brandt Report or the International Monetary Fund, one of whose major functions is to secure the integration of countries, to the greatest extent possible, into the capitalist world market. As it is, there is every sign that the IMF is fully in favour of the extremes of rough exposure to the cold blasts of domestic and international competition favoured by, for example, Thatcher and Pinochet, accompanied by the partial dismantling of the industrial base in their countries. Never mind that, intent on sending to the wall any industries unable to compete in times of recession, they may find that they have eliminated their countries' capacity to meet any demand that may arise from world recovery, supposing that takes place. They share with the IMF a doctrinaire allegiance to the resolute application of the principles of free trade and free competition.

In the late 1970s and early 1980s, there appeared to be some recognition of some of these problems in the IMF. There was talk of the 'supply side'. The June 1980 issue of the IMF *Survey* stated:

> As to the policy approach to be followed by the Fund, this must endeavour to create conditions conducive to improvement in the supply of resources and broadening of the productive base. Such developments will require, of course, supportive measures on the demand side directed to the reduction of excessive budget deficits and government consumption expenditures, to the adoption of appropriate monetary and credit policies, and to various external issues of problems.

But the prospect of moving from the IMF's traditional reliance on the restraint of aggregate demand was obviously daunting to the Fund; thus an internal Fund paper, in convoluted style, stated:

> Questions will undoubtedly arise as to the compatibility of these concerns with supply aspects with the guidelines directing the Fund staff to avoid micropolicy performance criteria. In discussing this issue, it is important to be clear about the role of performance criteria. They are intended solely [?] to trigger further discussions between the Fund and the authorities of the members and are therefore confined to policy variables reflecting overall developments. It is generally inappropriate to treat micropolicy actions in

this way – all such actions have some macroimpact but normally other microactions can be taken to ensure the appropriate macro-outcome. Particularly as the choice between alternative microactions is frequently influenced by political considerations, on which it is inappropriate for the Fund to take positions, it is not normally suitable for the Fund to include microactions as performance criteria.[47]

Do the writers really believe that the other demands made by the Fund are free of political implications? In any case the partial solution reached seems to have been to engage in closer collaboration with the World Bank, itself also professedly debarred from any expression of political bias. A World Bank official is now normally attached to IMF missions, with the function of looking at the government's investment programme (see below, p. 113). But none of this implies any real change in the content of Fund conditionality. In fact the closer links with the World Bank effectively reinforce the Fund's conditionality, since the Bank's function is to advise on how the government's investment plans can best be accommodated *within* the Fund's ceilings (see below).

Somewhat less problematically, the Fund embarked on a policy of greater 'flexibility'. In 1979 the Executive Board issued a guideline to the effect that conditionality should be applied in a flexible and appropriate manner, taking into account the domestic, social and political objectives and economic priorities of members and the fact that their balance of payments problems may have had external causes outside their control.[48] The IMF was prepared to provide more money for slightly longer periods. It also seemed prepared to accept a slower pace of adjustment. As Killick says:

> One informant suggested to me early in 1981 that 11 of the 15 most recent stand-by programmes would have been rejected as inadequate by 1970s standards; and industrial-country Executive Directors grumbled about the new 'laxity' in the Fund's approach and its willingness to accept at face value programmes unlikely to be implemented.[49]

The IMF also, apparently on the initiative of its Managing Director De Larosière, dropped much of its insistence on devaluation, and became willing to accept alternatives such as export subsidies and import duty surcharges which would have been 'anathema' not long ago and 'would have been ruled out by the Fund's lawyers as inconsistent with a system of free multilateral payments'.[50]

The question was whether these moves were more than tactical; on devaluation, Killick notes: 'During 1980 the decision was taken to "soften" the Fund's stance on this issue, as part of a campaign to give the Fund a more favourable image on conditionality and to encourage governments to make greater use of its facilities'.[51] With the collapse of the Bretton Woods system of fixed exchange rates when Nixon abandoned the dollar's fixed link with gold, the Fund was in danger of losing its role. And, in spite of the acute balance of payments difficulties experienced by most countries in the 1970s as a result of rising oil prices and falling prices for other commodities, the Fund's resources were actually being under-utilised. Two-thirds of IMF lending in the years 1974–78 was 'low-conditionality' finance drawn under the Oil Facility and Compensatory Financing Facility and in the late 1970s there were net repurchases of the Fund's resources: in other words repayments of past loans exceeded new drawings.

But this shortage of clients, and the accompanying need for greater 'flexibility', was short-lived. In a speech in October 1980 De Larosière was already saying:

> our response to the new rise in oil prices has not been to establish a facility, like the oil facility, offering assistance with a low degree of conditionality. Our new borrowings next year are intended for relending on what we call upper credit tranche conditionality. This reflects our belief that members must respond with appropriate policies to the present situation; financing and adjustment must go hand in hand.[52]

Simultaneously, new private bank lending virtually disappeared, and the banks demanded that agreement be reached with the IMF before they would agree to reschedule existing debts, so that avenue of escape was closed off.

The Fund's 1981 Report was able to report with apparent satisfaction that as a result of their acute balance of payments and debt problems, governments were coming to the IMF in increasing numbers. The total volume of resources made available to all countries during the year ended April 30 1981 amounted to SDR 9.5 billion, of which SDR 7.0 billion was for developing countries, up from a low point of SDR 1.2 billion in 1978. This meant that net purchases from the Fund were positive for the first time for four years, at SDR 1.9 billion. 32 new standby and extended arrangements were made in 1980-1, compared to 28 in 1979-80. Since 1979, about three-quarters of the finance from regular Fund resources had been made available under programmes of upper credit tranche conditionality.

The IMF had found a role – with a vengeance. From being an organisation designed to deal with governments' short-term balance of payments problems, it had become the major instrument for bailing out banks which had engaged, it was now recognised, in imprudent lending. As one European central banker put it: 'With the benefit of hindsight . . . it does seem to me a colossal mistake that the commercial banks were allowed to leap into the breach to recycle the oil surpluses, for the fact is that these banks do not have any hold over a sovereign borrower.'[53] In Peru in 1976 a consortium of six US banks had actually got together and attempted to impose IMF-type conditionality on the military government, which had been borrowing on a large scale on the Euromarkets in order to carry on with its reformist programme. The banks negotiated an orthodox stabilisation programme, including concessions to foreign companies and the Peruvian private sector. But this was the only attempt by the private banks to do this, and it was unsuccessful from their point of view. The following year they called on the IMF, saying that they would not re-finance Peru's debt unless Peru made an agreement with the IMF; an IMF mission went to Peru in March 1977 and was eventually more successful in imposing austerity.[54] This foreshadowed the generalised use of the IMF, from 1980 onwards, as the instrument for imposing discipline on the borrowers in the interest of the banks.

Increasing the size of the Fund's resources so that it could come to the rescue of the banks became an urgent priority, dominating discussions at the Fund-Bank Annual Meetings in Toronto in 1982 and in Washington in 1983. Before the Fund's resources could be replenished under the agreement reached at the IMF's interim committee in February 1983 to increase Fund quotas by $47\frac{1}{2}$ per cent, the Fund was already running out of money to fulfil its new obligations. Thus the IMF was reported in August 1983 to be facing a 'liquidity crisis' of between $6bn and $7bn by the end of the year; unable to raise further loans directly from governments, it was therefore left with no alternative to raising large sums of money on private capital markets, which it was unwilling to do.[55]

The problem was complicated by hostility in the US congress to quota increases for the IMF. The measure was passed initially, in August 1983, in the House of Representatives with a majority of only six votes and then only with a string of amendments unacceptable to the administration: that the IMF must not lend to South Africa, that it must not lend to Communist countries, that the private banks must bear a larger share of the burden of adjustment through a reduction in their profits and increases in their provisions for bad debts. The left and right united to condemn the bailing-out of the big banks, to which there is much historical hostility in the United States. The whole episode seriously embarrassed the Reagan administration, which ended up having to make concessions to the Democrat internationalists who were the only real supporters of the IMF bill. The Reagan government itself had begun its period of office with considerable hostility towards public multilateral institutions on the grounds of their interference with market forces, as well as the burden on public finances. But eventually, in the face of opposition from many of its own supporters, it had no alternative to backing them, in the interest of the survival of the capitalist world order, and the banks in particular.

Meanwhile, in a complicated game of threats and promises, the European and Saudi Arabian governments announced they would not bail out the Fund until the US administration got its bill through congress, and the Fund announced that it was suspending new commitments. Thus Nigeria had its application for an IMF extended loan held up, even though it was $4 bn in arrears on trade payments. This meant that it was likely to have to borrow under new Fund regulations, due to come into force in January 1984, under which its access would be reduced from 450 per cent of its old quota to 125 per cent of the new quota, or from a maximum of $2.6 billion to a maximum of a little over $1 billion.[56]

The IMF was nevertheless generally acknowledged to be a solitary bastion against default and huge weight was attached to its success in this endeavour. The Fund, while it was said to be putting pressure on the banks to make new loans to the major debtors, did nothing, in public at any rate, to persuade them to improve their terms or write off their debts. All of its pressures were on the side of the full repayment of debt. Its officials justified this position on the grounds that the IMF 'had no mandate' to put pressure on the banks to reduce the burden of debt or to take their share of the burden of adjustment. Its mandate, apparently, is to force individual governments to adjust to the appalling 'realities' imposed on them by external forces. But, whereas it has been critical of protectionism in the North and the limits this imposes on the ability of Third World countries to increase their exports, the Fund has not publicly suggested that the burden of debt should be reduced in any way, and continues to issue complacent statements about the situation being under control and its packages being effective. In response to a proposal at a press conference at the 1983 annual meetings that the banks should convert their debt into longer-term debt and should lend new money to invest in the growth of productive capacity in the debtor countries in order to convert their worthless assets into something that was worth something, De Larosière merely asked derisively whether the questioner had any plan for where the money was to come from.[57]

At the 1982 annual meetings, the focus was on Mexico. By 1983, the problem of Mexico having apparently been 'solved' without any mass explosion of popular protest, the limelight switched to Brazil. Brazil is showing some signs of being a tougher nut to crack. It failed to meet the terms of the previous IMF package. Practically everybody appeared to agree that the new IMF target for the reduction of inflation in Brazil was unrealisable. On the question of wage cuts, the IMF got itself into a corner, pronouncing them to be the keystone of its programme. Its credibility was on the line. If it backed down and dropped the demand for an overall wage cut of 20 per cent, its effectiveness elsewhere as a guarantor for the banks and final arbiter of international financial respectability would be diminished, or worse. If it refused to make an agreement without the approval of the Brazilian congress for the wage cut, the financing package for Brazil, meant to cover its debt servicing until the end of 1984, would fall apart, Brazil would have $3 billion of interest arrears by the end of 1983, and the banks would 'have to conclude in their 1983 accounts that at least some of their money in Brazil is irretrievably lost. If this occurs there is no way of predicting how bank depositors and bank shareholders will react.'[58]

Some of the IMF measures, including a 30 per cent devaluation in

February 1983 and the abolition of subsidies on oil and wheat, gave a further powerful push towards hyper-inflation and thus contributed to 'the universal conviction in Brazil that the IMF-inspired adjustment is simply impossible'.[59] And the $1\frac{1}{2}$ per cent rise in interest rates in the spring of 1984 made even the Brazilian authorities issue somewhat defiant statements to the effect that the rises were in danger of wiping out all of their painful efforts to comply with the IMF's demands for 'adjustment'.

During the same period, the Argentinian government of President Alfonsín, elected at the end of 1983, made repeated statements to the effect that IMF-imposed austerity was not in the interest of the banks, which would never get their money back if growth was systematically choked off. Partly because Alfonsín was willing to make the banks miss their accounting deadlines while he failed to reach agreement with the IMF, his views began to find some echo in the creditor countries. In May 1984 central bankers and a few commercial bankers met secretly in New York to discuss the possibility of long-term solutions. At the same time Martin Feldstein, retiring head of Reagan's Council of Economic Advisers, said: 'The time has come to shift from crisis management to a policy of promoting Latin American growth.'[60] All this called into question the 'short leash' policy applied by the IMF. A 'senior official in Washington' said: 'The real question is whether IMF conditionality as applied now is conducive to economic recovery in indebted countries.'[61] The problem appeared to be how to retain the IMF's 'credibility' and the value of its 'seal of approval', and to ensure that the IMF was not 'left on the sidelines'.[62] However De Larosière, at a seminar at St. Gallen shortly afterwards, continued obstinately to maintain that governments were making progress in adjustment and should continue to cope with this 'burden'; there was little hope, he said, of fresh initiatives to ease countries' debt service burden; and he 'stressed the orthodox line on debt rescheduling and adjustment'.[63]

The Fund has clearly not yet proved its effectiveness in its current role as saviour of the banks, let alone any ability to deal with the long-term balance of payments problems of developing countries. And as for the alleviation of poverty, that is over the horizon and out of sight and conscience.

Part II

The World Bank

4. The nature of the beast

Size and nature of lending

The International Bank for Reconstruction and Development (IBRD, or World Bank), like the IMF, was set up at Bretton Woods in 1944. In theory the IMF is responsible for short-term balance of payments equilibrium, the Bank for the long-term development of productive resources. Although the World Bank is dominant among the institutions that provide so-called 'aid', it tends to play second fiddle to the Fund. It is usually obvious that the rich governments which control the two institutions attach more importance to the IMF, presumably because they are more concerned with stability than with growth and are not convinced that the former depends on the latter. The IMF also attracts a good deal more attention from the media; for example, there are roughly three times as many journalists at the Fund's press conferences at its annual meetings as at the World Bank's. The main negotiations at Bretton Woods revolved around the creation of the IMF, and the World Bank was almost an afterthought.

The World Bank was supposed, however, to complement the activities of the IMF. It was to do so by promoting a steady flow of international capital for the promotion of productive investment; it was thought that the Bank would thus contribute to international stability and, by sharing risks, would ensure that countries with a balance of payments surplus invested this surplus abroad. The Bank's Articles of Agreement state that the purposes of the Bank are to assist in post-war reconstruction; to promote private foreign investment and if necessary supplement it from its own resources; to promote trade and balance of payments equilibrium by encouraging international investment; to ensure that priority projects are dealt with first; and to conduct its operations with due regard to the effect of international investment on business conditions in its members' territories. Membership of the World Bank is conditional on membership of the IMF, thus securing members' willingness to submit themselves to IMF supervision.

The World Bank now consists of three distinct financial entities: the IBRD, the IDA and the IFC. The original Bretton Woods institution, usually referred to in the Bank's publications as the IBRD in order to distinguish it from its more recently created 'soft loan' affiliate the IDA (International Development Association), has from the beginning made loans at near commercial rates of interest. These are included in the DAC's statistics under the heading 'non-concessional flows' (see p. 7). In 1981 the average rate of interest on outstanding IBRD loans was 7.6 per cent, but the rates charged on new loans have followed the general rise in interest rates, and from September 1981 the rate was 11.6 per cent, higher than the rate charged on some commercial export credits. In 1983, the Bank decided to make loans at variable interest rates, in line with the commercial banks. The loans generally have a grace period of five years and are repayable over a period of 20 years or less. The Bank is strict on repayment and claims never to have suffered a default or a deferral; governments which renegotiate their debts to private banks nevertheless pay their debts to the World Bank on time.

In 1983 the IBRD disbursed $6.8 billion (the Bank's fiscal year runs from July to June; thus FY 1983 refers to the period between July 1982 and June 1983 and references to years in this book in relation to the Bank are always to fiscal years). The Bank raises the bulk of its money in private capital markets; in 1983, its total borrowings from these markets amounted to $10.3 billion. Its ability to lend is supplemented by the capital subscriptions of its member governments. But only 10 per cent of the original capital subscriptions, and 7.5 per cent of the increase in the Bank's authorised capital agreed in 1980, is paid in and available for lending. The Bank's total subscribed capital in 1982 was $43.2 billion, of which the uncalled portion was $39.1 billion.[1] This constitutes a massive guarantee that the Bank will not default on its borrowings. Together with the Bank's reputation for conservative lending policies and its very conservative one-to-one ratio of capital to lending (unlike private banks many of whose loans exceed their capital base by 15 to 20 times), it accounts for the Bank's high credit rating in the markets from which it borrows. A further attraction to these markets is that voting rights on the Executive Board of the IBRD are related to capital subscriptions. Thus in 1982 the United States had 20.6 per cent of the votes; Britain had 6.1 per cent; these countries plus, say, West Germany, France, Japan and Canada held a majority of voting rights, or 50.2 per cent.

The IBRD's cumulative loans, up to June 1982, amounted to $78.5 billion.[2] Its commitments to lend increased rapidly during the 1970s, from $2.1 billion in 1973, to $8.8 billion in 1981 and $10.3 billion in 1982. Disbursement likewise rose from $1.2 billion in 1973 to $5.1 billion in 1981 and $6.8 billion in 1983. Its professional staff, excluding secretaries, has similarly increased in size, from 1,654 in 1973 to 2,689 in 1982.[3] But recently the rate of increase has slowed to no real increase in fiscal years 1983 and 1984. Because, under its Articles of Agreement, the Bank cannot lend more than the total of its subscribed capital and reserves and this ceiling has been reached, it cannot expand merely by expanding its borrowing in private capital markets; it has to go to governments for an increase in subscriptions. The Bank is asking for a selective increase in line with the current IMF increase, to be followed by a general increase in government quotas. It is proposing a rate of increase in lending of 5 per cent in real terms from 1985 onwards, which is considerably less that the hectic rate of increase up to 1982.[4]

The International Development Association (IDA) was set up in 1960. It is administered jointly with the World Bank. Whether a government receives loans from the IBRD or from the IDA depends not on the purpose for which the loan is to be used but on the income per head in the country concerned. The IDA's loans are on concessionary terms, with a nominal service charge of 0.75 per cent on disbursed and 0.50 per cent on undisbursed portions of its loans, grace periods of 10 years and 50-year repayment periods. They are of course included in the DAC's figures on Official Development Assistance. In 1983 disbursements from the IDA were $2.6 billion.[5]

The IDA derives its resources from its member governments' subscriptions, subsequent replenishments and special contributions from its richer members, and transfers from the earnings of the IBRD. It was set up in 1960 to provide loans, or credits as they are usually called, on softer terms to the least developed countries which were not creditworthy from the IBRD's point of view. Since 1977 over 80 per cent of IDA funds have gone to countries with annual per capita incomes of less than $411.[6] The decision to set up the IDA was made partly in response to demands from Third World governments for a lending agency under the control of the United Nations (SUNFED – Special UN Fund for Economic Development); their demands were opposed in particular by the United States, which was not willing to support a fund outside its control and eventually decided to support a soft-loan affiliate to the World Bank as a means of defusing the demands. As Eugene Black, then President of the World Bank, said, the IDA 'was really an idea to offset the urge for SUNFED'.[7]

Voting rights on the Executive Board of the IDA, as in the IBRD, are related to the size of subscriptions; in 1982 the United States had 18.97 per cent of the votes, Britain had 7.10 per cent, West Germany had 6.99 per cent, Japan had 6.67 per cent. It has 130 members, all of them members of the World Bank, divided into Part I, or developed members, and Part II members. Part I members pay all of their subscriptions in convertible currencies, Part II members only 10 per cent of them, the rest in their own currencies. By June 1982, the total of subscriptions and supplementary resources was $28.6 billion.[8] The cumulative total of IDA credits was $26.7 billion (compared to the IBRD's $78.5 billion).[9]

There have been six replenishments of the IDA. The sixth, supposed to amount to $12 billion for the three-year period 1981–3, was held up by United States delays and the initial unwillingness of other countries to exceed their pro rata contributions. In 1982 the IDA had only about $2.6 billion available for commitment, which was about 37 per cent lower than the programme approved by its executive directors;[10] and the IDA's commitments to lend have declined from $3.8 billion in 1980 to $3.5 billion in 1981 and $2.7 billion in 1982, although its disbursements, under past commitments, are still rising: from $0.5 billion in 1973 to $1.9 billion in 1980 and $2.6 billion in 1983.[11] There is therefore crisis talk of the collapse of IDA. The decline in the availability of IDA funds has been partially compensated for by a rise in the rate of IBRD commitments above the projected level, accompanied by attempts to persuade countries such as India that, in spite of its per capita income level of $190 in 1979, it should 'graduate' from the IDA to the IBRD. Attempts were also made to continue with some agreed IDA projects by making co-financing arrangements with other donors.[12]

The seventh replenishment of the IDA has encountered even greater difficulties, mainly because of opposition from the Reagan administration. The World Bank originally asked for an enlarged replenishment of $16 billion. It appeared to be willing to settle for $12 billion; but the Reagan administration refused to offer more than its 25 per cent share of $9 billion, or $750 million a year, claiming that Congress would not agree to more. Britain's contribution, partly as a result of quota changes, was due to be cut by more than half from $1.212 billion over the last three-year period to $585 million over the next.[13]

Although the two institutions, the IBRD and the IDA, are financially separate, their loans are administered in the same way and by the same staff. Over 90 per cent of the World Bank's loans have been for projects. The projects are more or less identical, whether they are financed by the IBRD or the IDA: they are subject to the same kinds of scrutiny, and are supposed to provide similar rates of return; there is not much difference in their distribution between sectors, although a somewhat higher proportion of IDA loans than IBRD loans goes to agriculture and rural development: 33.4 per cent and 21.1 per cent respectively in 1982, for example, partly reflecting the predominantly rural nature of most of the countries receiving money from the IDA.[14]

Up to 10 per cent of Bank lending has not been tied to specific projects. The Bank has from time to time made what were originally called programme loans: money which is available for general imports, usually to favoured clients in difficulties. Since 1980, it has engaged, more prominently, in what it calls Structural Adjustment Lending. Structural Adjustment Lending is still a small part of total Bank lending: 5.8 per cent of commitments in 1980, 8.2 per cent in 1982, and perhaps $8\frac{1}{2}$ to 9 per cent in 1983.[15] By June 1982, structural adjustment operations had been approved for 13 countries: Kenya, Turkey (three times), Bolivia, the Philippines, Senegal, Guyana, Mauritius, Malawi, Ivory Coast, South Korea, Thailand, Jamaica and Pakistan. Six of the programmes, those for Turkey (I and II), Kenya, the Philippines, Malawi and Mauritius, had been 'satisfactorily implemented'. Those for Bolivia,

Guyana and Senegal had encountered 'implementation problems'. The rest were too recent to assess.[16]

The Bank's other affiliate the IFC (International Finance Corporation) is administered separately from the IBRD and the IDA. Its activities are less prominent than those of the other two. The IFC is the only part of the Bank which directly invests in and makes loans to the private sector, without government guarantees. It also tries to help raise finance from other private sources and to support the growth of private capital markets in the Third World. It can make more or less any kind of investment, including equity, and it claims to rely on its commercial judgement, rather than government guarantees, to ensure the 'safety and profitability' of its investments. It aims also to act as an intermediary and to 'foster better understanding' between governments and the private sector. A total of just over 700 investments amounting to $5.5 billion have been approved since it was set up in 1956. Its 124 member governments subscribe paid-in capital of $54 million, and it has accumulated earnings of $203.8 million, and the authority to borrow up to four times the total of these. Investment commitments by the IFC in 1983 were $845 million, out of the total committed by the three parts of the World Bank of $15,322 million.[17]

Management

The World Bank has a Board of Governors, each representing one member government, which has joint annual meetings with the IMF. It has no powers of decision on the day-to-day running of the Bank. In the meantime decisions, particularly on the approval of loans put up by the Bank's staff, are taken by the executive directors, five of them representing the United States, Japan, Britain, West Germany and France, the rest representing groups of countries, increasingly large as the financial power of the countries they represent diminishes. The number of votes they can wield is related, as has been said, to the size of governments' financial contributions. In practice even the executive directors, apart from the US director, have limited power over the running of the Bank and are, for example, denied access to many of its documents. According to Mason and Asher, 'a project loan recommended by the President and staff of the Bank has never been rejected'.[18] The president of the Bank, after an initial period of power struggles between the President and the United States executive director, has come to exercise considerable autonomy in the day-to-day running of the Bank, and semi-dictatorial powers over the Bank's staff. The World Bank, say Mason and Asher, 'has, almost from the beginning, been a highly centralised organisation with decisions made in Washington rather than in the field, and made by the president and his close advisers without any considerable delegation of authority.' And, they say,

> The Bank is a highly centralised institution not only in its headquarters operations but also with respect to overseas activities. All stages of the project cycle are managed from Washington, and field operations are carried on by short-term missions. Except in one or two cases, country economic reports are prepared in Washington, again with the help of short-term missions to the field. Even in the countries and areas in which the Bank has permanent representatives, headquarters holds these representatives in most cases on a very short leash.[19]

Even in India, which has a big resident mission, its role is mainly confined to the supervision of projects; all large projects are initiated and appraised from Washington, and local Indian staff are frustrated by their inability to communicate directly with Washington, where they know that real power lies. This policy, Bank officials say, is pursued deliberately in order to ensure that they do not lose their (Washington-based) perspective.

The relative autonomy of the Bank's management in Washington does not in itself mean that the World Bank is any less an instrument of United States foreign policy. In fact since the United States does not have any power of veto over lending decisions on the Executive Board and needs the support of at least five other major countries to get a majority, it is potentially a further safeguard for its interest; it may merely encourage the US to ensure that loans that it opposes do not get as far as the Board. Thus, according to a Bank official:

> My understanding is if the US is against a loan it does not go through. The reason that this has rarely happened at a Board meeting is that the informal process works. Objection

from the US influences the Bank's willingness to send projects to the Board. Indeed loans are put before the Board, only when management has determined that the US will loudly object in comments but abstain in voting.[20]

The Bank and the IMF both have their headquarters in Washington. US government officials are known to lobby their staff individually on important issues.[21] Whereas the President of the IMF has traditionally been a European, the Presidents of the World Bank have all been United States citizens, their appointments approved by the US government – in the case of the current President, Clausen, who took over in 1981 and was previously head of the Bank of America, both by President Carter and by his then probable successor, Reagan. With the exception of McNamara and McCloy, they were all bankers. McCloy, who was a lawyer, 'modestly described himself as "a bankers' amanuensis" '.[22]

McNamara, who was President of the Bank from 1968 to 1981, presided over what, in retrospect, appears the apogee of reformism in the World Bank (see below, chapter 9). McNamara was President of General Motors before he was put in charge of the Pentagon and played a major role in the Vietnam war and in organising the bombing of North Vietnam. There have been occasions when even the decisions of these Presidents have been overruled, or even unsuccessfully opposed by the United States government; but mostly they can be relied upon to act in the interests of the United States in particular and the West in general.

As for World Bank officials, they are predominantly North American and North European.* Unlike in the United Nations, there are no national quotas for staff recruitment. When the Bank was first set up, staff were recruited rather haphazardly among contacts of its North American presidents; some are still there.[23] During the McNamara period, an attempt was made to recruit more Third World nationals and also more women, but the domination of male WASPs was not much diminished, especially at senior levels in the Bank. Of the 20 most senior staff members listed in the 1983 *Annual Report* with the rank of Vice-President and above, the Third World was represented by two Turks, two

---

* Catharine Watson provides a complementary account and much additional local colour in her account of life at the World Bank. See Appendix pp. 267–75 below.

Pakistanis, one Latin American and one African; and only one was a woman. In 1978, only 11 of the 65 'principal officers' of the Bank were nationals of the Third World.[24] Of the Third World nationals who do work in the Bank, the overwhelming majority have post-graduate degrees from major North American and European universities, Harvard, MIT, Chicago, Oxbridge and so forth. A number of the Bank's senior staff come like their Presidents from private US banks and some of them, like Irving Friedman, now resident ideologue at Citibank, return to them.

The Bank's staff is now probably somewhat more politically heterogeneous than it was in its first 25 years. During the McNamara period in particular, the Bank recruited a number of liberals and even the odd Marxist. It also continued to recruit, predominantly, ambitious young neo-classical economists (see Appendix). The power of the World Bank to assimilate even the less orthodox is very great. It is no doubt difficult to work with any satisfaction in a large bureaucracy without picking up some of the prevailing ideology. The inducements to do so in the World Bank are considerable. The pay and perks are exceptionally good: average salaries for professional staff in the Bank were about $46,000 in early 1982; Bank officials do not pay tax and they receive many additional perks, such as school fees.

The Bank is a notably hierarchical institution. Its staff, notoriously arrogant towards the government officials with whom they deal in the Third World, are subservient to the point of, as one of them puts it, 'arse-licking' to their superiors within the Bank.[25] Senior Bank officials also appear to be capable of very unpleasant behaviour towards their own subordinates; there are stories of mission chiefs reducing their female colleagues to tears, a senior official circulating scurrilous and wounding rhymes, and so forth. Indian economists employed by the Bank's resident mission in Delhi, while welcoming the high salaries by Indian standards, were resentful of their inferior status compared to the expatriates and of the fact that the latter, for example, never ate in the staff canteen. There are not many examples of Bank staff actually being sacked. But they can be put out to pasture (see Appendix). There are officials, thus banished, who are known to regret having taken a stand on an issue of principle. In order to rise within the institution, it appears to be necessary to conform; Vice-Presidents, said one official, are selected for their 'malleability'.[26] Only one or two individualists are cited at senior levels within the Bank. And to rebel is to risk either being ignored, or being put into parts of the Bank where it is impossible to influence any major decisions.

Bank officials are exceedingly nervous about talking to outsiders, especially those known to be critical of the Bank. The Bank justifies this reluctance, and also its unwillingness to allow access to its documents, on the grounds that it would violate the confidentiality of its discussions with governments. But a Third World critic of the Bank, Fawzy Mansour, in a mimeographed document entitled 'An Outsider's View of the Bank', concludes his analysis of the Bank as follows:

> Whatever merits such arguments may have, they provide no reason for keeping such documents secret *ad infinitum* . . . And in any case, the labels of confidential, secret, top secret, etc . . . can be removed from a sizeable class of documents without doing harm to anybody – except perhaps those who should be harmed. Most of the time, it is the peoples of the countries concerned, and their social scientists, who are kept in the dark regarding matters of vital importance to their well-being – and which can nevertheless be obtained by anybody else but themselves. As a matter of principle, opening windows for the entrance of light and fresh air should always be encouraged.[27]

The Bank has become increasingly nervous about leaks, and resorts to increasingly elaborate devices to stop them. But it has invited little success, partly because of the number of liberal/progressive recruits during the McNamara period who have become disillusioned but, unwilling to leave the Bank, and unable to put up an effective opposition within it, have assuaged their consciences by leaking documents.[28] A Country Program Paper on Haiti, dated May 20 1983, was marked thus:

> A Country Program Paper has a restricted distribution and may be used by recipients only in the performance of their official duties. Neither the reproduction of copies of this document nor distribution outside the World Bank is permitted. When the paper is no longer needed it should be sent to the appropriate Country Programs Division for disposal.

It was nevertheless leaked.

The instinct of World Bank staff for secrecy at times seems almost paranoid and must have something to do with the fact they are anxious not to displease their superiors. It may also, especially as far as unwillingness to talk at more senior levels is concerned, be related to the fact that the Bank, in its actual practice, diverges to an unusual extent from its public face. As Mason and Asher put it: 'It must be said that, to date, there continues to be a sizeable gap between the public pronouncements of some of the Bank's officials and its day-to-day practice.'[29]

5. The lenders' cartel

The Bank and the banks

The policies of the Bank are of course to a great extent determined by the sources of its finance. Unlike other channels of official 'aid', including the IMF, the Bank gets its money not just from governments, but from private capital markets. This has meant that it has always worked closely with the commercial banks and with private commercial centres, especially Wall Street. Eugene H. Rotberg, the Bank's vice president and treasurer for many years, is constantly trying to convince bankers that the World Bank is a sound institution which basically serves their interests, simply because his task is to raise money. 'The Bank is the largest non-resident borrower in virtually all countries where its issues are held.'[1] Its bonds carry a 'Triple A' rating on Wall Street. It sells around a third of its securities to governments and central banks; the rest are bought by private investors, mainly institutions: 'investors in the private investment markets through the medium of investment banking firms, merchant banks, or commercial banks'.[2] Rotberg is well aware that the Bank may be misunderstood; in a booklet published while McNamara was president, he writes:

> I would be less than frank, and indeed quite naive, if I
> assumed that [the Bank] was universally recognised by the
> investment community in, say, the United States as the only
> premier credit in the marketplace. Few people understand
> the Bank (it is often confused with the IDA); fewer still have
> any conception of its financial structure, liquidity,
> profitability, guarantees, the repayment record of its
> borrowers, or the quality of its lending operations . . . We
> are not a social welfare agency committed to making
> transfer payments to solve the problems of misery or

> poverty. We are a development bank using the most
> sophisticated techniques available to facilitate development,
> while providing unmatched protection and strength for
> creditors and shareholders.[3]

The Bank has always been strictly conservative in its attitude towards repayment of its own loans. It has also done what it could to ensure that others get their money back. Some of the Bank's earliest loans were in Latin America, and were preceded by demands that countries should re-establish their creditworthiness by settling their pre-war debts. Thus vice-president Garner told Chilean negotiators in 1947 that:

> the most difficult policy problem facing the Bank is where
> borrowers are in default on previous debt . . . The present
> management does not see how the Bank can make loans in
> the face of widespread dissatisfaction in financial and
> investment circles to whom the Bank must sell its own
> bonds. The principle applies, of course, not only to Chile
> but to all potential borrowers.[4]

Chile eventually reached a settlement with the Foreign Bond-holders Protective Council Inc. of the United States and the Council of Foreign Bondholders of Great Britain, among others, and on the following day the Bank announced two loans to Chile, noting in its press release that accommodation had been reached with the injured bondholders. Thus the role of debt-collector for unscrupulous Wall Street lenders became enshrined in the traditions of the Bank. The position was subsequently formalised in an internal memorandum, Policy Memorandum 204, which states that the Bank shall not lend to countries which default on debt repayments or servicing (without agreeing on refinancing), which nationalise foreign-owned assets (without adequate compensation), or which fail to honour agreements with foreign private investors (for example tax agreements). This Memorandum has been invoked against Egypt, Burma, Sri Lanka, Iraq, Indonesia, Brazil, Costa Rica, Peru, Algeria, Ethiopia and no doubt many other countries.[5]

Clausen, who was previously Chairman of the Bank of America, undoubtedly has some enthusiasm for 'partnership' between the

Bank and the banks. In May 1982 he devoted an entire speech to it.[6]

Addressing an audience of bankers, he said:

> I want to focus especially on what I believe can be a new era of partnership between The World Bank and international commercial banks for helping the economies of the developing countries . . . The World Bank's project lending is a strong complement to the lending that commercial banks do.

And in a speech in February 1983 at Harvard University, on the problem of debt Clausen said: 'We have no intention of "bailing out" commercial banks. Instead we want to encourage them to get involved more deeply in the important and profitable business of lending to developing countries.'[7]

This is in fact the World Bank's preferred solution to the debt crisis. It has indeed been accused by some of being partly responsible for the crisis, by insisting that countries should borrow more. Tanzania, Zimbabwe and China have all been told by the Bank that they were 'under-lent', even after the size of the debt problem had become apparent. In the case of the major Latin American debtors, the orthodox solutions involve them taking on yet more debt so that they can pay interest to the banks. The World Bank is fully behind these 'solutions'. Because of its sources of finance, it is in an even worse position than the IMF to do or say anything which might be construed as hostile to the banks, even supposing its banking presidents wished to. Throughout the 1982–3 debt crisis it was not, in public at any rate, in any way critical of the banks and of their self-destructive greed (see above, pp. 22–36). It did not suggest that the burden of debt repayment and high interest rates might be too great for the developing countries, or that it might be shifted from them. At the beginning of 1984 Clausen, rebuffed over IDA funding by the Reagan administration, did say that the outflow of funds to the banks was 'premature . . . on this scale'.[8] But any contemplation of default or non-payment of debt would go right against all of the Bank's traditions. It has gone out of its way to argue against default. Thus Mr Ernest Stern, the Bank's long-standing senior vice-president, speaking in Mexico City in August 1983, warned Latin American countries against declaring a unilateral moratorium on their external debts, saying that such a move would 'without doubt eliminate a country for many years from receiving credit', and praising Mexico's deflationary policies.[9]

While repeatedly pronouncing itself to be opposed to any formation of a debtors' cartel, the Bank is in effect part of what one of its own officials is said to have described as a 'lenders' cartel', whose function it is to extract the maximum debt servicing from the Third World through IMF austerity programmes. For example in 1983 the Bank's two loans to Brazil were submitted to the Board a few days after Brazil had come to terms with the IMF; loans from the World Bank are sometimes part of the 'rescue' packages and the Bank, like the commercial banks, does not lend to countries which fail to reach agreement with the IMF – thus falling into line with the general exhortations to developing countries to 'put their houses in order' as though it was they, rather than the authorities in the industrialised West, who were responsible for the crisis. The Bank, rather than putting forward any long-term solutions to the debt crisis or even recognising that they are necessary, has merely joined in the complacent chorus about the expected beneficial effects of the hoped for resumption of growth – in the North – and accepting, apparently without disapproval, that any increases in exports achieved by countries under IMF conditionality will go not into imports and growth, but straight into debt service.[10]

The World Bank, it appears, is not just against debt repudiation; it's against even 'responsible . . . restructuring'. Thus Barend de Vries, senior World Bank official for many years, writes:

> Given the enormity of the problems of adjustment some politicians in debtor nations have called for unilaterally stopping debt repayments, a position widely regarded as against the interest of both debtors and creditors as well as the international system of finance. But there are also more responsible calls for a restructuring of the debt of many developing nations including a consolidation of the short-term debts. Some observers, like Felix Rohatyn and Professor Kenen, have offered ideas for the refinancing of a major portion of the debt outstanding. Richard Weinert proposed that the World Bank refinance and assume part of the LDC debts on long and subsidised terms in return for

World Bank bonds to be held by the commercial bank. However, proposals of this kind have not been considered in detail, and indeed they could adversely affect new bank lending and there is widespread doubt that they could work.

For the time being, responsible officials, both national and international, are of the view that the situation in individual countries can be managed, assuming sustained recovery of the world economy and given the forthright short-term assistance provided by both national and international institutions, especially the IMF, and including the US authorities (the Federal Reserve and the Treasury), other central banks, and the BIS, all working in tandem with the large commercial banks which have assumed a constructive attitude.[11]

The Bank has of course not been heard to say that debt repayment is a burden extracted from the poor. Asked whether he saw any prospect of the burden of austerity programmes being reduced, Clausen replied that the international financial community had shown remarkable understanding of individual problems and had co-operated in ways not hoped for before in helping to support countries while they made a valiant effort to regain creditworthiness and acceptable debt service ratios.[12]

Asked whether in some cases there might not be a need for lower rates of interest and longer maturities, Clausen's answer was: co-financing.

Co-financing

Co-financing, in Bank jargon, means that the Bank associates other lenders, official and private, with its loans. About one-third of Bank projects now have an element of co-financing.[13] An increasing proportion of the Bank staff's time is devoted to the cause of co-financing; a 1980 memorandum estimated that co-financing increased a project's appraisal costs by 5 to 10 per cent and its supervision costs by 20 per cent.[14] Through co-financing, the Bank hopes both to increase the size of new commercial (and other) lending to the developing countries and to improve its terms. It does not claim to have any effect in lowering interest rates; only in lengthening grace periods and maturities. Co-financing has become central to much of what Clausen has to say about the Bank. In his 1983 speech to the Board of Governors, he claimed that the Bank was 'sound, profitable, innovative, know-ledgeable and respected'. Under the heading of 'innovation', there were two paragraphs. The question of accelerating disbursements and strengthening policy dialogue was dealt with in one sentence. The rest was devoted to the subject of co-financing. Of the two press conferences given by Bank officials at the meetings, one was on the subject of co-financing; it was given by Mr Teruyuki Ohuchi, the new Japanese vice-president in charge of co-financ-ing.

There are three types of co-financers: bilateral and other multilateral aid agencies; export credit agencies; and commercial banks. In the case of official agencies, the argument is that they can take advantage of the bank's professional development expertise; in other words the Bank's view of what a borrowing government ought to do is reinforced. The Bank is more hesitant about claiming that co-financing led to any increase in the amount of official aid provided. In all three cases the Bank claims to offer the assurance that the projects financed are well designed and appraised and will yield high returns and therefore repayment. In the 1970s official agencies supplied the largest amounts of co-financing with the Bank, but by 1983 private sources had increased in importance: $1.7 billion of co-financing came from official sources, $2.9 billion from export credit agencies, and $1 billion from commercial banks. The Bank's contribution was about $4.3 billion. Nearly a third of the Bank's operations in 1983 was associated with co-lenders.[15]

Clausen himself puts most emphasis on co-financing with the private banks and this is clearly where his enthusiasm lies. '"I call it Clausenomics,"' he says. '"I cannot help it if President Reagan agrees with me."'[16] Co-financing arrangements between the World Bank and commercial banks are not in fact new; Clausen, as President of the Bank of America, was involved in the first co-financing deal between the World Bank and a private bank in the mid-1970s;[17] and nearly two-thirds of a restricted World Bank report on co-financing, produced in 1980 before Clausen became president, was devoted to co-financing with the commercial banks.[18] This report noted that in the 1970s environment,

neither borrowers nor lenders saw much benefit in co-
financing with the World Bank . . . Banks were so eager to
lend to developing countries in the past few years that there
is no indication that past co-financing has added
significantly to the flow of funds to the beneficiaries, or
eased the terms on which such funds were available . . .
[But] tighter credit conditions . . . could make for a sharp
further increase in co-financing with the World Bank.

The report recognised that private bank lending was about to be
'constrained' by a number of factors, and claimed that by
'ensuring the soundness of the final assets, co-financing can
effectively contribute to bolstering the banking system and expanding its lending on a sustainable basis'.[19]

In order to convince potential co-financers, the Bank was
willing to make available to them confidential Bank documents,
such as project appraisal documents, and information on the
country's ability to service debt. The 1980 report concluded that:
'By ensuring the sound use of external capital and the overall
effectiveness of development and structural adjustment programs,
[co-financing with the World Bank] can serve as the catalyst
needed in critical cases for private capital inflows to occur, on
reasonable terms.'[20] The Bank must however be rather disap-
pointed at the rate at which co-financing with private banks has
increased, or not increased; although it did go up to a high point of
$2.2 billion in 1982 (from $1.8 billion in 1980), in 1981 it was only
$1.3 billion, and in 1983 it was down to $1.0 billion.[21] Hence,
perhaps, the rather frantic attempts under Clausen to advertise its
usefulness to all concerned. However much the Bank might like to
become more deeply involved in 'bolstering the banking system',
the banks clearly do not find its offers of help sufficiently attractive
to cause them to resume their lending to the Third World on any
scale.

The value of World Bank co-financing to other lenders is
supposed to be enhanced by the existence of cross-default clauses.
The 1980 Bank staff report describes them thus:

Cross-default clauses, a standard feature of commercial
banks' international loans, link the loans of several lenders
in such a way that a default on any associated loan is a
default on all associated loans. The Bank has accepted

optional cross-default provisions which give it the right, at
its option, to exercise its remedies in the event that the co-
financier suspends or accelerates [i.e. demands early
repayment of] its loan as the result of a default under its
loan agreement. Some private co-financiers . . . press for a
removal or reduction of the optional character of the clause
so as to increase its deterrent effect and its value to them.
The Bank has refused to commit itself in advance to
exercise its remedies . . . As for borrowers, they have shown
some distaste even for optional cross-default provisions.[22]

This is not surprising since the existence of the cross-default
clauses can in theory, as was confirmed at Mr Teruyuki's press
conference, give the Bank the right to 'invoke its remedies' (stop
lending or demand early repayment) if a country defaults on any of
its debts to the banks involved in co-financing, including those not
related to the co-financed project. There are also 'cross reference
clauses', covering the conditions set by the Bank, which are
supposed to govern the disbursement of the loan.

The value of the cross-default clauses to the co-financiers
depends on how much a particular government is concerned about
falling out of favour with the World Bank, as opposed to the
private banks, the IMF, and all the others concerned. The Bank's
claim that by associating other lenders with its own lending it is
automatically offering them 'comfort' rests on the fact that the
Bank itself has traditionally been extremely, and successfully,
strict in regard to the servicing of its loans. Thus Eugene H.
Rotberg, Treasurer of the Bank for many years, states:

The Bank has not had *any* losses on loans. The Bank has
never had a write-off of a loan. The Bank has never had a
non-accruing loan. The Bank has a firm policy against
rescheduling its outstanding loans. The Bank does not
change the terms of loans or stretch out principal payments
or 'refinance' a maturity. The Bank, in short, does not write
blank cheques, either for development, or to permit
countries to service their debt . . . Borrowers have, in fact,
seen fit to maintain impeccable financial relationships with
the World Bank.

There are substantial pragmatic reasons why borrowers
do not default on World Bank loans. In the event of a

default, no further disbursement would be made on that loan or any other loan outstanding but not yet disbursed to that country. And no new loans would be committed until the default had been made up . . . [Also] if, for example, principal or interest payments on loans are even 30 days late, the Executive Directors of the Bank, representing all 139 member governments, are formally notified of this delinquency.[23]

Bolivia, in 1984, was one of the rare exceptions to this general rule.

Clausen's claim to innovation, almost his only claim to innovation (no wonder one of his staff is said to have described him as a 'retail banker out of his depth'), is that the Bank has introduced, on an experimental basis, a new mechanism for co-financing, known in Bank jargon as B-loans. 'As the developing world looked for more commercial investment from the industrial world,' he said in his 1983 speech to the Board of Governors, 'the Bank moved to strengthen its role as a catalyst by introducing innovative new co-financing instruments in January of this year.' Until then, although the World Bank might have put forward suggestions about private co-lenders, the borrower reached separate agreements with the Bank and with the co-financiers, chosen in theory by itself. Under the new B-loans, as Teruyuki explained at his press conference at the 1983 annual meetings, the World Bank and other banks participate in principle on an equal footing in one syndicated loan. This was intended to give the banks a 'closer association' with the World Bank and also better protection by giving them preferential access, over the World Bank, to repayments if these fell short of the proper amount; and by applying the Bank's strict policy against rescheduling to all portions of the loan. Other 'comfort' to the banks was to be found in the cross-default clauses, although the Bank still reserved the right not to allow defaults elsewhere to trigger defaults on its own loans; compromise was necessary, said Teruyuki, between comfort to the private banks and the stability of World Bank lending.

By September 1983, the Bank had made B-loans to only two countries: Thailand and Hungary. The poorer developing countries, especially in Africa, have never figured very largely in the Bank's co-financing with private banks. Thailand was one of the most creditworthy of all developing countries at the time, so the Bank could hardly claim that it was giving it access to commercial bank lending which would not otherwise have been available. The only success it could claim for all the attention it had devoted to co-financing was that the terms were better than they had previously been, in the sense that grace periods and maturities were longer; it stated that a reduction in interest rates could not be expected as well. The other two B-loans were to Hungary. Unlike other countries in Eastern Europe, Hungary had a fairly high credit rating; again, the Bank's claim was that it had improved the maturities.

From the point of view of the borrowers, one of the effects of the Bank's new insistence on co-financing is to strengthen the united front of Western creditors, or creditors' cartel, with which they are increasingly confronted. The 1980 internal report on co-financing speaks of 'a mutual will for co-ordinated approaches among bilateral donors'.[24] The borrowers may feel that, rather than improving the terms on which they borrow, this actually limits their ability to find the best terms available. Thus the Indian Oil and Natural Gas Company (ONGC), for example, found that the Bank's insistence on tying together all of the finance for a project restricted its freedom of manoeuvre. From around the middle of 1982, the Bank had stopped financing the whole of the foreign exchange costs of energy projects. Instead of allowing the ONGC to determine for itself which source of credit it wished to use, it had tried to insist on working out in advance where the rest of the money was to come from and on incorporating this into the agreement. The ONGC was annoyed by this, and speculated that the purpose of the new arrangement was to safeguard the interests of suppliers. Similarly, the Indian newspaper *Business Standard* reported that a World Bank loan of $450 million for rural electrification had been cancelled because the Bank had insisted that the government should accept a Canadian loan offer tied to the purchase of aluminium rods from Canada; the government had rejected this on the grounds that the cost of the rods was 45 per cent above the ruling market price and that it would therefore be cheaper for India to buy on the open market with Eurodollar finance; the World Bank had called off the project, saying that its foreign aid requirements were not properly tied up.[25]

In general co-financing represents, as of course is publicly stated, an ever closer association of the World Bank with the interests of the commercial banks. There is currently the possibility that this association will be further reinforced by the creation of a new World Bank affiliate. According to the *Financial Times*,

> Outlines of the proposal are vague . . . It is clear, however, that any affiliate will not be used to take developing countries off the books of commercial banks, nor to guarantee these loans. Neither would it subsidise interest rates charged on commercial bank loans. Mr Rotberg [the World Bank's Treasurer] said the main purpose of such an affiliate, if approved, would be to work with commercial banks, encouraging more joint lending to developing countries with the World Bank.[26]

The question remains whether this is merely a formalisation of an existing situation, and therefore greater openness about it, or an actual change in the situation confronting the developing countries. Probably it is a bit of both.

The Bank and foreign private investment

The promotion of inflows of private capital into the Third World has been the other major constant in the Bank's activities. In this it has been entirely faithful to its original statutes. The injunction to governments to improve the climate for private investment, especially foreign private investment, is almost as routine a recommendation in its reports as import and exchange liberalisation is for the IMF, and quotations to this effect from published and unpublished Bank sources would fill a book.[27] The obvious justification is the simple one that the better the treatment of private capital, the greater the flows; as Mansour says:

> there is hardly a recommendation, a policy statement or even a theoretical speculation emanating from the Bank that can be construed as throwing a shadow of doubt on the validity of this basic – and clear cut – article of faith for, like many articles of faith, it is based on a superficially irrefutable reasoning: poor countries are poor because they lack capital resources . . . hence any inflow of capital is bound to speed up development. History has proved it . . .[28]

The Bank also of course supports the private sector within developing countries, although it is sometimes accused of being biassed in favour of metropolitan-based multinational companies (see below). Thus a senior Indian official, closely involved in negotiations with the Bank, said that the Bank's general remedy was to increase the role of the private sector, 'especially the foreign private sector': 'the more we moved to a market-oriented system the better off we would be'; it was 'something like a gospel', propounded 'every morning'.[29] Such examples could, again, be multiplied ad nauseam.

The Bank has not, as its Articles of Agreement imply that it should, operated directly and solely as a guarantor for private capital inflows and, except through the IFC, it has not lent directly to the private sector without government guarantees. In his public statements, however, Clausen currently puts a good deal of emphasis on the IFC and promises that it will increase in size and importance. He has also said that the idea that the Bank should set up a multilateral insurance scheme to attract more private investment to developing countries has long been close to his heart. But the major activity of the Bank has been as a lending agency, making loans from its own resources. From the beginning it lent, usually for projects, to governments or with government guarantees. This has sometimes led staff to tell its left-wing critics, and its right-wing critics to allege, that it is in effect biassed towards the public sector. But this is far from true. The Bank's early loans were overwhelmingly in what is called the economic infrastructure, in sectors in which the private sector is unwilling to invest but which it nevertheless needs for its profitable operation: roads, railways, ports, electricity supply, telecommunications. These are all sectors where public ownership is the norm in advanced capitalist countries because the private sector is unable to operate them at a profit and they have therefore often been taken over and run by the state.

The US Treasury's report on the multilateral development banks (MDBS) commissioned by sceptics in the Reagan administration (see below, pp. 196–8) set out to refute these allegations by the right:

available evidence on MDB lending does not support the contention that MDBS have sought to support the public sector at the expense of the private sector.

The high proportion of MDB loans which is judged non-competitive with the private sector is explained, in part, by the emphasis in MDB lending on infrastructure investment, e.g., water supply and sewerage, much of which is considered to be traditionally either a public sector activity or a regulated private sector activity in the United States. Such lending can in fact indirectly promote the private sector by providing services essential to its development.[30]

Where these operations do exist in the private sector, the Bank lends to them, with government guarantees. Loans to agriculture, now around a third of the total, have of course been mainly in the private sector. The Bank has, on the other hand, clearly been unwilling to lend for industry in the public sector, and has frequently turned down requests to do so. In general, the Bank has a marked preference for financing by private foreign investment, especially where the only alternative is investment by governments, which may in turn be financed by foreign private banks and export credits. This preference is now also frequently expressed in reaction to the debt crisis. Governments are told that it would have been so much better for them if only they had financed their development through foreign private investment because then there would have been no question of debt repayment (or non-repayment). The habitual response of Bank officials to requests for loans for projects in the public sector is to ask why they cannot be in the private sector, which often means, in effect, the foreign private sector. There is no known example of them taking the opposite position.

For example, interviews with Indian officials were frequently dominated by accounts of the Bank refusing requests to finance projects in the public sector, and of the government therefore going elsewhere, or occasionally, during the 1970s, persuading the Bank to change its mind.[31] The Indian government engaged in protracted struggles with the Bank over the question of whether its fertiliser plants, which both parties agreed were necessary, should be in the public sector or financed by foreign private investment. In the 1960s the Bank wouldn't budge. By the 1970s its position had changed because, one public sector chief cynically suggested, the private sector was no longer interested. Shortly afterwards the Bank began to finance projects in the state oil sector (see below) because, suggested the same official, it was at the time in the interest of the developed countries to invest in new sources of supply, irrespective of ownership, in order to undermine OPEC. Now that India plans to invest in the petrochemicals sector, again the Bank's 'first question' is why the government wants it to be in the public sector; 'we refuse to answer'. 'It is out of order,' said the Indian official, 'for the Bank to raise this issue; it may decline to give a loan, but it is not within its rights to ask why the project should be in the public sector.' Clausen's belief, the same official said, appeared to be that the Bank should be 'a lender of last resort' (it should lend only if the private sector was unwilling to invest); 'if that is what Clausen wants, the sooner the Bank is wound up the better'.[32]

Many Indian officials now feel confident that, unlike in the 1950s and 1960s, they can win some of the arguments. For example, the Bank agreed to finance the cement industry in the public sector, apparently accepting the argument that only the state-owned Cement Corporation would go into certain areas unprofitable for private enterprise. But it could be argued that this in fact only meant that the Bank was fulfilling its function as 'lender of last resort'; and, in any case, the Bank eventually refused to lend for a cement project on the grounds that the Indian government refused to raise the rate charged sufficiently to cover costs. Algerian officials had similar stories of battles with the Bank. The political situation in Algeria has similarities with that of India: a powerful state sector in industry with many allies within their central governments, as well as members of both governments who are interested, together with the World Bank, in promoting a larger role for the private sector, and whose influence has recently been on the increase (see below, pp. 209–14).

During the McNamara period the Bank, as has been said, became somewhat more willing to finance activities which previously it had maintained should be reserved for private investment. State-owned development banks, making loans to industry, came to be considered suitable recipients for World Bank loans after 1968.[33] An Indian official suggested indeed that in India's case, the Bank had developed a sophisticated understanding that the public sector was performing the role in support of the private sector which had been envisaged for it in the Second Plan, and that it was not therefore perceived as a threat to the private sector. But when the Bank lends to public enterprises, it frequently attaches conditions designed to ensure that they operate more like private enterprises, especially in their pricing policies. Quotations of the following type could no doubt be found in every Bank report: 'Considering the distortions resulting from widespread government interventions, which in many state-owned enterprises reached a degree that left management virtually without any meaningful authority and financial responsibility, the Government should pursue a vigorous policy of decontrol, decentralisation, and devolution of economic decision-making to the company level. Price controls and regulations should be progressively dismantled and price formation left to the market subject to appropriate anti-monopoly and anti-dumping safeguards'.[34] Elsewhere in the same report, the recommendation is repeated and coupled with the injunction that: 'Systematic efforts should be undertaken to attract foreign investors.'[35]

The Bank at times has its own proclivities reinforced by direct pressures from the private sector, usually the US private sector. This has been most notably the case in the matter of oil investments. In response to the balance of payments crises in many Third World countries in the 1970s, partly induced by the rise in oil prices, and the difficulties they have had in servicing their debts, the Bank has put much emphasis on investment in greater self-sufficiency in energy, and currently about a quarter of its lending is for energy projects, including oil. It also appeared willing to contemplate assistance to state-owned oil companies in the Third World and to argue that an investment in oil extraction in a given country, which might not be viable from the global perspective of the major oil companies, might nevertheless be desirable for an individual country, given the rising cost of its oil imports. The Bank's proposal to set up an 'energy affiliate' was however sabotaged by the oil companies. Much of the Bank's lending for oil consists in assisting Third World countries in exploration, helping them to revise their investment codes to make them more attractive to the oil companies, and leaving the profitable business of oil production from proven reserves to the private (foreign) oil companies.[36]

In the special case of India, the Bank has so far persisted, against US opposition, in lending to the ONGC (the Indian state-owned Oil and Natural Gas Company). But its $400 million loan for the development of Bombay High, already explored by India which hired its own technology after the Bank had refused to help, was associated with a marked reversal in Indian policies on 'self-reliance' in oil; thus, according to the Bank's project appraisal,

> Until recently [the Government of India's] policy regarding foreign oil companies has been hesitant, and not encouraging to the oil industry. The Government has recently announced a major policy change in this regard, and intends to enter into oil exploration agreements with foreign oil companies.[37]

There is a possibility that this was window-dressing for the Board; as an Indian official, otherwise hostile to the Bank, put it, the Bank did appear to be more sympathetic than the US towards the needs of the ONGC and had made a contribution to its growth. The Bank had, for example, lent $200 million, a third of the total cost of exploration, for Krishnagodavari, and the loan had gone through the Board against the opposition of the United States. But by 1983 US pressures were so strong that whether or not the Bank would continue to lend to the ONGC was said by Indian officials, including senior officials favourably disposed to the World Bank, to be potentially 'a major block'. If the Bank responded to US pressures for joint development with the foreign oil companies, said one of them, it would be a 'real operational concern'. An official in the Prime Minister's Office said it was not up to the Bank to decide whether a project should be in the public or the private sector; he rejected the US argument that the Bank should only lend for projects which were not profitable for the private sector; on the contrary, the Bank should lend to ONGC precisely because the projects which it puts forward are profitable. As an ONGC official said, 'No country in the world leases out acreage where oil has already been found', yet this was what the US wanted India to do, and India had in fact been persuaded to offer some blocks to foreign companies where oil was known to exist. The Bank, he said, was telling the ONGC 'not to embarrass us by asking for more'. However it was clear that, if the Bank refused to lend to the public sector, India could raise commercial finance, as it had done in the past.[38] If this happens, it will be following the path trodden by Algeria which, having failed to persuade the Bank to finance oil projects in the public sector, built up its oil and gas industries without having recourse either to official assistance or to private foreign investment (see below, pp. 210–12).

The question of public sector versus private sector is also related to whether local or foreign technology is used. A publicly owned industry is in theory free to make use of local manufacturing capabilities. Of course it need not do so; the government may merely buy turn-key factories, with no input from local manufacturers, as the Algerian government was frequently criticised for doing. An Indian official in the Ministry of Steel and Mines made plain that the inflow of foreign technology was 'the country's choice', not just the fault of the Bank:

> We are subjected to very high pressure salesmanship from firms and banks; the department is flooded with Germans and British and, in the last few years, masses of foreign bankers; the Germans come with the Dresden Bank, Davy Jones with Lazard Brothers; for Hindustan Steel the British come with Williams and Glyn; the French with the BNP . . . they are infinitely more powerful than the World Bank because they have more freedom to operate, to buy up certain people, which the World Bank can't do, or doesn't do. Although the World Bank insists on imports, the others are 100 per cent worse.

Nevertheless he added that 'the stultifying of local manufacturing capacity is the greatest disservice done to us by the foreign aid agencies. If IDA stops, that will be the greatest service they can do to us.'[39]

6. The Bank and leverage

The Bank now publicly acknowledges, even advertises, its involvement in the general economic policies of Third World governments. This is a recent development; Bank publications in the past rarely alluded to such involvement. But the idea that aid agencies could do more to promote economic development through 'policy dialogue', 'leverage', 'performance criteria' and so forth gained ground over the 1960s and 1970s. Economists in the US produced quantitative evidence to back this idea:

> although there are severe difficulties of measurement, an increase in the supply of capital and in labor of unchanging quality does not explain at a maximum more than one-half of the estimated growth of gross national product (GNP) in the many countries studied.[1]

The World Bank was an influential, if covert, operator in this new fashion in aid. Its demands on governments, to increase the prices paid to peanut growers, say, or to reduce borrowing from commercial banks, or to devalue, became increasingly frequent. It began to boast, at conferences of like-minded people, that its recommendations were included in the speeches of Finance Ministers.[2] Where there existed 'elements in the government [who] are both eager and capable of taking action to improve economic performance', the World Bank could and should act to reinforce their positions within governments.[3]

It is not usually difficult to discover who the 'World Bank's men' are in any particular country. Often they have worked for the Bank, or would like to do so, and have direct or indirect links with it. They share the Bank officials' arrogance and gloss of technical fluency, in addition to the requisite ideological attitudes. In Peru, for example, the Bank's resident representative said in 1982 that he expected Peru to become the biggest recipient of the Bank's lending in the following year, not just in proportion to its national income, but in absolute terms.[4] One of the (unstated) reasons for his expectations was that the Belaúnde government which had recently taken office was dominated by the World Bank's men. Belaúnde's party, *Acción popular*, although it had won the elections, lacked membership and party organisation. Belaúnde resorted to hiring people whom many Peruvians thought of as 'practically foreigners'. Four of the key members of the economic team, including the minister of energy and mines, the president of the Central Bank and the vice-minister initially in charge of the import liberalisation programme, had worked for the World Bank. Several others, including the minister of finance, Ulloa, were associated with US private banks. Others, including the minister of labour and Belaúnde himself, had connections with the Inter-American Development Bank, a regional multilateral bank which is modelled on the World Bank. Some of them, having taken a cut in salary, obviously thought of themselves in much the same way as any aid official might: their stints in the Third World were of a temporary nature, lasting only as long as they could afford, given their 'need', for example, to put their children through Ivy League universities in the US.

In the Philippines, after President Marcos had appointed a cabinet consisting almost entirely of World Bank-orientated 'technocrats', the tide of nationalist opposition was joined by one of the President's own allies, Teodoro Valencia, who said:

> The government's worst enemies are on the side of the President. They are the ones sinking the economy to please the Americans . . . Only the small-fry Filipinos will be left to suffer the consequences of the decisions made in the midst of crisis. After we go under, they can always go to the IMF and the World Bank as officers.[5]

Indian officials, lamenting the unwillingness of their colleagues to stand up to the Bank, blamed it on the fact that they were hoping for a few years in the Bank in order to save up money to buy themselves a house for their retirement. A similar story was told by a Pakistani official; the Bank, he said, offers subtle inducements. The Bank's Economic Development Institute is specifically intended to train Third World officials in the Bank's methods; the aim is that they will go back to their own countries and apply them.

'So infiltrated with strategically-placed EDI alumni are the governments of certain less developed member countries,' say Mason and Asher, 'that some representatives of the new left profess to see in the situation evidence of neo-imperialism, of a system whereby the Bank can influence or dominate policymaking.'[6]

Clausen, clearly in response to right-wing criticisms that the 'Bank had not been aggressive enough in making its clients change their policies in return for aid' makes the fully justified claim that the Bank 'has always done many of the things which its critics now urge'.[7] There are now many statements to be found in Clausen's speeches that the Bank's project financing and its 'policy dialogue' are of equal importance. 'Policy dialogue' is the euphemism most frequently used in the Bank to describe its attempts to change governments' economic policies, especially their macro-economic policies. The Bank's 1983 *Annual Report* puts it thus:

> the transfer of resources to developing countries is only one – albeit the most visible – aspect of the Bank's development role. Its role as a partner in the dialogue with governments on overall economic policy and sectoral strategies, and as a source of technical assistance and advice is as important as its role as a lender. The deterioration in the economic climate in many of the Bank's developing member countries has increased the importance, as well as the visibility, of this advisory function. The Bank responded . . . in several ways. These have included increases in staff time spent on country economic and sectoral analyses.[8]

But up to now the invisibility of the Bank's policy dialogue has been such that even outsiders who are quite knowledgeable about the workings of the Bank have denied its existence, except in relation to Structural Adjustment Lending. This is partly because the Bank, however ardently it may desire to play a major role in the decisions of governments, cannot always get governments to listen to a mere project-financing agency and must often content itself with, for example, playing second fiddle to the IMF. It is partly also because the Bank itself has in the past been extremely unwilling to admit any involvement in attempting to influence the economic policies of governments, other than those directly connected with its projects. Thus in 1967 the Bank tried to suppress research on the subject even before it knew what the conclusions would be: 'the

Bank felt that it could operate less effectively if it was publicly known to be engaged in the business of leverage; an analogy was drawn with "secret diplomacy"'.[9] As recently as 1980, a World Bank official in Pakistan professed incomprehension at questions about the Bank's involvement in the government's economic policies.[10] Many officials believed, and some still believe, no doubt correctly, that if the actual nature and extent of the Bank's intervention in the policies of Third World governments were known, then all its treasured pretence of ideological neutrality (see below) would have to be dropped, with a corresponding diminution of its ability to promote the interests of the West. Hence the secrecy, by which many people are deluded. Hence also the fact that, even though the macro-economic policies of the World Bank are virtually identical to those of the IMF, it has so far escaped some of its unpopularity.

It remains true that the World Bank is best known as a project lending agency. This in itself partly accounts for some people's belief that the Bank changed significantly under McNamara. For the most obvious change under McNamara was in the nature of projects financed by the Bank (see p. 234). But, as Lipton and Shakow guardedly point out in an article on 'The World Bank and Poverty', in the Bank/Fund publication *Finance and Development*,

> The Bank's program, however, finances less than 2 per cent of total investment in the developing countries, and individual projects normally affect only a minority of a country's poor people. Government policies, on the other hand, have an impact on vast numbers, and on the success of projects. This makes the Bank's economic dialogue about poverty with borrower governments especially significant. Experience suggests that the Bank has been more successful at incorporating an emphasis on poverty in projects than in policy dialogue.[11]

This cautious statement allows its readers to infer that the Bank tried, in its 'dialogue' with governments, to get them to do something about poverty, but was unsuccessful. The reality is that concern in the Bank's 'policy dialogue' about the effects of government policies on poverty is, as it was in the 1960s, and as it is in the programmes of the IMF, an afterthought, something that should be attended to in the future, after the government has dealt with the more immediate problems of debt, deficits and inflation.[12] Whether in the projects themselves, marginal as they are in most countries in their effects on the poor, the Bank is 'more successful at incorporating an emphasis on poverty', is another question (see below).

The Bank's usual method of providing finance, in the form of a contribution to the cost of specific projects, does not enable it to be formally involved in the larger decisions of governments. The IMF's standby and EFF loans are specifically conditional on the adoption of certain policies and they are disbursed, in tranches, only if the IMF considers that its conditions have been adequately met. On the other hand, the Bank's project loans take an average of two years to negotiate; this in itself gives the Bank the opportunity to become involved in wider questions. Once the projects have been accepted by the Board and disbursements have begun, the Bank generally stops disbursing only if there are overdue service payments or if the conditions attached to the project are not met. But it has also been known to do so when it considers a project is 'falling apart' or that a country is 'about to go bankrupt', for example because it is following left-wing policies, and the Bank therefore wishes to 'reduce its exposure'. What it usually does is to stop negotiating new loans, or at least submitting them to the Board for approval. To give itself additional 'leverage', it relies to a great extent on the influence it hopes to have on other donors, which is one reason why it is enthusiastic about co-financing.

There have also been discussions on whether the Bank should become more deeply involved in programme lending, or quick-disbursing money which can be easily switched on and off and is also more attractive to governments because it is available for urgently needed general imports of food, raw materials and spare parts. But programme lending initially encountered hostility from the executive directors of advanced capitalist countries who foresaw a decline in exports of capital goods. The Bank agreed that they would not exceed 10 per cent of total lending.[13] The Bank, which has a large investment in the skills required for detailed project work, also presumably does not wish to abandon it. It can exercise considerable influence through the projects themselves; the conditions attached to projects frequently extend beyond the immediate project and into the sector as a whole. For example, a loan for the purchase of railway locomotives may have as a condition that rail fares are increased and the institutions responsible for running the railways are reorganised.

Shortly after the Second World War the Bank made some programme loans to European countries, and in the 1960s it made a few such loans to India and Pakistan. In the 1970s, the Bank made programme loans, in amounts ranging from 2.6 per cent to 8.8 per cent of its annual commitments, to a number of countries, including Nigeria, Bangladesh, India, South Korea, Pakistan, Romania, Egypt, Guatemala, Tanzania, Zambia, Jamaica, Lebanon, Guyana, Peru, Turkey, the Dominican Republic, Nicaragua and Uganda. Conditions were not attached to these programme loans very systematically. A 'restricted distribution' staff study on programme lending, addressed to the executive boards of the Bank and the Fund, says:

> Countries receiving program loans have normally been expected to have an acceptable medium or long-term development program . . . But increasingly . . . the Bank has been satisfied with a limited action programme . . . the loan to Peru in FY79 supported a four-year public investment program, while the loan to Turkey put particular emphasis on export promotion . . . Frequently, the existence of an economic stabilisation program formulated in the context of an IMF standby or Extended Fund Facility has helped in establishing the measures needed to achieve the objectives of the program loan . . . Several of the loans have been released in tranches, the release of the second or subsequent tranches depending on the fulfilment of undertakings specified in the program. An example is the first program loan to Jamaica in FY78 which was approved on the basis of an Emergency Production Plan, but with the requirement that a three-year public sector investment and financing program should be adopted before the second tranche was released.[14]

The Bank's programme loans were insignificant in comparison with the IMF's loans, ranging from $15 million for Tanzania to $200 million for India. But by the end of the 1970s, the deficits of developing countries were rising at an alarming rate. The Bank therefore decided it needed a more substantial instrument to deal with the problem, in the form of Structural Adjustment Lending. Structural Adjustment Lending, says the staff report:

> should not be isolated and episodic. To be effective, [the loans] should be seen to be clearly in support of fundamental adjustment policies adopted by countries . . . While the Bank's policy dialogues with its member governments are conducted in the context of overall country lending programs and not of individual operations, a country may hesitate to adopt measures involving a risk to the balance of payments (e.g. restructuring tariffs) without the assurance of additional aid disbursements extending over several years . . . a project lending usually disburses too slowly to provide the support required . . . If steps are not taken now to meet the emerging problem, there is a serious risk that domestic resource constraints in many countries will erode the very basis of the Bank's traditional project and sector lending.[15]

Another confidential document from the president and senior staff of the Bank to the executive directors, dated 9 May 1980, on the subject of 'implementation procedures', said that the agreements would contain formulations both of long-term policies and of 'those specific actions' to be undertaken within the year or other stated period, with their expected results normally to be specified in quantitative terms. 'Specific items would be identified which would serve as the basis for an interim review.' But, 'the interpretation of performance would not be mechanical . . . the major safeguard for the Bank is that satisfactory policy performance under an agreed program of action would be a precondition for subsequent structural adjustment lending.' Sometimes, 'longer term technical assistance may be required. For instance, in Kenya the Bank has seconded an economist to the Government to assist in the study of tariff reforms and export promotion.'[16]

The Bank acknowledges in the earlier document that 'the likely amount of such lending available from the Bank will be small compared to the total amount of external capital required', but hopes that 'the Bank's initiative may encourage the provision of similar assistance from other sources to those countries which are seen to be implementing appropriate policy reform measures.' And it continues:

We expect that there will be opportunities to co-finance our structural adjustment loans with both official and private sources of finance but, more important in terms of volume, we expect that sound programmes of structural adjustment, acceptable to the Bank as a basis for lending, will encourage bilateral aid agencies to expand lending for this purpose and complement and sustain lending from commercial banks for general purposes.[17]

Thus the Bank was aspiring to a role similar to the IMF's in providing a 'seal of approval' on the basis of which other lenders are to decide whether or not to lend. It is not always clear whether Bank offers of Structural Adjustment Lending constitute a promise or a threat. There are indications that Nicaragua was 'offered' a SAL in 1981 and that the Sandinistas' refusal to enter into SAL-type negotiations provided the Bank with a pretext to stop its negotiations on project lending.

The Bank's involvement in macro-economic policies is not confined to the countries which receive Structural Adjustment Lending, although the absence of SALS may indicate unwillingness by governments to get themselves too deeply involved in 'policy dialogue' with the Bank. Thus, defending itself against the charge that the geographical spread of its new structural lending had been limited, the Bank in its 1982 *Annual Report* notes:

Such limited coverage . . . reflects the fact that this form of assistance is appropriate only in those cases in which there are not only structural problems that help create balance of payments problems, but also a government that is both able to formulate and implement a credible program of reforms and wishes to have Bank financial and technical support for its program.

In cases where a government is willing but not able, the Bank will help:

As a matter of Bank policy, no country is ineligible for structural-adjustment lending only because it lacks the technical capacity to work out an adequate reform program. In such cases, the Bank remains ready to step up its country economic and sector work to assist in the design of suitable reforms. Furthermore, most structural-adjustment lending operations have been buttressed by a technical-assistance loan or credit to assist governments in both formulating and implementing programs of reform.[18]

In the absence of Structural Adjustment Lending the Bank will, as has been said, attempt to influence policies by supporting sympathetic elements within governments. It has also, as Bank officials frequently point out, accumulated considerable 'country knowledge' over the years; by which they mean such knowledge as is to be derived from the perusal of government statistics and the bullying of government officials to supply them with more statistics. The Bank produces, annually for its major clients, what it calls Country Economic Reports which usually cover the whole range of governments' economic policies. Although the Bank originally justified the reports' existence as an aid to itself in the selection of projects, they obviously have wider uses. They are not usually published. But once they have reached their grey-cover, somewhat sanitised, version, they are fairly widely available to governments, official institutions, and some libraries, and they are frequently leaked, to journalists and others. There would be little point in the Bank staff putting the effort into producing them if they were not intended to have any influence.

The reports do, in fact, contain numerous recommendations, commendations and criticisms of various aspects of governments' policies. The Bank's aim is, its officials say, to remove some of the criticisms in early drafts as a result of changes made by governments. But since the reports are sometimes written by outsiders or in any case not by the Bank officials directly involved in negotiations with governments, they may not accurately reflect the actual demands made in negotiations and may at times display more flexibility and sensitivity. Thus the Bank's 1980 country economic report on Peru implied that real wages there might have fallen too far; but in the central bank this was viewed as further evidence of the Bank's 'rhetoric' diverging from its practice; the position agreed in negotiations with the government was that wage increases should not exceed the rate of inflation.[19]

The reports contain much statistical material, sometimes more comprehensive than the governments' own statistical compilations. The Bank's staff also produce what are called Country Program Papers which are written by operational staff and restricted to circulation among senior officials within the Bank, excluding the executive board. They contain usually highly political evaluations of a government's policies and of the role that the Bank can play in influencing them. From time to time they, too, are leaked.

The economic reports are used as the major background material for the meetings of consortia and consultative groups which are organised and chaired by the World Bank. These are set up to co-ordinate and perhaps increase official aid to the Bank's favoured clients. They usually meet in Paris. In 1981–2 the Bank chaired 12 such meetings: for Bangladesh, the Caribbean Group for Co-operation in Economic Development, Colombia, India, Kenya, Madagascar, Nepal, Pakistan, the Philippines, Sri Lanka, Uganda, and Zaire; it participated in a thirteenth, for Indonesia, which was sponsored by the Netherlands. At other times meetings have been organised for other countries, for example, Peru. The Bank's economic reports provide estimates of the external financing needs of these countries. Since they also express approval or disapproval of the government's policies, governments have an incentive to act in such a way that the report presented to the aid co-ordination meeting shows them in a good light. The meetings are used as occasions for bilateral donors, sometimes reticent in their normal dealings with governments, to air their prejudices. Frequently these coincide with those of the Bank, and reinforce their impact. As the us Treasury report on the multilateral development banks puts it, 'the Bank has sought to influence borrowers' policies indirectly through the establishment of inter-governmental Consultative Groups on particular borrowing countries. Through these groups, the Bank attempts to rally other donors around its recommendations.'[20]

Rehman Sobhan, in his book on foreign aid to Bangladesh, says that the Bangladesh Planning Commission, of which he was a member from 1972 to 1974, was reluctant to get involved in a Bank-chaired aid consortium, believing that it would do nothing to increase the level of aid and was

more of a ritual to appraise the Bank's report on the Bangladesh economy. Those donors who would not dream of making comments on Bangladesh's policies during bilateral negotiations tended to feel much freer in the consortium to ventilate their grievances and prejudices. The tone for this was set by the Bank's document. If this was

favourable then the consortium became a laudatory ritual
. . . Since the Bank was hardly a disinterested observer of
the Bangladesh scene and was a very integral part of the
international and national dialectic being played out in
Bangladesh, it merely infused less conscious donors with the
Bank's particular prejudices.[21]

An example of a very favourable Bank introduction to a consultative group meeting is provided by its 1981 'consultative group
presentation' on Peru which, as Peruvians said, was so complimentary it 'might as well have been written by the government'.[22]

There have been times and places where the Bank has virtually
assumed the economic policy-making functions of governments.
Sobhan's book is about aid to Bangladesh in general. But the
whole of Chapter 7 of the book, from which the following
quotations are taken, is devoted to 'The role of the World Bank in
Bangladesh'. It demonstrates clearly the 'ascendancy' of the
World Bank in the aid process and the 'Godfather'-like eminence
of World Bank staff who set themselves up as authorities on the
politics and economy of Bangladesh. Sobhan explains that the
initial reluctance of the Bangladesh authorities, after the liberation
in 1972, to concede hegemony over its economic affairs to the
World Bank was partly the result of the Bank's identification with
the Ayub regime in Pakistan during the 1960s where,

> along with the Harvard Advisory Group, they conceived
> and underwrote Pakistan's development strategy . . . During
> this period, the Bank occupied an honoured position in the
> external relations of the Ayub regime and its representatives
> enjoyed the privileges of a visiting head of state, waited
> upon hand and foot by the Pakistan Planning Commission.

When McNamara first came to Bangladesh, he was met with
'humiliation':

> Here was he, the President of one of the most powerful
> international institutions in the world, coming personally to
> this destitute, shattered country as an angel of mercy
> anxious to take Bangladesh under the Bank's bounty. He
> expected the overwhelmed Government to lay down a red
> carpet for him and his Bank. Instead he was met at the
> airport by the Governor of the Bangladesh Bank . . . When

asked by McNamara what the Bank could do for
Bangladesh, Tajuddin Ahmed, with tongue in cheek . . .
said, 'We need bullocks, I wonder if the Bank can supply
that.'

But, 'Bangladesh was no revolutionary China or Vietnam determined to pull itself up by its bootstraps . . .' After initial resistance,
Bangladesh, too, succumbed to what Sobhan calls 'the aid
narcotic'.

The Bank, for its part, resorted to writing a series of 'potentially
damaging and frequently tendentious reports':[23]

Bank missions went around eliciting their own information
and then wrote a preliminary report which was known as a
'Green Cover' by the colour of its jacket. This was
submitted to Bangladesh for comments before it was put
out in a final form as a 'Grey Cover'. The problem arose
from the fact that the 'Green Covers' were informally
obtained by the concerned agencies of the
consortium/donor countries resident in Bangladesh or with
direct access to the Bank in Washington . . . The 'Green
Cover' reports really became political tracts designed to
castigate the policies, institutions, personnel and politics of
Bangladesh. For example [one] report . . . was loaded with
polemical and unsubstantiated observations about industrial
policy and its administration . . . a statement saying 'New
men had access to political power for the first time with
little conception of how to use it for purposes other than
self aggrandisement'[24] would make good copy for an
opposition leader writer . . . The relevant issue was not
whether there was not some basis of truth in the Bank's
report but why the Bank abdicated a decade of practice in
writing reports on the Pakistan economy to embrace the
idiom of the political opposition to the regime. There has
been no lack of corruption or inefficiency in Pakistan,
Indonesia, Kenya, Thailand or other favoured Bank clients.

Eventually, however, the government made 'surrenders on the
policy front': devaluation, and concessions to the private sector.
The Bank still had both allies and enemies in the government:

Whilst some in the administrations welcomed [the Bank's]
interventions to reinforce their position, others resented the
fact that the Bank projected itself as a source of original
wisdom . . . when elements within the administration had
already made these points in internal debate . . .
    The new Planning Minister was an old friend who had built
up intimate contacts with the Bank during his tenure as
Finance Minister of East Pakistan during the Ayub regime
of the 1960s. In the top echelons of policy-making, as
advisers and heads of ministries, were people who had not
only worked closely with the Bank in the 1960s but had
retained their links even in the post-liberation period. No
longer was there any attempt to contain Bank intervention . . . The Bank and Fund have now, under cover of
their multilateral format, emerged as highly effective proxies
for the Western powers. Their staff are chosen for their
ideological commitment to the prevailing Bank philosophy
and deployed to infiltrate or impose their will on dependent
regimes. The inroads made by the Bank could, however,
only become effective because of the structural weaknesses
within the regime which compel them to turn to external
sources rather than their own people to resolve their
endemic economic crises. In such regimes it is not difficult
for the Bank to pick up elements within the regime and
polity who are bound to them by ideological and material
interests, who are willing to act as surrogates for the Bank's
position in domestic debates, and to use the Bank's
influence as a political resource to bolster their own
positions within the polity.

Another book, *Development Debacle: The World Bank in the
Philippines*, is devoted to the World Bank and based on massive
quantities of leaked World Bank documents.[25] It shows, in even
greater detail, the extent of World Bank involvement in the
policies of a particular country, described in Bank documents as a
'country of concentration' set to receive, after the imposition of
martial law in 1972 and the scope which that gave for the exercise
of 'almost absolute power in the field of economic development',
amounts of money from the Bank 'higher than average for
countries of similar size and income'. By 1976 it was possible for

the Bank to assert, in its confidential Country Program Paper, that 'The Bank's basic economic report proposes a framework for future development, which the government has accepted as a basis for its future economic plans'. The process culminated in the creation of a 'World Bank cabinet', composed of technocrats close to the Bank and the IMF, and with almost unfettered power to impose the economic solutions favoured by the Bank.[26]

There are many other countries in which the Bank's involvement in general economic policies, usually alongside the IMF, is considerable. For example, a leaked Country Program Paper (CPP) on Haiti, dated May 20 1983, (from which the quotes that follow are drawn), requests a real increase in IDA lending to Haiti in the years 1984–8 of 20 per cent over the preceding four years' lending. It justifies the request on the grounds that Haiti

> has chosen a more liberal approach to economic and political management . . . Technocrats in increasing numbers have been included in cabinets . . . Haiti's present economic policies represent a definite improvement over a long tradition of chaotic management of economic and fiscal affairs and contempt for the needs of the Haitian population.

There is now, the Bank says, 'a pronounced receptivity to external advice'. In 1982, 'a major fiscal reform was executed at the prodding and insistence of and with technical support from IDA and IMF'.

However the government subsequently, in response to the destruction wrought by Hurricane Allen, resorted to

> highly expansionary fiscal policies relying heavily on central bank financing. Such a combination led to strong pressures on the balance of payments, pressures that were exacerbated by the confidence factor as Haiti exceeded the limits of an EFF Arrangement with the IMF.
>
> Under strong pressure from the international financial community and from governments of traditional donor countries, the President of Haiti and the group surrounding him were made to understand that continued aid to Haiti would require major policy corrections. As a result, President Duvalier appointed a strong and responsible

economic cabinet – notwithstanding the replacement for political reasons of a key finance minister after only a few months – that realised full well that, because of its openness, its limited productive capacity, narrow export base and low level of exchange reserves, the Haitian economy cannot afford excess demand pressures. Extremely tight fiscal and monetary policies were adopted in May of 1982 under a new stand-by arrangement with the IMF.

The Haitian authorities' affirmative response to the position taken by the international community on this occasion was encouraging; more recently, the Government has also responded in an equal manner to external recommendations related to development policies and institutional reforms. This attitude is strongly conditioned by the intensity of the policy dialogue the main international donors are conducting with Government – a dialogue which needs to be sustained even during times of economic improvement in order to strengthen the Haitian long-term commitment to economic and social reform.

On the occasion of the first Subgroup Meeting on Haiti within the framework of the Caribbean Group for Co-operation in Economic Development [one of the consultative groups chaired by the Bank] on June 15 1982, the Haitian delegation outlined the measures and policy changes that were to be implemented under its Stand-by Arrangement.

During the same Subgroup Meeting, the Haitian delegation announced medium and longer term policy measures that had been discussed earlier with the World Bank . . . In order to support this program, the Government has repeatedly asked IDA to consider a SAL. The idea behind this request is to create the financial capability to continue with the economic reform program after the termination of the IMF Stand-by Arrangement.

In the co-ordination of foreign aid, which is apparently encouraged by the government, the CPP claims that 'IDA leadership is looked upon as a source of technical and managerial expertise . . . Only IDA and IDB are able to sustain long-term sector involvement and efficient institution-building.' USAID works with private volunteer groups, and 'Germany ánd France increasingly channel their capital development assistance as co-financing support to IDA projects. With both Germany and France, aid co-ordination is very successful . . .' The Bank also hopes to achieve co-financing arrangements with the EEC, OPEC and IFAD (International Fund for Agricultural Development).

> A Country Economic Memorandum . . . will be used for a probable aid-coordinating exercise . . . in the context of the Haiti Subgroup of the Caribbean Group for Economic Development . . . In general, IDA's involvement in Haiti will continue to be the traditional project approach complemented by strong technical assistance. But sector credits and/or structural adjustment operations may prove to be indicated to support particularly strong, longer-term Haitian efforts to redress sector or structural imbalances.

There are of course many other cases of Bank involvement in governments' policies. It is clear that the Bank does in fact intervene wherever it can in the economic policy-making of governments, and that it is particularly pleased when it encounters 'a pronounced receptivity to external advice', as the Haiti CPP put it. Its ideal situation is probably a receptive government, staffed with 'technocrats', although one Bank official interviewed did express some reservations about the value of working with such people, who are unlikely to have a strong political base in their own country.[28] In repressive dictatorships, however, this does not matter so much: for example in both Chile and the Philippines, Bank documents welcome the virtually unlimited power their governments possess to carry out 'sound economic policies'.

7. The Bank and ideology

A basic code of conduct

The Bank's view of what constitute sound and desirable economic policies is still not as well known as it ought to be. For example, in 1982 the British Labour Party published a report entitled *Development Co-operation*. It contained some powerful criticisms of the IMF, including a case study on Jamaica, which quotes complaints in internal IMF documents that the government was abandoning 'the basic tenets of the [IMF] programme, viz, reliance on the market mechanism and on the private sector to effect recovery', and concluded that 'the Fund was no longer playing neutral finance or even political economy but straight politics'.[1] In its section on the World Bank, however, the Labour Party says it needs to decide whether to make a substantial increase in its contribution to multilateral institutions. The report continues:

> Ten years ago, Teresa Hayter produced a damning report
> . . . which suggested that [the Bank's] contribution to the
> Third World was 'negative'. There was a good deal of
> evidence to support this claim – the Bank strongly
> encouraged 'free enterprise' and especially the use of private
> foreign capital . . . Since then, however, the Bank has
> produced a much more radical approach to the problem of
> the poorest countries, and is now concerned to improve the
> position of the most disadvantaged section of the
> population through a policy of 'redistribution with growth'
> . . .
>
> In the light of these developments, IDA's claim for
> additional resources seems to be a strong one. The
> American commitment to the bank is now very suspect, so

that its progressive initiatives will require the strongest support, both financial and intellectual, from other industrial countries if it is to be maintained. We should therefore make an appropriate contribution to its funding, and use our influence on its board of directors to support the progressive policies which it has been developing, and also encourage it to support forms of socialist organisation where these can make a visible economic contribution to Third-World development.[2]

This is flying in the face of all the evidence of what the Bank is and can be expected to be, so long as the sources of its finance are what they are. There are some basic tenets of Bank philosophy which have been consistent throughout its history and undented in its last ten years. These are: support for reliance on market forces and the private sector; encouragement to foreign private investment and good treatment of existing foreign investments; support for the principles of free trade and comparative advantage; aversion to the use of controls on prices, imports and movements of capital; aversion to subsidies and support for the principle of 'full cost recovery' on the projects it finances and public investments in general; support for financial stabilisation policies to be achieved by austerity programmes of the IMF variety, including overall reductions in demand and devaluation; and the requirement that debts be serviced and repaid.

A Bank official, writing in 1968 to say that 'a major revision' to my draft would be necessary, identified 'a sort of code of conduct' demanded by the Bank, to which he thought it was 'difficult to take exception', including: 'measures conducive to a larger flow of private capital and public funds'; 'not . . . too much inflation'; 'full-cost pricing of projects to which [the Bank] lends'; 'not . . . large and rapidly growing administrative expenditures'; 'not . . . administrative controls over production and prices'; 'a financial plan for [public investment programs] which does not call for too much suppliers credit financing or too much printing of money'; and 'service payments on . . . external debt'.[3] The list remains valid. Requirements concerning the alleviation of poverty or the distribution of income were not, and still are not, part of this basic code, except in relation to projects, and then only formally and with dubious effect (see below).

An attempt to summarise the Bank's concerns is also made in the US Treasury Report which says:

> While it is difficult to summarize the wide variety of policy reform urged upon developing countries by the World Bank, a review, such as that submitted for the record in 1981 at the request of the Subcommittee on Foreign Operations of the House Committee on Appropriations, of the individual country reports prepared by the Bank staff reveals that the advice is generally along neo-classical economic lines. On the external side, the reports emphasize the need for open international trading systems, realistic exchange rates, and the use of world market prices to reflect real opportunity costs. On the internal side, there is an emphasis on appropriate resource allocation (i.e., in accordance with true costs and benefits), realistic pricing policies, cost-recovery, and the maintenance of sensible fiscal and monetary policies.[4]

The priority attached by the Bank to the repayment of debt has been described (see above, pp. 77–81) as has its attachment to the supposed virtues of foreign private investment (pp. 87–93). But perhaps the clearest demonstration of the true nature of the Bank is to be derived from the fact that it differs so little from the IMF in the basic policies it supports.

The World Bank and the IMF

The Bank's co-operation with the Fund has recently become more intense, and somewhat more institutionalised. But it is not new. The two institutions originally shared a building in Washington. When this building became too small for them, the IMF built a new one across the road, and the Bank subsequently built another one next to it. They have always co-operated closely and shared information; and 'since 1963, however effective or ineffective staff co-operation may have been, relations at the top have been close and amicable'.[5]

With the formalisation of the Bank's attempts to exercise leverage in Structural Adjustment Lending, the Bank's relationship with the Fund has become even closer. The Bank is aware that this may be thought to imply an incursion into IMF territory and is anxious to ensure that the policies demanded by each of them do not conflict. In its 1982 *Annual Report* the Bank says that a recent staff report had noted that 'experience over the past two years had shown that the Bank's structural adjustment lending operations and the IMF programs were, in practice, both complementary and mutually reinforcing'. A 1980 unpublished staff report to the Boards of Governors of the Bank and the Fund says:

Since lending for structural adjustment would normally address macro-economic policy issues related to the balance of payments, the need to consult the IMF is readily apparent . . . Fund staff have co-operated closely in processing program loans. In several cases a Bank staff member joined the Fund consultation or review team (e.g., Turkey, Jamaica and Guyana). In other instances, the Bank's program loan appraisal mission overlapped with the Fund's consultation or review mission in the field (e.g., Sudan and Zambia). It is normal practice for the Bank and the Fund staff to consult each other closely in Washington and share information and views. *The Bank usually regards the success of the short-term economic stabilisation or recovery program (on which the IMF standby arrangements are based) as important for the fulfilment of a government's medium-term investment or development program.* For its part, the IMF relies on the Bank's judgements on the appropriateness of a country's medium-term investment program which provides a context for stabilisation measures and is particularly relevant to Extended Fund Facility (EFF) programs (emphasis added).[6]

This co-operation has continued, and it is now usual for a member of the Bank's staff to be attached to Fund missions with the formal purpose of pronouncing on the government's investment programme, its 'appropriateness', and how it can best be cut. Similarly, the Bank is supposed to consult with the Fund before it makes recommendations and demands in fields which are clearly recognised to be in the competence of the Fund. This applies particularly to devaluation, a measure beloved of both institutions. Mason and Asher say:

Although this understanding has been violated on a number of occasions, with a resulting protest from the managing director of the Fund, these violations are exceptional. Discussions of

> exchange rate policy in the Bank's country reports are cleared
> with the Fund, and in general there is a pooling of views of
> Bank and Fund staff members on aspects of exchange rate
> policy of interest to both organizations. It is understood that
> the actual negotiation of changes in exchange rates is a
> prerogative of the Fund and must be conducted in strict
> confidence.[7]

This did not prevent the Bank, in the late 1960s, claiming
devaluation in India as its major achievement in the field of
'leverage'.

Bank and Fund officials are unwilling to talk about cases where
there have been conflicts between them. De Larosière, asked after
one of his press conferences at the 1983 Annual Meetings whether
the Bank had been critical of the severity of IMF programmes, said
he had always found the Bank 'very co-operative'.[8] What is fairly
certain is that there are no consistent ideological differences
between the two institutions. Both are committed to the usual list
of orthodox neo-classical desiderata: reliance on market mechanisms and the price mechanism, no controls, and especially
import liberalisation (see below).

On perhaps the most important question that might arise
between them, that of the relationship between short-term financial
stabilisation and long-term growth, the potential differences have
been simply resolved by the convenient fact that the Bank shares
with the IMF the view that short-term stabilisation is an essential
prerequisite to long-term growth. Indeed in 1959 a Bank official
wrote that the 'Bank might be even more interested than the Fund
in a diligent search for stabilisation measures outside the field of
investment if only to minimize the cutback that might be necessary
in the size of the investment program'.[9] Mason and Asher
categorically endorse this: 'Indeed the Bank has generally accepted
the Fund proposition that stabilisation is a necessary though not
sufficient condition for growth'. They are moreover critical of it.
Whereas the Fund, they say, is supposed to be concerned with
short-term matters, the Bank

> has no such defense . . . If the Bank and the Fund have not
> moved further away from relatively short-term considerations,
> it may be the result of an overemphasis on stabilisation as a
> necessary, though not sufficient, condition of growth – to the

neglect of the equally important proposition that, in many situations, growth is a necessary, though not sufficient, condition for effective stabilisation.[10]

The Bank's concern with public investment, or the 'supply side', is usually *within* ceilings imposed by the Fund, possibly after discussions with the Bank. Officials are unable, or possibly unwilling, to supply specific evidence that these ceilings are contested by the Bank, even though they may at times feel that their own projects are threatened by them. They have responded in part to this latter problem by what the Bank calls its Special Action Programme under which the Bank is willing, as a temporary measure, to provide a higher proportion of the projects' costs itself.

To the extent that there are differences between the two institutions, the differences are probably random: they depend on the personalities of individual mission chiefs and directors of departments, rather than on any systematic differences in institutional ideology. There may well be cases where World Bank officials take a 'softer' view than that of their IMF counterparts, especially outside the notoriously reactionary Latin American and Caribbean departments of the Bank.[11] Tanzania was said to be such a case, although Bank officials were unwilling, or unable, to supply any evidence that this was so,[12] and the Bank's position on Tanzania has clearly hardened (see below, p. 208). Elsewhere, the reverse may equally be true. A senior Bank official, answering questions in 1981 about the nature of conditionality in Structural Adjustment Lending, said that it was often linked to (more quantifiable) agreement with the Fund. Where the government had an agreement with the Fund, he said, there was no need for the Bank to make its own separate agreements covering the same ground. But it would offer comments: sometimes the Fund was 'less stringent'; the Fund was 'a little bit too easy-going these days'; its Managing Director had 'an expansionist approach'.[13] According to another source,[14] the Bank's staff 'viewed with dismay' the relaxation of the Fund's attitude on devaluation in the late seventies and early eighties; but of course the Fund's attitude has since hardened (see above, pp. 59–60).

An IMF official tells the story of being invited to a meeting with Bank country economists. He embarked on a defence of the thesis that IMF stand-by programmes are not damaging to growth. He was told that the Bank was much more worried that the Fund was giving countries too much leeway and was thus 'pulling the rug from under their feet.' Other IMF officials have said that there have been 'some cases where we have given countries more leash – and *vice versa*', and other cases where the World Bank has insisted that the IMF insist on devaluation, and 'then done something messy themselves and made us look foolish'. Bolivia, Ghana and Senegal were cited, in 1981, as cases where 'Bank/Fund co-ordination was falling apart'. In another case, that of Guyana, the problem was simply that the Bank 'changed its mind' about the advisability of financing a project on political grounds: the project was located in a disputed border area and somehow neither the Bank nor the Fund had realised that this was so. But the Fund lamented that its 'whole programme had been based on the assumption of the Bank's programme and a lot of assurances from the Bank that it would be heavily involved, and it all came to nought after a couple of months'.[15]

Since the IMF's involvement in the destabilisation of the Manley government in Jamaica is well known and well documented, it is interesting to note that the Bank too played its part, or feels that it did. In the 1980 staff report quoted above, pp. 98–9, the Bank explains the tying-in of its programme lending in Jamaica with that of the IMF as follows:

The possibility of linking the Fund's credit tranche conditions with the Bank's program loan disbursements was discussed by the Executive Directors in April 1977, but the only instance in which this was attempted was the first program loan to Jamaica. In this case it was stipulated that the first $10 million of the loan would be disbursed only if Jamaica met the eligibility criteria for drawing down the second tranche of the IMF standby, and disbursement of the remaining $20 million of the loan was to be conditional on Jamaica being eligible to draw down the third tranche. However, the standby arrangement was replaced shortly afterwards by a three-year Extended Fund Facility, so that the link became inoperative.

The extended facilities offered by the IMF are aimed at establishing conditions which ensure sustained development. EFF operations have been mounted in two of the countries which have received program loans from the Bank in the period under review (Egypt and Jamaica), and experience has shown that the activities of the two institutions, so far from competing with each other, tend to be mutually supportive . . . short-term stabilisation measures have generally been necessary for the success of the longer-term development programs which the Bank's lending has been designed to support.[16]

The Bank's linking of its programme loan to the Jamaican government's compliance with IMF conditions in 1977/8 came at the time when, as already mentioned (p. 49), the IMF used a technical infringement of one of its conditions as the opportunity to impose a drastic change of policies on the Manley government. Bank officials who were working on Jamaica confirmed that although the Bank 'went along with a number of things' in Jamaica, it was 'not more supportive of Manley' and not 'softer' than the Fund. After Jamaica's break with the Fund in 1980, the Bank also ceased to have a close relationship with the Manley government, and there were no new project commitments from May 1979 until April 1981, after Seaga took office, although processing of loans continued so that the projects would be ready to submit to the Board 'when things were okay'; there was no formal decision not to submit to the Board, but it was 'difficult to support a programme which was built on the assumption of increased commercial arrears'; it could not be considered a 'consistent' programme. Manley's decision to break with the Fund in 1980, the officials considered, was a political rather than an economic one; the hard decisions had all been taken, the Fund expected agreement to be reached, and was taken aback when the government broke off negotiations. The Fund was 'incredibly flexible' in Jamaica, 'incredibly soft'. However, when Seaga took office, he 'put together a very substantial package of foreign aid'; Manley's claim that Seaga had got a better deal from the IMF than he had was 'by and large correct'. The new government had changed very little but 'the confidence of the private sector was increasing fast'.[17]

As for the question of basic needs, they did not figure in the Bank's dialogue in Jamaica. 'Manley introduced a number of social programmes which probably went beyond what Jamaica could afford'.[18] Hugh Small, the Jamaican who took over as

Finance Minister after the break with the IMF, held up a copy of the Bank's *World Development Report*, which was all about 'basic needs', at the 1980 Bank/Fund Annual Meetings, and said, 'Look, this is not consistent with what the Fund is recommending; why don't you two get together?' The reality is that the two institutions do get together, and they agree that while attention to poverty is all very fine, now is not the time. 'The vast majority of ldcs [less developed countries] have a serious balance of payments problem', as Bank officials put it, 'which means there is less for social expenditures'.[19] There always is; except in Cuba, Grenada (before the US invasion), Nicaragua . . .

In the key case of Chile, there were no very important differences between the two institutions. As was the case for the IMF (see above, pp. 52–6), Chilean free market policies under Pinochet came close to the World Bank's ideal. When Allende was elected, negotiations on projects which had been far advanced under Frei were stopped. They were resumed later as a result, Bank officials say, of 'political pressure from the Scandinavians'. But the projects did not get to the Board until after the coup. According to one official, 'within 60 per cent of Bank opinion, Allende's policies had gone beyond an acceptable range of minimal rationality; the magnitude of atrociousness of the economic policy-making was such that the Bank could not lend to Chile'. The same official volunteered, however, that a case could be made that the Bank had resumed lending in a big way to Turkey at a time when things were equally 'out of control'.[20]

When Allende was overthrown, the Bank enthusiastically welcomed Pinochet's 'hard decisions'. In its 1975 report on Chile it said:

> The Chilean government has made the hard policy decisions required, given its precarious balance of payments and international reserve positions, and has met its international debt service obligations, while at the same time introducing certain fundamental reforms that lay at the basis for resuming economic growth. It has gone a long way towards rationalising the public sector budgetary process, and opening the domestic economy to the opportunities and competition of the world economy. It has implemented a major reform of the tax system and instituted significant steps towards the

modernisation of the financial system. These measures are consistent with the recommendations made repeatedly by the Bank and other international institutions over the past decade.

After describing the Chilean government's economic objectives, stressing the establishment of the base for market-orientated, 'outward looking' growth and policies including divestment of most expropriated assets, sharp reduction of government expenditure and reduced import tariffs, the same report concludes categorically: 'These objectives and policies, essentially consistent with the recommendations of both the Bank and the Fund, have been steadfastly pursued since September 1973'.[21]

The criticisms of human rights violations under the Pinochet regime, especially in the United States under Carter, caused a temporary pause in Bank lending to Chile in the late 1970s. But the Bank made two loans, amounting to $60 million, to Chile in 1977 *after* the US Congress had cut US bilateral and military aid to Chile, and by 1981 its lending was up again.[22] Moreover it did not allow the mounting criticism of violations of human rights, in Washington as well as elsewhere, to diminish its enthusiasm for Chilean economic policies: 'In terms of economic efficiency', said a senior Bank official in 1981, there was 'no question' the Bank should be lending more, but it was not lending as much as it would like to 'because of pressures from Board members'; 'whatever you may say about the politics, there have been remarkable achievements in efficiency', he added.[23] Possibly the most important member of the Chilean economic team known as the 'Chicago boys' was Jorge Cauas; he was Minister of Finance from late 1974 and given the rank of 'superminister', in charge of centralising all fiscal and monetary policy, in 1975, in time to preside over the famous 'shock treatment'. Cauas was formerly a senior official in the World Bank. Another Bank official, currently in a senior operational position in the Bank, who was among those who claimed to have struggled, unsuccessfully, for the Bank to lend to Allende, nevertheless in 1981 described Allende's policies as an 'economic disaster', quoting Chou en Lai to the effect that the wage increases under Allende were unwarranted, and then spoke of the 'very impressive economic team' and 'great economic successes' of the Pinochet regime; admittedly, he said, they were accompanied by hardship, but it was quite difficult to see any alternative, given that everything had been destroyed under Allende. And in any case, there was less hardship now.[24]

These are the views of somebody on the 'left' in the Bank, relatively speaking, and there is little doubt that these views were and are widespread in the Bank. The Bank published a 582-page Report on Chile in January 1980; unusually, since the Bank's country economic reports are not now written for publication. In the Report's Summary and Conclusions it said, in what sounds like a litany of Bank desiderata:

> The Pinochet Government, which took power on September 11 1973, made a clear break with the development approach of the preceding four decades. The import-substitution model of the past was rejected in favour of opening Chile to the world economy. The present authorities view the proper economic role of government as one of setting the overall rules of the game and otherwise facilitating the allocative decisions of the private sector. The State is to play a 'subsidiary' part, intervening only where there exist clear divergencies of social and private benefits and costs or to attack the causes and relieve the effects of 'extreme poverty'. Preferred policy tools are those which are general and indirect and minimize distortions to the price system. At this stage the goal of improved economic efficiency is given highest priority. Improving the efficiency of government programs – particularly that of social programs – is an important objective. The present poverty emphasis is directed towards reducing absolute poverty.

> Accordingly, since September 1973, virtually all prices, including interest rates, have been progressively freed; most tax and subsidy distortions to relative prices have been removed; tariff and non-tariff barriers have been drastically reduced, the exchange rate massively devalued and a crawling peg re-established, exchange controls have been largely eliminated, and foreign investment is being actively encouraged. In addition, reforms have been introduced in the tax structure, public sector budgetary process and banking legislation; land expropriations were ended and by mid-1978 individual titles had been issued to some 37,000 peasant farmers; and most of the enterprises taken over by the Allende

government have been returned to the private sector. In one of the few exceptions to the general aversion to subsidies, a massive reforestation program was undertaken which will approximately quadruple Chile's long-fiber forest resources by the late 1990s. Programs in the social area are being restructured in an effort to better identify and more efficiently reach the truly needy while eliminating subsidies to the middle and upper income groups . . .

In the mission's judgement many of the policies introduced since 1973 have opened the door to a more rapid and sustained growth of output and employment and to a steady reduction of Chile's historical dependence on a single primary export commodity. *Many of these structural reforms are consistent with advice long offered Chile by the World Bank and other international institutions* (emphasis added).[25]

The Report could not ignore the increasingly massive concentration of wealth in Chile, and suggested 'a review of the adequacy of existing anti-trust law and its enforcement, with particular attention to the interlocking ownership of industrial, financial and commercial enterprises', while noting that: 'the Government places greater reliance on the elimination of market distortions and the opening of economy to foreign competition'. Bank officials say that the criticisms of 'asset concentration' were stronger in the original report, and were toned down as a result of protests by the Chilean government. And, since attention to the problems of poverty and income distribution were obligatory in reports written during the McNamara period, the Report has something to say about them. Its comments on these subjects come, as usual, at the end of its Summary and Conclusions. They are critical of previous governments' efforts to alleviate poverty which, the Bank says, resulted in 'severe distortion' and benefitted the urban middle class. They applaud the present government's strategy of 'remedial services carefully targetted at identified groups or individuals rather than on general programmes of price controls or subsidies which distort market incentives and are available to everyone'. They say that 'lack of data' makes it impossible to determine what effect recent policies have had on the distribution of income. But 'significant and promising innovations have been introduced', and more needs to be done. Unemployment is a 'nagging problem' but should be improved with faster growth; the 'education and training components' of the emergency employment program 'could be enriched'.[26]

In the main body of the Report there is also a final section entitled 'The distribution of income' (pp. 274–80), which has more of the same. It adds that the Pinochet government, like Thatcher's, has a 'preference for contracting the actual delivery of services to the private sector on the basis of competitive bidding. In implementing this new approach, significant and promising innovations have been introduced . . .' And the Bank, like the IMF, thinks that wages should be lower. Under the heading 'Wage and Employment Policies', the Report notes that:

> One important exception to the general policy of non-intervention in pricing decisions is the continuing legal adjustment of economy-wide wages and salaries . . . This effort to protect and improve the earnings of the employed may have come, however, at some cost to employment . . . It would seem propitious to begin the transition toward a market determination of wages through a revitalised process of collective bargaining.

The Bank thus appears to believe that, now that unemployment and repression have taken their toll of the Chilean working class, leaving wage bargaining to the unions might result in lower wages than 'legal adjustment'.

Finally, the Report notes that the present system of taxation, 'must have had a very adverse impact on Chile's poor'. The Report hopes that when, in future, the burden of taxation can be reduced, 'first attention [will] be given to lowering the very high burden of indirect taxes, principally, the VAT'. However, 'the mission does not now recommend any major changes of the tax system towards greater progressivity' (p. 280).

By the time the Bank's 1983 *World Development Report* was published, the Bank could comment that 'rigid adherence to policy prescriptions can be hazardous: Chile has provided an example of this danger' (p. 70). But the failure of the Chilean experience was by then plain for all to see (see above, section on IMF, p. 55).

In Chile, even though both institutions wanted the government to go further in the reduction of real wages, there was not much need for them to impose 'hard decisions' on the government: it was taking them of its own volition. Elsewhere, the Bank and the IMF have co-operated in trying to impose 'discipline'. They worked together in Turkey, helping to bring about another 'dramatic turnaround' in the sense of re-imposing financial equilibrium through austerity, at the price, again, of harsh military dictatorship and declining real wages, employment and investment (see p. 45). More recently, Nigeria has been, as a Bank official put it, 'touted as a wonderful example of Bank/Fund co-operation'.[27] It is clear that it is also an example of co-ordinated pressures. Both the Bank and the Fund were determined that the re-elected Shagari government should devalue the *naira*. According to the *Financial Times*, virtually all Nigerian officials, including the newly appointed team of 'technocrats', were bitterly opposed to the idea, whatever its merits, mainly on the grounds that it would give a further twist to the inflationary spiral.[28] According to a World Bank official, the IMF asked the Bank what they thought about the size of devaluation required; the Bank, which had 'done the work', suggested a figure; the Fund said 'that seems okay to us'.[29] '"The World Bank is doing the dirty work for the IMF", says one top official, only half seriously. "I think they are engaged in a conspiracy."'[30] The *Financial Times* claims that deals with the IMF and the Bank are crucial to resolving Nigeria's debt problems and that:

> the key question is what conditions will be attached . . . In addition to the $2bn Nigeria hopes to get from the IMF as extended credit, officials here also hope to qualify for a loan from the compensatory financing facility . . . From the Bank, Nigeria is seeking a structural adjustment loan of up to $500m, although Washington officials suggest $350m would be more realistic. Both institutions are clearly taking tough negotiating positions.[31]

The other demands of the two institutions, apparently less problematic for the Nigerian government than devaluation, included the reorganisation and privatisation of public enterprises (a particular concern of the Bank), cutting public expenditure and stopping most new public investment projects, including the planned investment in steel.

One IMF official, asked whether the Bank was at times tougher than the Fund, thought it was, and gave the case of the Philippines as an example. He had been extremely impressed, he said, with the rigour and thoroughness of the import liberalisation programme which the Bank had caused the government of the Philippines to adopt.[32] It appears that the Bank succeeded where the IMF had failed. The IMF, which negotiates with the Central Bank, came up against a brick wall: the then President of the Philippines Central Bank was an economic nationalist, with close connections with the Philippines business community, and was not willing to inflict on them the bankruptcies that would result from an import liberalisation programme; the Bank, however, which was able to negotiate over a longer period with a number of different ministries and officials, managed to achieve the result desired by both institutions.[33]

This is, again, borne out by a quotation in a *Financial Times* article by Anatole Kaletsky:

> Mr. Ernest Stern, the Bank's senior vice-president for operations, summed it up like this: 'The differences in procedures reflect differences in the nature and scope of each institution's operations. The Fund's involvement is restricted to a single type of operation – balance of payments support – with relatively infrequent and limited staff visits to a country, while the Bank has many missions relating to a wide range of operations. Fund support is generally – though not always – seen as a rescue operation in response to a crisis. In these circumstances failure to a Fund arrangement [sic] is likely to have grave consequences for a country's creditworthiness.
>
> 'The Bank's individual SAL [structural adjustment lending] operations have a much lower profile and are negotiated at a less intense pace. The consequences of failure to reach agreements are therefore much less serious. In these circumstances negotiations tend to be less confrontational and it may be possible to achieve a more fundamental government commitment to reform.'[34]

There is no doubt that governments are increasingly confronted with what Kaletsky calls 'this two-pronged approach'. The Bank may often exaggerate its role; its pressures may be insignificant compared to those of the IMF. For example, whereas the Bank's role in the devaluation and import liberalisation measures in India in 1966 were prominent and notorious, it did not play any leading role in the negotiations between the IMF and the government of India over the SDR 5 billion EFF agreed in 1981. But its officials claimed that the IMF's initial report was largely based on the Bank's 'country economic knowledge', since the Fund had little experience of India. And the Bank, unlike the left in India, had no criticisms of the IMF agreement and fully supported the moves towards import liberalisation which were a major feature of it. Similarly, a Peruvian who had been much involved in negotiations with the Bank and the IMF during the 1970s, asked whether the Bank was more willing to be sympathetic to the difficulties of governments, said they 'always try and give that image, and stay off fiscal and monetary questions, but actually they work it all out with the Fund beforehand'.[35]

As for Mr Ernest Stern's claim that negotiations with the World Bank are less 'confrontational' than those with the Fund, officials in the Third World might not agree. Like a very senior Indian official, they might say that World Bank officials in a bunch, however sympathetic they may be as individuals, are 'poisonous'.[36] This comment was made in a country where the Bank does have a large resident mission, some of whose members accumulate considerable knowledge of the country and some sympathy with the problems. But in many cases Bank officials are renowned for the arrogance and superficiality of their views partly because, in ways not so dissimilar from their colleagues in the Fund, their method of operation is to make fleeting visits. A two-week stint in the best hotel in the capital city, travelling by car to government offices, is not the best way to begin to understand the realities of the countries they are dealing with. Staff turnover is high. Both the Bank and the Fund have a considerable capacity for remarkable ignorance about fairly elementary aspects of local reality.

As for IMF officials themselves, they have little but praise for the rigour and toughness of the Bank's approach. The closer contact between the two institutions has probably if anything reduced any friction there might have been. Far from undermining the Fund's commitment to rigorous austerity, the Bank has undoubtedly reinforced it.

The Bank and free trade

Within its overall advocacy of market forces, the Bank is and always has been an advocate of the benefits of free trade. In this its enthusiasm at least equals the institutionalised enthusiasm of the

IMF. Together with the IMF, it insists on overall limitations in demand and on devaluation, which discourage imports by an across-the-board increase in their prices, rather than selective import controls or tariff increases, as the means of controlling balance of payments deficits. One of the earliest major examples of the use of 'leverage' by the Bank was in India in 1966, where it was involved in pushing for both devaluation and import liberalisation.[37] The Bank is systematically enthusiastic about programmes of import liberalisation, welcoming them when, as in Chile, they occur, and is itself sometimes largely responsible for their introduction, as in the Philippines (see above, p. 124), and in Peru.

In the case of Peru, the World Bank hired a Peruvian economist, Roberto Abusada, who had been on a 'major' Bank mission to Argentina in 1978 directed by his friend Enrique Lerdau of the Bank's Latin American and Caribbean department, to do preparatory work for the Bank's 1979 programme loan to Peru; import liberalisation was part of the conditionality for this loan. Then, under the terms of the programme loan, he was hired by the government of Peru, with his salary paid from Washington, (which meant, he said, that he received in $1\frac{1}{2}$ days the equivalent of his previous salary from the Universidad Catolica). He worked in the Ministry of Industry on further proposals for import liberalisation and wrote a report on the Peruvian manufacturing sector, arguing for the removal of protection and other controls.[38] But he had difficulty in persuading the military government to adopt the proposals. When Belaúnde took office in 1980, however, and hired his economic team from Washington and Wall Street (see above, p. 95), Abusada was made Vice-Minister in charge of Trade in the Ministry of Economy and Finance. He was able to write out decrees embodying a programme of substantial tariff reductions which were immediately put into effect, without any attempt to get them passed by congress. It was 'practically the programme that the Peruvian government had asked the World Bank technical assistants to shape up'.[39]

Free trade, and its accompanying theory of 'comparative advantage', clearly favour established producers and manufacturers. The theories were developed by British economists in the nineteenth century at the time of British industrial ascendancy, challenged by its now industrialised competitors such as the United States and Germany, and reasserted by the United States when it had achieved industrial supremacy for itself after the Second World War. The theory of comparative advantage does not take account of possible changes over time. The World Bank has been opposed to the setting up of major new industrial capacity in the Third World, on the grounds that the products in question can be more cheaply obtained from abroad, and no doubt also on the grounds that they would compete with established industries in the West. (It would be interesting to know whether its reports on Japan in the 1950s contained advice against Japan embarking on the motor-car industry, and the usual solemn invocations on the economic unsoundness of the required protective measures.) Its reports on South Korea in the 1970s did advise the South Koreans not to 'go into heavy industry', i.e. make ships.[40] In Pakistan in the 1950s, 'The Bank opposed investment in heavy industry and initially even discouraged the establishment of jute-processing mills'.[41] Every country that contemplated manufacturing steel must have been advised not to do so by the World Bank.

Even of Brazil, a NIC (Newly Industrialising Country) with a potentially vast internal market, the Bank's 1983 *World Development Report* says with some scepticism:

> Since the mid-1970s the government has expanded its share of industry and played a bigger role in the choice of new investment. It has promoted a new wave of import substitution in the few activities where this remained possible. Some sectors (such as steel) may have been overexpanded, and many of the new industries (such as sophisticated machine tools and computers) have complex and rapidly evolving technology; being capital goods, their cost and quality will affect the whole economy. Whether these new activities will become internationally competitive remains to be seen.[42]

In the Bank's own projects, the question arises as to which inputs are to be procured locally and which from abroad. As Mason and Asher put it:

> The IBRD has two interests of central importance to be served by this choice: (a) to minimize the cost of the project by procuring inputs from lowest-cost sources, and (b) to encourage the development of borrowing countries by assisting their industries in producing inputs for Bank projects.[43]

The Bank has plumped heavily for the former. The Bank is, in its statutes, debarred from financing local costs, 'except in exceptional circumstances'. Although it has interpreted this rather widely to enable it to finance projects with unavoidably low import content, such as its rural development projects, it has insisted that wherever possible, the parts of its projects to be financed by itself must be open to international competitive bidding. In its early lending to industrialised countries, the Bank naturally found that local suppliers were often able to submit the most competitive bids, and it was nevertheless willing to finance them. It wondered whether this was 'fair' in view of the fact that local bidders benefited from various forms of protection, but decided there was nothing it could do about it.[44] However, as it began to lend more to under-developed countries, and as these countries increased their industrial capability, the Bank decided that their industries benefited from protective barriers that were too high. The Bank, according to Mason and Asher,

> recognised that industrialisation was difficult without some degree of protection of industrial 'infants'. However, it wanted to make sure that the infants it encouraged by its procurement policies had some reasonable chance of growing into industries that would eventually be capable of standing on their own feet. After much discussion in the Bank's staff and board of directors, it was decided in 1962 that local producers should be entitled to a maximum level of protection of 15 per cent in bidding on Bank projects. Henceforth either the existing tariff rate or 15 per cent, whichever was lower, would be accepted.[45]

Rather curiously, Bank officials nowadays produce this 15 per cent 'preference' accorded to local suppliers as evidence of the Bank's willingness to promote local industry, failing to mention that this preference is a substitute for, not an addition to, tariffs. It is nevertheless clear that the 'preference' was introduced as a means of reducing, rather than increasing, the protection accorded to industries in the Third World, and there are many complaints that it is far too low and effectively excludes local bidders. Attempts by the governments of Third World countries to get the level of preference raised to 25 per cent, still quite a low level of protection, were defeated explicitly on the grounds that it would limit the opportunities of the major powers for export. Mason and Asher say that:

> the Bank continued to lend for local procurement in developed countries without any extensive enquiry into the question of tariff protection. The problem of the degree of preference to be permitted a domestic supplier apparently was raised only in connection with loans to less developed member countries.[46]

If borrowing governments want to reserve certain parts of projects to local suppliers, they will not be financed by the Bank. The situation provides an inducement to governments to open up a larger portion of projects to international competitive bidding than they might otherwise do.[47] Moreover even though the Bank has been willing to finance a substantial amount of local costs especially in Africa and other 'low income' countries in cases where there is clearly no question of materials and skills being provided from abroad, it has been known to manipulate project design so as to facilitate 'competition' from foreign suppliers, for example by insisting that a road project should be put out to tender not in the usual small sections suitable for local contractors, but as a lump, suitable for foreign bidding.[48]

But while the Bank has been opposed to import-substituting manufacturing and the protection that it requires at least in its early stages, it has become an advocate of exports of low-technology manufactured products destined for Western markets and taking advantage of the Third World's 'comparative advantage' in the possession of cheap labour. During the 1970s the Bank took from other economists and itself espoused and developed a theory that programmes of import liberalisation can lead to growth in exports, including manufactured exports. It has been a consistent advocate of the greater integration of all Third World economies into the capitalist world economy and of greater 'openness' to and reliance on international trade. In particular the work of Bela Balassa, a professor at Johns Hopkins University and a consultant at the World Bank who has more than a dozen publications listed in the 1983 World Bank *Catalogue*, has been 'immensely influential', according to a Bank official.[49] Rejecting the 'pessimistic' theses of Prebisch, the first Secretary-General of UNCTAD, and others on the externally imposed difficulties for developing countries in increasing their exports, his major thesis is that:

> the export performance of a number of developing countries was adversely affected *by their own policies*: the bias against exports in countries pursuing import substitution policies led to a loss in their world shares in primary exports and forestalled the emergence of manufactured exports (emphasis added).[50]

The Bank has persisted in its advocacy of import liberalisation, export promotion and an increase in countries' dependence on trade in the face of developing countries' drastic loss of markets and export revenues resulting from depression and protectionism in the industrialised countries. In fact the emphasis it attaches to such policies has been reinforced by the appointment of Anne Krueger as vice president in charge of economics and research, in succession to Hollis Chenery, who directed much of the Bank's research on basic needs and income distribution in the 1970s. Krueger is said by her staff to have 'right-wing instincts'. Her academic specialisation is the economics of trade and she is very much an advocate of free trade. She is said to be mainly interested in using the Bank's research capabilities, which have themselves been reduced by about a third, to prove the thesis that developing countries can be turned into export platforms, exporting labour-intensive manufactured products and other 'non-traditional' products such as fruits and flowers to the West, as well as their more traditional raw materials and primary products. The Bank's *Report on the World Bank Research Program*, published for restricted distribution in March 1983, under the heading 'The evolution of the present program and emerging priorities', lists 'international trade and finance' as the first of four subjects for new research.

Krueger gave one of the two press conferences by Bank officials at the 1983 annual meetings (the other was on co-financing; see above); its subject was 'Trade and Protectionism'. A briefing issued to the press argues that, although 'recovery is under way', it might be put at risk by protectionism. It then puts forward the Bank's credo on developing countries:

> Developing countries have an important stake in an open and expanding trading system . . . Outward-oriented strategies are

characterised by the maintenance of realistic exchange rates,
the provision of similar incentives for domestic and export
production and the relative tolerance of import competition
(= good). In contrast, inward-oriented development strategies
are typically characterised by extensive protection against
imports that extends well beyond infant industries; a bias in
incentives in favor of import substitution and against exports;
wide variation in degrees of import protection across
industries; and greater reliance on administered allocative
mechanisms than on relative prices (= bad) . . .

[The outward-looking] countries have generally fared
better in terms of growth of output, income and employment,
and have also been able to adjust more rapidly to external
shocks.[51]

At her press conference, Krueger recommended that developing
countries should join the GATT and submit themselves to its rules.

While it might perhaps be true that developing countries'
interests would be better served by a genuinely open and expanding
trading system, the fact is that such a system does not exist. While
the Bank does advocate less protectionism by the industrialised
countries, it has no power whatsoever to achieve this objective. Its
financial clout is of course effective only in the Third World. But to
advocate import liberalisation and an attempt to rely on increasing
exports in the absence of expanding markets in the industrialised
countries seems to have mainly theological value, as far as the
peoples of the Third World are concerned. For them, it can be
desperately disruptive, with the 'long term gains', on which the
Bank explicitly relies, nowhere in sight. In the short term, both the
exporters of industrialised countries and Third World elites, for
whom the luxuries of the West suddenly become available, do
nicely. Thus one Bank official, recognising that the import liberalisation in Peru was bound to lead to an influx of Mercedes, etc.,
because of 'repressed demand', said 'if we took a moral position,
we wouldn't be lending to any of these countries'.[52]

What Bank statements and publications usually fail to mention
is that the 'outward-looking countries' that are supposed to have
'fared better' are most of them virtually city-states: Hong Kong,
Singapore, even Taiwan have small internal markets; South Korea
is possibly the only one of them that is both of fair size and not in

acute balance of payments and debt crisis. It is in any case doubtful whether South Korea should be counted as a show-case for liberalisation, the price mechanism and the free market, since its government pursued a highly interventionist policy, and promoted heavy industry against the advice of the World Bank. The idea that these countries' experiences as export platforms for the West could be replicated throughout the Third World seems far-fetched, even supposing there was a new sustained recovery in the West. China, following a policy of somewhat greater outward-orientation, as recommended, incidentally, in the World Bank's report on China, is already threatening to swallow up what markets there are for cheap textiles produced in the Third World.[53] Would the West tolerate the extra millions in the dole queues that would be the result of an export drive from India, Pakistan and Indonesia similar to that of South Korea and Singapore?

Sometimes it seems unclear whether the Bank really believes that concentration on labour-intensive manufactured exports is a feasible policy for all countries, or whether it simply believes that developing countries should 'stick to what they are best at': the export of primary commodities and raw materials. In Peru, Abusada (see above, p. 126) was said by one of his fellow economists to have believed initially that the import liberalisation programme which he successfully promoted would lead to labour-intensive manufactured exports, and that incentives should be provided for such exports.[54] 'Taiwanisemos' (Let us Taiwanise), he is said to have said. But Abusada's 1981 report, written while he was working for the Bank, and on which the Belaúnde government's liberalisation measures were based (see above), argues instead that 'an appropriate basis for an effective long-term strategy of industrial development of Peru is to exploit the country's comparative advantage', and claims that, 'in the past Peru has not followed this principle, but rather has provided strong support to industry at the cost of other sectors and, within the industrial sector, has promoted capital intensive forms of manufacturing. Both aspects of the past strategy are not in accordance with the country's resource endowments, which are mainly abundant skilled labour and natural resources, including minerals, agricultural and fishery products'. Because, says the report, the exports of traditional products and oil will be high, 'there should be no need to promote non-traditional exports at any cost . . . and a balanced reduction of both import protection and export incentives can be implemented as the key industrial policy instrument to promote efficient industrial development'. Moreover, the report recognises that, 'for a substantial part of export products, where Peru could utilise its comparative advantage of abundant and well-trained labor (mainly garments, footwear, consumer durables), Peruvian exporters will be late-comers on highly competitive markets . . . Trade restricting measures . . . by the industrial countries . . . provide additional obstacles. Thus, while manufactured exports will play a major role in the long-term industrial development of Peru, it appears improbable that the example of export-led high industrial growth set particularly by East-Asian countries under favorable world economic conditions prevailing during the 1960s and early 1970s can be repeated.'

Nevertheless, the report claims that: 'If the trade policy suggested in this report is implemented in successive steps, the manufacturing sector will be thoroughly restructured toward higher labor intensity and increased export orientation'.[55] Interviewed in 1982, Abusada waxed enthusiastic about the 'immense variety of new things, fruits, flowers', that Peru could export: Colombia, he said, exported more than $100 million of such products and Peru had a better climate.[56] But the increase in Peru's exports of agricultural products had led, he admitted, to some diminution of production for local consumption. It could in fact be argued that at a time of shrinking world markets it is suicidal for developing countries to increase their dependence on trade, and that India, for example, has actually fared 'relatively well' during the recession precisely because the dependence of its industries on external trade, as opposed to its internal market, is relatively low, and because its moves towards import liberalisation, much welcomed by the World Bank and the IMF, have been minor compared to those of the Latin American countries.

While import liberalisation may well fail to produce the desired rapid expansion of exports, it usually has a devastating effect on existing import-substituting industries. This is clearly partly intended by the Bank, which argues that such industries are inefficient and wasteful, and that they produce monopoly profits for local businesses. Thus, in the Philippines, the Bank complained of 'heavily protected and inefficient manufacturing industries, controlled by politically well-connected Filipinos, which were gradually increasing in importance despite their inefficiency and the existing [sic] of some foreign competition'.[57] Similar complaints were made by the Bank about import-substituting manufacturers in Peru and India. There is of course much truth in these attacks on Third World business elites; sometimes high profits are made from screwing together imported components, in Peru in particular. But there are ways of dealing with them other than by destroying their industries through import competition; for example they could be taxed, or nationalised, and perhaps induced to carry out more of the manufacturing process internally. There is also the possibility that this concern about 'inefficiency' and excessive profits is a cloak for other fears. For example a panel of representatives of US government and business at Georgetown University's Center for Strategic and International Studies said in 1971:

> As Filipino enterprises have grown and moved into new activities, Filipinos and American businessmen have become competitive and the former . . . have taken political action to minimise the threat of American competition. As the most influential political group motivated to limit access to Philippine resources and markets, they have provided a respectable nucleus around which diverse nationalist elements have coalesced . . .[58]

The import liberalisation policy itself has the effect of driving such people well and truly into the nationalist camp; it may even cause them to form alliances with the left. In the Philippines it has brought them out onto the streets. In Peru business interests affected by the liberalisation programme were vocal in their opposition to it, expressed partly through an extremely critical national daily newspaper, *El Observador*. But of course the people who suffer most from the destruction of import-substituting industries are not the business elite, who are likely to switch to making fat profits as importers, but workers and the owners of small workshops who lose their jobs. It is not, for example, clear why it is in the interest of the people of the Philippines that small, typically very labour-intensive manufacturers of leather shoes should be put out of business by liberalised imports of plastic shoes from Taiwan. In the Philippines, the Bank itself estimated that roughly 100,000 people in 'inefficient' garment and textile firms, or 46 per cent of the workforce in those industries and about

5 per cent of total employment, would lose their jobs. As in other cases,[59] the Bank seemed little concerned about what might happen to them: 'Reabsorbing those who may be displaced in the process – and who would be best placed and qualified to compete for new jobs – is a minor task in comparison to solving the fundamental employment problem.'[60]

The Bank, in its advocacy of export-orientated industrialisation, does claim as one of its virtues that it is labour-intensive. One of the Bank's criticisms of import-substituting industry is that it has been excessively capital-intensive (because 'overvalued exchange rates' and 'excessive wages' have created a bias in favour of imports of capital equipment). The inducement being offered to the multinational companies which make use of the Export Processing Zones proliferating, partly at the urging of the World Bank, throughout Asia and Latin America, is cheap labour. The Bank is a consistent advocate of lower wages on the hoary right-wing argument that workers are 'pricing themselves out of jobs'. It shows little sign of concern at the methods by which low wages are achieved: suppression of trade unions and other extreme forms of repression which are common in the Third World. The conditions of super-exploitation that exist in these export processing zones are well known: extremely low wages, and extreme exhaustion of the workers, the majority of whom are young women considered to be both 'dexterous' and docile and who are habitually got rid of when they are worn out with over-work. While these activities may add to the number of people who are employed, government policies of 'wage restraint' also add to the number of people who need work, to the extent that they make wages too low to support families. It is not uncommon for wages to have declined by 25 to 30 per cent during the seventies in countries under IMF/World Bank supervision.

Another benefit of export-orientated industrialisation for its proponents is that it avoids the classic Keynesian dilemma: high wages increase costs, but if wages are cut too much, industry loses its markets. The markets for the export platform industries are abroad, so wages can be cut with impunity. This is one reason why left-wing opponents of the policy in the Third World, while recognising the limitations of import-substituting industry, particularly since it is currently largely based on the limited internal markets for luxury consumption provided by Third World elites, advocate a radical redistribution of income and an enlargement of internal markets as a way forward from the industrial stagnation experienced by some import-substituting economies. The export-orientated industries are usually enclaves, with few connections with the rest of the economy, and dependent on imported inputs, so that their foreign exchange benefits, like those of the import-substituting industries before them, are often illusory. They are also often merely the labour-intensive part of some total manufacturing process, the more skilled and technologically advanced components of which are performed in the industrialised countries.

The policy of export-orientated industrialisation appears to have been on the whole acceptable even to liberals within the Bank, on the grounds presumably that some industrialisation is better than none. In the case of the Philippines, and possibly elsewhere, one confidential Bank document does recognise that 'in a fiercely competitive and fickle international market, Philippine handicrafts will be in fashion today, and tomorrow [sic]. The bread and butter and the basis of a modern manufacturing sector will always be at home.'[61] There was apparently some debate within the World Bank and even between the World Bank and the Bank-orientated Filipino 'technocrats' (although they all agreed that protection on imported consumer goods should be reduced) on whether there should not be some encouragement for import-substitution in intermediate and capital goods industries. The Filipinos proposed a range of such industries, attempting to justify them on the grounds that part of their production would be for export and that some of them would be 100 per cent foreign-owned. But even these projects were effectively torpedoed by the Bank, and the export-orientated free traders appear to have won the day.

The Bank's wholesale espousal of the export-orientated industrialisation strategy has coincided, fortuitously or not, with the outward drive of multinational companies in search of new sources of cheap labour and ways of getting round the high wages and strong trade union organisation that exist in the advanced capitalist countries: what the first Brandt Report delicately described as 'in a sense a new frontier, with fewer of the special economic difficulties and social and political constraints operating in the North'.[62] The same kind of point is sometimes made about the Bank's prescriptions for agriculture, which include the expanded use of fertilisers, improved seeds and other inputs available from the currently powerful and expanding agribusiness firms. The extent to which the Bank acts directly in the interests and at the behest of multinational firms is debatable. But what is clear is that its emphasis on making use of the abundant reserves of cheap labour that exist in the Third World does not run counter to the interests of multinationals based in the North, and has also been of benefit to Northern consumers of cheap textiles and cheap electronic goods.

In addition, while the concentration on manufacturing for export is justified on 'free trade' arguments, there is some sophistry in this, as in most such apparently technical arguments. The export processing zones offer a number of inducements which are in fact the result of large-scale government intervention. First, and most importantly, a workforce which is as cheap and docile as government repression can achieve. But there are also very substantial tax concessions and other incentives; very expensive provision of infrastructure facilities such as power and water; and notional charges for land, in which the Bank's principles of market determination of prices and 'full cost recovery', so zealously pursued when the poor are having to pay, go by the board.

All this is justified on the grounds that countries have to earn foreign exchange somehow. But calculations which offset the increases in foreign exchange earnings against the increases in imported inputs, repatriated profits,and the cost of infrastructure, tend to come up with a negative sum. The result – continuing balance of payments crisis through dependence on imported inputs – is not necessarily different from the effects of import-substituting industry. And there are, as always, ways of dealing with balance of payments crises, such as income redistribution, different priorities for consumption, greater self-reliance, refusal to pay extortionate interest rates to the banks, which would fall less heavily on the backs of the poor and, incidentally, be of less benefit to the multinational companies and banks of the North.

Except in a very few East Asian cases, the policies of the World Bank and the IMF have failed to achieve even the limited objective of resolving balance of payments crises. The fact that they might have been rather more successful if there had been no capitalist recession in the North does not excuse the renewed vigour with which the policies are currently being pursued in countries throughout the world.

Markets, the price mechanism and privatisation

The underlying rationale for many of the Bank's favoured policies is that the 'market' should be allowed to work. Thus much of the argument for import liberalisation is based on the supposed gains in efficiency that are to be achieved through the introduction of competition. The Bank now harps greatly on the need for 'efficient pricing policies' and the need to avoid 'price distortions'. Removing subsidies and price controls has for the Bank the double advantage that it supposedly reduces such 'distortions' and cuts down government expenditures.

The second subject listed in 1983 as an 'emerging priority' for Bank research was 'Issues in the area of government intervention', and the main issue seems to be 'pricing policies'.[63] Like the IMF, the World Bank has put a good deal of emphasis on the need to raise the prices of goods and services such as food, petrol, public transport and so on. Governments habitually subsidise services and the prices of some essential goods in order to protect consumers, many of whom may be poor. But the Bank is committed to the concept of 'full cost recovery', for its own projects in particular, although it does not always achieve it. Many of the Bank's most bitter battles with government officials are on the question of whether it is desirable to cover the costs of, for example, a water supply project by charging for the water. Its arguments for financial autonomy for public sector institutions include the argument that they should finance themselves by charging higher rates, and that this will provide an inducement towards greater efficiency.

The Bank appears to be somewhat more willing than it has been to recognise that there may be equity considerations involved. Often its arguments have some weight: for example the Bank argued that the West Bengal government (Communist Party-Marxist) should raise the fares on public transport because the massive subsidies on fares were a misallocation of scarce resources; many of the government's own supporters are inclined to agree. Bank officials will also argue that, for example, there is no reason why the mainly better-off users of telephones should not pay the full costs of the telephone service. The Bank's document on research says that it will evaluate

> the costs and benefits of institutional and policy reforms, particularly pricing policies, under competing objectives like economic efficiency, redistribution and poverty alleviation, increasing fiscal revenues, as well as such non-economic objectives as maintaining political support . . . Work in this area has become increasingly important as the result of many countries experiencing a decline in external and fiscal resources which has increased pressure [from the World Bank?] for a rationalisation of pricing policies and other interventions such as quantitative restrictions of various kinds, particularly those which involve large subsidies.[64]

One of the Bank's major prescriptions for agriculture is that the prices paid to producers should be raised. The Bank sometimes argues that this will redress the pro-urban bias in income distribution. But it remains unclear whether the Bank pays adequate attention to the fact that many of the producers are likely to be rich landlords and that many of the consumers are not only the urban poor, but also the rural landless and near-landless, who often constitute a majority of the rural labour force.[65] Attempts to raise the prices of food have been the major factor in what have become known, since the popular protests that took place in Egypt in 1977 when the government attempted to increase the price of bread, as 'IMF riots'. They could be described as 'IMF/World Bank riots', for the World Bank is fully behind the policies that cause them. In January 1984 the Tunisian government's attempt to double the prices of basic foodstuffs was met with such strong popular resistance that the army was brought in, a number of people died, and the government retracted the measures. A week or two later, similar price rises were similarly retracted in Morocco after popular protests. A World Bank official spoke of 'necessary rationalisations in food grains subsidies in North Africa'.[66] And in Morocco the increases were 'prompted by austerity measures demanded of the government by the International Monetary Fund', according to the *Financial Times* of January 24 1984. Yet subsidising the prices of the basic food consumed by the poor is one certain way of helping them, especially in countries where there is much unemployment and landlessness. Opposition to such subsidies is to a great extent inspired by ideology. The Bank's predilections clearly lie in the direction of the neo-classical principles of full-cost recovery and market pricing, together with the view that those who can pay, should pay, rather than the principle of free provision of services to all.

The Bank's 1983 *World Development Report*, in a chapter entitled 'Pricing for efficiency', produced a remarkably imaginative negative correlation between growth rates and 'price distortions' in a pretty picture with five different colours and shadings thereof and a box which states that: 'The regression equation relating growth to the composite distortion index shows that price distortions can explain about one-third of the variation in growth performance'.[67] There is a good deal more besides on 'weights' and the relative importance of different distortions in the total mix' and 'the exchange rate distortion being the most significant' which all tends to go to show that the Chicago-trained Third World Bank official who said the whole exercise was 'simplistic' and 'analytically incorrect', was right.[68] The report also claimed that there was 'virtually no correlation' between price distortions and equity: 'the distortion index explains hardly 3 per cent of the variation in equity, when the latter is measured by the proportion of income going to the bottom 40 per cent of the population'. In other words, the Bank feels that governments which alleviate hardship through, for example, a free rice ration, as the government of Sri Lanka did before the World Bank and the IMF got to work on it, or through indexing wages to the rate of inflation, don't *really* help the poor.

Each year's *World Development Report* takes up a particular issue. For the 1980 report this was 'Poverty and human development'; in 1983 it was 'Management in development'. The Bank's 1983 report on its research programme says that efficiency always was 'an overriding concern of Bank research and operations', and that renewed emphasis on it does not imply the abandonment of research on 'distribution and poverty issues'.[69] But the 1983 *World Development Report* effectively embodies the prevailing wisdom of the Bank, what one former member of Chenery's research department described as the view that 'the universal application of neo-classical economic theory holds the key to economic efficiency'.[70] The Report attempts to define 'the concept of efficient pricing' as though it was somehow a question of objectively measurable fact; thus differing from, for example, the *Financial Times*, which at the end of a long article on the arcane ramifications of public sector pricing policies in Britain, says: 'None of this, however, is likely to deter the politicians since setting prices in state-owned industries is, by definition, political'.[71] As Mason and Asher put it,

> The moral code for the Bank's top leadership is provided by the 'laws of economics'. A conscious effort is made to give the status of natural law to this flexible code. 'We ask a lot of questions', said Eugene Black [McNamara's predecessor], 'and attach a lot of conditions to our loans. I need hardly say that we would never get away with this if we did not bend every effort to render the language of economics as morally antiseptic as the language the weather forecaster uses in giving tomorrow's prediction.'[72]

One Bank official described the 1983 *World Development Report* as 'a political and compromise document, negotiated between different interests and views'. It is certainly political. Thus the section on 'The search for efficiency' starts with some patronising remarks about 'weak institutions and management' and says:

> large organisations place greater demands on management than do small ones. Governments tend to be involved in the management of big organisations, such as running state farms and marketing boards, rather than relying on peasant farmers, small traders, and individual truckers. And the mistakes that big organisations make have serious consequences.[73]

Therefore, presumably, such things should be left to the private sector. But what about the very large private ranching concerns, for example, that the Bank often ends up supporting (see page 163 below)? And what about the Bank itself, undeniably a large organisation, whose inefficiencies many beleaguered Third World officials irritably point to? Perhaps it should be split up, as the Bank tells Third World governments their public sectors should be, into smaller independently operating units, with less centralised rigidity in its bureaucratic structures.

The Report goes on to say that, throughout the world, the role of the state has been increasing and productivity has (therefore?) been declining. Its chapter on 'The role of the state' reads like a political manifesto. Not quite so extreme, perhaps, as the 1979 Tory manifesto in Britain, but with many similarities. Gestures towards political impartiality are instantly qualified or contradicted. For example:

> The key factor determining the efficiency of an enterprise is
> not whether it is publicly or privately owned, but how it is
> managed. In theory it is possible to create the kind of
> incentives that will maximise efficiency under any type of
> ownership . . . But there is a great difference between what is
> theoretically feasible and what typically happens . . .[74]

Or again: 'Markets may not perform perfectly . . .' But: 'All too often the attempted cure has been worse than the disease.' And so on.

Again and again the Report eulogises the gains to be derived from private competition to state services or contracting out: private bus services in Buenos Aires, Calcutta and Thailand; private management contracts for water supply in the Ivory Coast; the 'rural production responsibility system' in China which, the World Bank does not say, has reintroduced inequalities between households in rural areas.[75] The discussion on 'the role of the state' concludes:

> This chapter has suggested that government interventions can
> result in large losses of efficiency and should therefore be
> selective. In the face of compelling political and social
> pressures, governments will always be tempted to do more
> than can be accomplished efficiently. Yet today's widespread
> re-examination of the role of the state is evidence of a new
> realism. In the search for greater cost-effectiveness in the
> provision of services, governments are exploring ways of
> tapping private initiative and simulating competitive
> conditions. The most common approach is to use private
> contractors in a variety of fields, from road maintenance to
> garbage collection. This serves to mobilise new managerial
> resources, and if well supervised, can greatly improve the
> quality and reduce the cost of services.[76]

Chapter 8, 'Managing state-owned enterprises', continues in the same vein:

> In theory [whose theory?], efficiency is highest when an
> enterprise strives to maximise profits in a competitive market,
> under managers with the autonomy, motivation, and

> capability to respond to the challenge of competition.
> Inefficient enterprises would not be able to compete and
> would go bankrupt.[77]

There is more of the same in every succeeding chapter. Thus on 'Project and program management' there is a box on 'Contracting maintenance to the private sector': 'One main reason contractors are cheaper is their flexibility. They gear up more easily for peak demand and slim down [i.e., sack workers] faster when demand slackens'.[78]

The Report does not suggest that the only way to improve the public sector is to get rid of it, or make it smaller. It recommends decentralisation to other parts of the public sector as well as to the private sector and greater accountability in general. And it is undoubtedly true that many bureaucracies are centres of privilege, corrupt, excessively concerned with minor regulations, and over-staffed. The Brazilian Ministry of Debureaucratisation, if it is true as the Report says that it 'has simplified and reduced red tape, by starting at the point where the bureaucracy meets the public', must be good. A Cuban official in the Ministry of Education said in 1969 that one of their first acts when they took over was to carry a lot of the desks out into the street and burn them.

But, in general, the Bank's report evidently reflects the views of one of the senior officials involved in its preparation:

> Evidence supports the view that the capacity of governments
> is very limited, and the general level of government
> administration is so low . . . that there is a lot to be said for
> relieving the burden on government and allowing the private
> sector to do it . . . Nigeria is a very entrepreneurial society,
> people are brought up in the tradition of making money;
> money incentives are more effective than ideas of public
> service.[79]

The Bank and 'capitalist efficiency'

The World Bank's favourite word is 'efficiency'. It demands it in others, and arrogates it to itself. Criticisms of the waste and inefficiency of development projects, including those financed by bilateral aid agencies and United Nations specialised agencies, is widespread (and justified). The World Bank is sometimes held out as a shining exception to the general rule. Proposals are made for more aid to be channelled through the Bank, or associated with Bank lending, for example in co-financing arrangements, on the grounds that it would then be more efficiently used.

In bank terminology, the word efficiency is often simply a euphemism for capitalism. The Bank equates efficiency with capitalism, or with allowing market forces to operate more freely. Thus when, for example, it says in one of its reports on Peru that: 'The principle of efficiency should then reach all sectors, but in particular agriculture' it simply means that market forces will be allowed to operate, marketing will be privatised, agricultural co-operatives will be broken up into small private plots.[80] As one of its own, more open officials claimed, the Bank's aim could be said to be to promote 'capitalist efficiency'. Given that this is so, it might perhaps be argued that it is doing as good a job as could be expected.

It would be easier to give the Bank credit for this if, in its public face, it was not so arrogant, complacent, and prone to seeing the mote in the eyes of others while ignoring the beams in its own. The Bank does sometimes make gross mistakes even in its own terms and attempt to cover them up with phoney statistics. Some of its officials are reputedly more concerned with the statistics of their expense accounts than with those of wider application and value. Nevertheless there are also Bank officials who are hardworking, competent, dedicated, and passionately concerned with the promotion of what can reasonably be called 'capitalist efficiency'.

Any attempt to evaluate the success, in their own terms, of Bank projects is likely to be almost impossible, even though the Bank itself now attempts it, in its annual project reviews, which however are not published (see next chapter). But, as well as the failures, which may or may not be covered up, there are likely to be examples of the following sort, as reported in Mason and Asher:

> Early in the Bank's history, a Latin American member
> requested a sizable railway loan, primarily to finance the
> purchase of some large, speedy, and highly efficient
> locomotives. The Bank's investigation showed that
> locomotives as heavy as those requested could not be borne by

the country's railway tracks and roadbed. Moreover, if the locomotives did manage to cross the bridges without crashing into the waters below and travelled at the speeds expected of them, they would derail themselves on the curves. Instead of rejecting the loan proposal, the Bank helped the borrower choose a different type of locomotive.[81]

Nowadays the Bank is often involved in evaluating not just its own projects, but the whole of a government's investment programme. A number of its strictures and recommendations are likely to have value of the railway-engine type. Many new government projects, especially big ones, undoubtedly are badly evaluated and have mainly prestige value, whereas existing projects are under-utilised and badly maintained. The Bank tactfully gives the example of 'the Anglo-French Concorde, where the only two airlines that bought the aircraft have difficulty covering even their operating costs, and none of the development costs (several billion dollars) will be recouped'.[82] 'Embarking on fewer projects,' it says bluntly, 'would also help'. It acknowledges that all this is partly a 'donor' problem. Donors, the World Bank included though its Report does not mention this, normally finance only the initial foreign exchange costs of new projects; they do not pay for maintenance or the importing of spare parts and current inputs. In general many of the Bank's comments on better evaluation, accounting procedures, and so on, have obvious validity and are relatively free of ideology. Third World officials, though often infuriated by the slowness of negotiations with the Bank and the 'bureaucratic red tape' with which they say the Bank surrounds itself, also at times express appreciation of the demands it makes for thoroughness.

The irony is that many of these strictures could well be applied to some of the Bank's own projects. It is sometimes said that Bank projects have deteriorated in quality, recently in particular, because, under McNamara, the pressure on loan officers to meet their higher lending targets was so great that standards of evaluation and supervision fell. Bank officials also say that, with the greater importance attached to macro-economic questions, officials with technical competence in the Bank feel under-valued, and some have left. The US Treasury report takes up this question. In one of the few sections that is at all critical of the Bank, it says:

The World Bank's audit of more than 500 projects evaluated in the past 5 years reveals that 94 per cent of the investments turned out to be worthwhile. *However, the audit covers only a fraction of the lending undertaken in recent years* . . . anecdotal information – both solicited and unsolicited – from World Bank staff indicate that the emphasis placed on achieving lending targets has had a definite and adverse impact on loan quality. The frequency of these assertions, and the highly professional character of the sources, strongly suggest that the Bank needs to accord greater priority to assuring the high quality of all projects (original emphasis).[83]

The 'problem' projects are likely to be mainly in the new sectors, in rural development in particular (see following chapter). One Bank official, responding to the question of whether there would be a change of emphasis under Clausen, said that as the project evaluations came in, they were providing 'a lot of ammunition' to those who were opposed to the basic needs type projects. Many of these were, of course, projects whose results had not yet officially come in by the time the US Treasury report was written. Agricultural economists not working for the Bank corroborate this, saying that a project which is designed as a result of a six-week mission has no chance of success.[84] It is in fact dubious whether outsiders, even when their missions are more protracted, have the capacity to bring about real improvements in rural areas, particularly in countries whose governments are not committed to the goal of eliminating poverty in rural areas. The problems apply also to the Bank's health and education projects in rural areas. The Bank is by nature a capital-city institution. There is a story of the Bank engaging a construction company based in Port-au-Prince, the capital of Haiti, to construct a duplicate of an existing building that had already been constructed with local materials and labour for a fraction of the cost. But the fact that Bank staff normally make fleeting visits, and that staff turnover is high, must cause problems with many of its projects, including its traditional type of projects in the economic infrastructure. The Bank itself can be accused of fanciful accounting procedures and inadequate supervision of its own projects; its big internal evaluation of its experience in Colombia (see below, p. 177) shows that much of its work on 'institution-building' merely caused Colombian bureaucrats to devise tactics of evasion. In some countries monuments to the Bank's enthusiasm for institution-building are to be found, small replicas of the spacious air-conditioned luxury of the Bank's headquarters in Washington, and equally remote from the under-privileged and overcrowded reality of the regular central government buildings.

An even more serious question is whether the Bank's claims to 'capitalist efficiency' are not vitiated by bias towards First World capitalism. It is possible that, in some limited ways, the Bank staff does take a broader view of the interests of capitalism than its executive directors. It has made some attempt to resist the pressures of the oil companies, and has consistently opposed the massive Majes and Olmos irrigation works in Peru even though, and even perhaps partly because, some European suppliers were making fat profits out of them. Attempts in 1977 by the US executive director, in accordance with the wishes of Congress, to veto two World Bank loans, one to Malaysia for oil and one to Swaziland for sugar, failed. 'Review of minutes of discussions surrounding the two negative votes shows not only a lack of sympathy for the US position but a counter-productive reaction on the part of other executive directors to US efforts to inject political and/or protectionist attitudes into the loan discussions'.[85]

Even the Bank's view of 'comparative advantage' is not a wholly static one. The Bank takes a broader view of where it currently lies than the governments of some of its major shareholders. Now that it has decided that cheap labour counts as a 'comparative advantage', it argues, together with many liberals in the advanced capitalist countries, that the governments of these countries should abandon labour-intensive, low-skilled industries to the Third World and shift to more capital-intensive, high-technology industries. However, it would not go so far as to admit that the developing countries are entitled, yet, to the latter as well. It is at times hard to interpret its opposition to potentially efficient industrial projects as being motivated by anything other than a desire to protect the interests of First World producers. Thus when the Bank, as for example in its 1984 economic report on India ('circulated privately to Government Ministers and to foreign countries involved in next month's annual meeting of aid donors'), tells a government that it 'should concentrate its future major investments on improving the performance of its outdated and inefficient industries rather than indulging in expensive new ventures', and that 'Protectionist and bureaucratic policies – including price controls – which "no longer serve well their original objectives and have adversely affected incentives . . ." should be abandoned',[86] its lecturing is likely to be tainted with the ideology of comparative advantage.

In relation to its own projects, the Bank can undoubtedly be accused, at times, of favouring foreign technology over the development of local technological capacity, for motives which are no doubt mixed. The Bank's argument, of course, is that the technology is proven and readily available. Thus in the early 1980s the Bank engaged in a long-running dispute with the Indian government over a proposed large loan for the modernisation of the Indian railways. The point at issue was whether a computerisation system, which both sides agreed was necessary if the new equipment was to be fully utilised, should be imported ready-made from abroad or developed in India. The Bank's representative in India argued with passion that it made no sense for India to develop its own system since a number of systems already existed for use on railways, that for India to develop its own system would take too long and would in any case be of strictly limited usefulness, since India would not be able to market it abroad in competition with established technologies. Indian officials argued that it was a good opportunity for India to develop its own capacity in computer systems, that the process of adapting foreign systems for use in Indian conditions was often difficult and expensive as experience in the oil industry had shown, that it would in any case take time to train railway employees to operate the new system, that the system could be phased in as training proceeded, and so on. There are usually good arguments on both sides of such questions. The problem is that it is entirely predictable which side the Bank will be on when such disputes arise, and that they arise with some frequency. The Algerians, for example, were engaged in a similar type of dispute over a proposed loan for the fishing industry. The Algerian government was proposing to include in the project an industry to build fishing boats, as well as port and repair facilities; the Bank was proposing credit to the private sector for the acquisition of fishing boats from abroad. An Algerian official suggested that this represented support for shipyards in the North.[87]

There is the related question whether the technology with which Bank officials and technicians, trained in the West, are most familiar, is in fact the technology that is likely to be most efficient in the countries to which the Bank lends. There are not many accusations that Bank officials are directly corrupt. But they have the major say in the choice of consultants, which in turn virtually determines the choice of suppliers. Indians in particular complain that in designing projects, Bank officials ensure that their specifications are suitable for certain contractors, and imply that there may be at times be a corrupt relationship.[88] And Escott Reid, former official of the World Bank, wrote in his book *Strengthening the World Bank*, that the executive directors of rich countries

> will take up on behalf of companies in the countries they represent complaints that these companies have been discriminated against in the award of contracts financed from Bank Group loans. They will do their best to ensure that the appropriate authorities of their governments receive information . . . about contracts for goods and services likely to be awarded during the next few years, so that their governments may in turn inform the firms that might be interested.[89]

Even Mason and Asher, in their semi-official history of the World Bank, referring to left criticisms including 'a more moderate but still severely critical account of Bank lending policy . . . presented in Teresa Hayter, *Aid as Imperialism*', say:

> As one reviews the history of the Bank, taking into account the predominant ideology of the directors representing countries having a majority of the votes (and for much of the first twenty-five years, the ideology of management as well), one must in all fairness concede a measure of validity to the left-wing criticism . . . International competitive bidding, reluctance to accord preferences to local suppliers, emphasis on financing foreign exchange costs, insistence on a predominant use of foreign consultants, attitudes towards public sector industries, assertion of the right to approve project managers – all proclaim the Bank to be a Western capitalist institution.[90]

The Bank is not merely a capitalist institution, disinterestedly devoted to the goal of 'capitalist efficiency'. It is also a 'Western capitalist institution', necessarily biassed towards the interests of its major shareholders. Seen in this light, the Bank's strictures on efficiency have at times a hollow ring.

8. The Bank and agriculture

The Bank's general strategy

It is often hard to discern exactly what the Bank is trying to achieve in its lending for agriculture, and it is possibly a mistake to ascribe too much theoretical consistency to the Bank's activities in this field. One such attempt, however, reaches the following conclusions:

> The World Bank's new strategy of rural development and income redistribution is largely rhetoric. It appears as if it is addressed to the social-democratic consciences of the practitioners of the business of rural development, and to defuse the radical critics of the practice of development. Its logic is to intensify the 'compulsive involvement' of small farmers in the market. It legitimates the World Bank's long-standing commitment to liberal trade and exchange policies, by arguing that these promote the welfare of the worst off. It finances, on a greatly expanded scale, a continuation of the various forms of rural development undertaken, with more or often less success, by colonial governments. These forms of rural development contradict the declared objectives of rural development. They do serve other purposes, providing employment to experts, or markets for firms, subordinating rural producers to the requirements of agro-industrial firms, enriching the better off, and extending networks of political patronage.[1]

Until the 1970s, the Bank lent very little for agriculture and such loans as it did make were mainly for large commercial under-takings, particularly in livestock. The Bank was criticised for its neglect of agriculture, partly on the grounds that poverty is concentrated in rural areas.

In the 1970s, under the presidency of McNamara, Bank lending for agriculture increased at a much faster rate than other sectors of Bank lending. By 1980, it amounted to nearly a third of total Bank commitments (see table, p. 234). The Bank's claims that it had a new 'poverty orientation' were based largely on its lending for projects in rural areas, where, according to the new rhetoric, the 'poorest of the poor' were to be found. It is nevertheless probably a near-universal phenomenon of Bank rural development projects that their benefits are appropriated by the better-off peasants and landowners. Thus, according to Cheryl Payer,

> In Guatemala the Bank solved the problem of reaching 'small farmers' by defining them as anyone with less than 45 hectares of land (108 acres) – a category which encompasses 97 per cent of all Guatemalan farmers. Half of the funds would go to 'small farmers' thus defined, while the other half would go to 'medium' and 'larger' farms in the top 3 per cent. 'I don't care what country you take', an agricultural specialist with wide experience in Latin America told me, 'if you follow World Bank money down through the distributing institutions, it's all going to the wrong people'.[2]

McNamara, however, emphasised in his speeches the need to support small farmers. In theory the Bank seems to be well disposed to the principle of private ownership of small, but not too small, plots of land. Some at least of its officials are aware of the possible political advantages in the creation of a conservative, kulak-type peasantry. It is in any case clear that the Bank's projects do little or nothing, as its officials will sometimes admit, for the landless. They may in fact add to their number; this has happened on a considerable scale in areas where the Green Revolution, a phenomenon for which the Bank claims some credit, has been 'successfully' implanted and has provided an inducement to landowners to evict their tenants.[3]

But it is not even clear how small the Bank would like its farmers to be. The Green Revolution has often had the effect of increasing the size of larger landholdings. The Bank has continued to lend for large commercial undertakings. It depends, in practice, on a theory about 'progressive' farmers which amounts to a rural version of the 'trickle down' theory upon which McNamara's advisers were supposed to be casting doubts (see p. 228). In Northern Nigeria, the Bank insisted on making the subsidised fertiliser to be provided under its loan available to selected 'progressive' farmers who were to provide an example to the rest, to whom its benefits would 'trickle down'. This actually provoked a reaction from the poorer farmers who were not thus favoured, and who did not need examples, just cheap fertilisers. As a result, the Bank had to change its project guidelines to enable wider distribution of the fertilisers.[4]

The Bank is of course opposed to the public ownership of land. Its reports welcome the termination of land reform programmes, when this occurs. For example, its laudatory presentation to the consultative group for Peru says with evident approval that 'the Agricultural Promotion Law . . . ends the agrarian reform expropriation process – an important measure to instil investor confidence'.[5] Another report on Peru describes the failures and 'negative effects' of land reform under previous reformist military governments[6] and a report on the Peruvian agricultural sector states that: 'This entire period (1970–80) from its start has been characterised by ill-conceived and mal-administered sweeping land reform and economic control measures'.[7] The sector report tells, at length, the sad story of an expropriated coffee grower, 'a highly respected professional living in Lima', apparently on his uncorroborated evidence. 'Having acquired 360 hectares in four parcels of land in the Tingo Maria area in 1957, the idea was eventually to develop coffee production as a long-term private investment that would also benefit the local economy'. A number of improvements were apparently made, 40–60 workers employed, '40 stable families' housed on the land. Then along came an official communication from the agricultural reform authorities, announcing that the property was under expropriation procedures; payment would be made with 30-year 4 per cent bonds 'representing about 10 per cent of the property's value'. Most of the experienced labour force 'departed': 'the workers did not want to take over individual parcels of land in a property which they knew how to operate as a unit'. Efforts to recruit replacement families were unsuccessful (in a country with the degree of land hunger that exists in Peru?). Lower output ensued. And the poor 'developer' did not even get the 40 hectares due to him, because he was living in Lima.[8]

Bank officials have sometimes recognised that improvements in agricultural production would be difficult without land reform. A report prepared in the Bank's research department on the Brazilian North-East argued, with figures, that the Bank's money would be more effective in raising living standards if there were small, individually owned plots of land, rather than the large estates prevalent in the area; this was a delicate way of suggesting that land reform was desirable. But the Bank's projects department rejected the report on the grounds that there were some small technical errors in the calculations.[9] The response of senior management to such suggestions is sometimes, alternatively, that the matter is 'too delicate', or that the Bank must work through 'local hierarchies': 'it is not our job to start social revolutions', one official wrote in reply to criticisms of a Bank project in Nigeria.[10]

The Bank has, on the other hand, been involved in attempts to break up large-scale land reform co-operatives or collectives into small privately owned units. In both Peru and Algeria, the process was known as 'restructuration'. In Peru the Belaúnde government's policy was explicitly to provide inducements to workers on co-operatives to opt for individual ownership; the Bank was involved in major projects in support of this policy in two important areas: in the Puno region and in the sugar estates on the coast. In Algeria, the government was said, in 1982, to be studying the various possible options for reorganising state farms; the Bank was again much involved (see below, p. 213). In both cases, the arguments advanced were that state or co-operative ownership had been responsible for inefficiency and low levels of production.

There was no recognition of the external difficulties imposed on the co-operative or state farms. (See also section on Tanzania, p. 204.)

There are few positive references to land reform in Bank documents. There is no discussion of land reform in any Bank annual report and the first mention of it in a public Bank document seems to have been in 1972 in the Bank's *Agricultural Sector Working Paper.* As far back as 1965 the Director General of the FAO had asked the Bank and other development finance institutions to consider making money available for the implementation of land reform programmes. The Bank rebuffed this and other similar requests with the dubious argument that it did not want to help governments compensate landowners for their expropriated lands as the funds used in compensation would not of themselves have created any new productive capacities in the country, although it could be argued that land reform would have released the productive capacities of unemployed and landless peasants.[11] The Bank also declined to guarantee the bonds issued to compensate landowners who had had land expropriated as 'this would have had the paradoxical effect of giving land bonds greater stability than that enjoyed by the currencies of issuing countries.'[12]

McNamara spoke emotionally of the need for land reform in his 1973 annual speech but gave no real indication of how the Bank was to support it. In 1975 the Bank published its *Land Reform Sector Policy Paper*. In this cautious document, which has remained the Bank's policy on land reform until today, the Bank puts a sizeable distance between itself and land reform. The Bank will support land reform if it is consistent with the 'development objectives of increasing output, improving income distribution and expanding employment,' but the Bank 'cannot force structural change'.[13] The Bank's leverage is limited, says the document: 'Such political decisions [as land reform] are not amenable to ready negotiation with governments in the same way as are other institutional questions – such as, for instance, the setting of public utility rates.'[14]

The document lists 12 policy guidelines for the Bank's participation in land reform. Two of them reiterate the Bank's intention to support land reform and to help land reform beneficiaries if the country pursues broad-based agricultural strategies directed towards the promotion of employment, with special attention to the poorest groups. However, the Bank has not lived up to these guidelines in at least one country; in Nicaragua, the Bank preferred to lend to cattle ranchers and not to beneficiaries of land reform before lending was suspended, although the government's policies in theory fit the Bank's criteria (see p. 219).

Four of the guidelines say that the Bank will research various aspects of land reform and tenure and the costs and benefits of settlement schemes – which it has done to an extent. Two refer to the Bank's intention to foster equitable and secure tenancy arrangements; however, in at least two post-1975 Colombian projects, tenancy arrangements are extremely vague, allowing better-endowed colonists to obtain more land. And two of the guidelines say that the Bank will be alert in its country analyses to land tenure problems and, in general, to the impact of new technology on land ownership; however, in many recent Bank economic memoranda, including the latest on Colombia, land reform tends to be mentioned briefly, if at all.

The strongest of the guidelines would seem to be the two which follow, numbered 8 and 9. Firstly,

> The Bank will not support projects where land rights are such that a major share of the benefits will accrue to high-income groups unless increases in output and improvements in the balance of payments are overriding considerations; in such cases, it will carefully consider whether the fiscal arrangements are appropriate to ensure that a reasonable share of the benefits accrues to the government.[15]

This guideline, however, reflects more a general concern about the distributional effects of projects rather than a specific concern about land tenure and reform. And secondly, 'In circumstances where increased productivity can effectively be achieved only subsequent to land reform, the Bank will not support projects which do not include land reform.'[16] But with respect to this guideline, it is hard to imagine a situation, given the Bank's continuing confidence in technology like high-yielding seed varieties, in which the Bank would consider land reform to be the only way to increase productivity. It is doubtful whether the Bank has ever invoked this guideline.

One of the major successes in 'land reform' claimed by the Bank is the Lilongwe project in Malawi. But this is land reform in a peculiar sense: it amounts to the conversion of communally allocated land into private property. The Bank argued that this would give the farmers greater security, but contradicted this assertion by saying that it would create a market in land that would ensure that the land reached its commercial potential or was sold.[17]

The Bank puts more emphasis on production than it does on income distribution. In some 'Green Revolution' areas, and perhaps particularly in India, the Bank has been able to claim some success in increasing production, even though the effects on income distribution are probably the reverse of what is sometimes claimed. The Bank's report, *IDA in Retrospect*, published in 1982 as part of its bid for IDA replenishment, makes much of the fact that

IDA was 'closely involved' in the introduction of Green Revolution technology in India, Pakistan and Bangladesh. It says that: 'India, which was the world's second largest cereal importer in 1966 and 1967, reached basic self-sufficiency toward the end of the 1970s'.[18] There is some dispute whether this 'self-sufficiency' did not imply lower levels of consumption within India. But it is widely accepted that the Green Revolution in India, whatever its effects on income distribution, landlessness and actual deterioration in the ability of those displaced to feed themselves, did result in increases in production above those that would have taken place without it, and that the World Bank made a contribution to those increases. Elsewhere, it is doubtful whether Bank projects in agriculture contributed very much even to production (see above, pp. 146). For example, one of the Bank's own (unpublished) evaluations of its project results, the 1979 'Grey Cover' *Annual Review of Project Performance Results*, records that out of 21 projects, 14 had not reached the expected higher yields, and out of 25 projects, 20 did not achieve the expected higher production.[19]

The Bank is also at times accused of bias against production for local consumption of food. Clearly the Bank favours greater commercialisation of agriculture. It advocates the integration of rural producers into national and international markets, in ways which parallel its advocacy of the greater integration of Third World countries into the world market, and which carry similar or greater dangers of increased dependency and precariousness in their livelihood. Thus one of the reasons presented by the Bank for devaluation is that it improves the incentives for agricultural exports, and the Bank is frequently accused of putting pressures on countries to increase their exports of agricultural commodities, curiously at a time of plummeting world prices for such products, at the expense of their ability to use their land and resources to produce their own food. This is an accusation which is made also by officials within the Bank, and especially in regard to the so-called Berg report.[20] One junior Bank official, describing the 'general bias' in favour of the cash economy and production for the market rather than for local consumption, said that 'old colonial hands' working for the Bank in India 'cooked the figures' to show that irrigation projects would produce more for the market and thus made them acceptable to senior management in the Bank.[21]

Cheryl Payer's book on the World Bank describes what she calls 'the attack on self-provisioning peasantries'. She gives the following quotation from a World Bank country report on Papua New Guinea (PNG):

> A characteristic of PNG's subsistence agriculture is its relative richness: over much of the country nature's bounty produces enough to eat with relatively little expenditure of effort. The root crops that dominate subsistence farming are 'plant and wait' crops, requiring little disciplined cultivation . . . Until enough subsistence farmers have their traditional life styles changed by the growth of new consumption wants, this labor constraint may make it difficult to introduce new crops.[22]

Not all 'subsistence farmers' live in such an idyllic situation, but many are better off than other rural producers who are totally, or largely, dependent on the market. The Bank is not only averse to subsistence farming; it also exaggerates its extent.[23] Thus the Berg report, ignoring the past century or so of African history, says:

> as the postcolonial period began, most Africans were outside the modern economy . . . African labour was overwhelmingly concentrated in subsistence-oriented farming . . . The dominance of subsistence production presented special obstacles to agricultural development. Farmers had to be induced to produce for the market, adopt new crops, and undertake new risks.[24]

Elsewhere in the report, the Bank acknowledges that:

> All the evidence points to the fact that smallholders are outstanding managers of their own resources – their land and capital, fertiliser, and water. They can be counted on to respond to changes in the profitability of different crops and of other farming activities . . .[25]

The introduction of commercialised inputs into agriculture may raise yields and rural incomes. But it sometimes merely adds to the precariousness of rural producers by making them more deeply indebted, increasing the costs of failure, and adding to the inducements for landlords to throw them off their land.

And yet, in all its major publications on agriculture, and particularly in its 1975 sector paper on *Rural Development*, the

Bank has regularly argued the need to bring the rural population 'from traditional isolation to integration with the national economy', and therefore the international economy. This was of course a problem that exercised colonialists, especially in Africa. It has also been faced by many industrialising societies, including Britain in the nineteenth century and the Soviet Union in the 1920s: how to extract a surplus from rural areas to feed the towns and, in the case of most Third World countries, to keep urban elites, locally and abroad, in the import-dependent luxury to which they have become accustomed. It is clearly necessary, for most societies which wish to escape from poverty, either to produce or to import food to be consumed by those who do not grow it themselves. The problem is that, in nearly every case, this has been achieved at the cost of greatly increased hardship for the people who do produce the food. This was certainly the case throughout Europe and in the Soviet Union. It is no less so under the methods advocated by the World Bank and other supporters of the greater commercialisation of Third World agriculture under capitalism, especially those embodied in the so-called Green Revolution, as innumerable publications have demonstrated. If this type of agricultural modernisation did hold out the prospect of more security and well-being for most people in rural areas, as well as more products for the towns and for export and instead of more wealth for some landlords, then of course there would be nothing to criticise. But, up to now, the reverse is more typically the case, even though the Bank's projects in agriculture are advertised as a means of redistributing income to the poor.

Livestock loans in Latin America

> . . . the cattle fatten on the plains while the people often have to struggle for a bare existence in the hills.
>
> World Bank 1950[26]

The World Bank's first loans to Third World agriculture went to Latin America to develop livestock. They began in 1963–4 with loans to Chile and Paraguay and grew in number and size throughout the 1960s and into the 1970s. This section is largely based on internal Bank evaluations of these projects, so-called Project Performance Audit Reports (PPARS), produced by the

Operations Evaluation Department (OED) of the Bank, including documents on 13 projects in nine countries. The Operations Evaluation staff are independent of the projects staff; the idea is that they have no vested interest in making the projects sound better than they really are, unlike the projects staff whose success within the Bank depends on 'their' projects being good – having high rates of return, and so on. The OED has in fact produced some fairly damaging indictments of the Bank's livestock projects, none of which have been published.

The documents show that the projects were remarkably unsuccessful in most of their stated aims. The projects were not intended to help the poor, to create jobs, or to make the distribution of wealth more fair. But they strengthened the position of the rich to an extent far beyond that expected by the Bank. Moreover the projects *were* intended to increase productivity by lending to experienced ranchers, by establishing modern farming methods, and by funding useful research. In this, by and large, they failed. They did so because the Bank ignored the realities of the countries it was lending to and because the Bank was more concerned with lending money, and with the conditions attached to that money, than it was with the quality of its projects.

The projects made credit and technical assistance available to medium and large ranchers. The credit was intended to enable ranchers to improve their pastures and herds by investing in fencing, new grasses, salt-licks, vaccines, veterinary services and other inputs. And the technical assistance was to help ranchers to introduce new methods of farm management and to phase out unproductive traditional practices. The Bank believed that it was only the lack of money and know-how which prevented Latin American ranchers from abandoning traditional extensive ranching and becoming efficient producers in the mould of Australian ranchers.

The institutional arrangements were the same for most of the loans. Loans went usually to the country's Central Bank and from there out in sub-loans to ranchers. Occasionally they were disbursed through private banks like Chase Manhattan, as in the Dominican Republic project. Usually a Livestock Project Division (LPD) was set up in the Central Bank to assess ranchers' requests for credit, to grant the sub-loans, and to give technical assistance. Most of the projects had research components – either to study technical issues such as the transfer of Australian grasses to Brazilian soil, or to study marketing problems such as the lack of hygienic slaughter houses. Many of the projects had training components which provided for 10–20 technicians to go on courses in the developed world, usually New Zealand.

The Bank believed that medium and large commercial farmers were ideal loan recipients because they were educated and entrepreneurial, and because they controlled most of the land generating the bulk of agricultural production anyway. During this period the Bank did not lend to smaller producers; an inter-agency agreement decreed that they were the domain of the Inter-American Development Bank and the US Agency for International Development. The subsistence sector, on the other hand, was not a serious option, as one Bank report explained, because it 'employs a primitive technology that is difficult to modify because of the problems of communicating with numerous, dispersed and generally illiterate producers.'[27]

The projects were similar in design, and they were also similar in the ways in which they failed and in the ways in which they differed from what was expected of them at appraisal. Thus the projects, already targeting a small population, reached fewer people than anticipated. The size of both sub-loans and ranches tended to be larger than expected. And the ranches tended to be sited on flat and fertile land which both the Bank and governments maintained should only be used for intensive crop production. Moreover, the ranchers tended to use sub-loans to expand their land holdings through purchase or renting and to create new pasture rather than improve existing pasture. They expanded their herds through purchase rather than improving the health of their herds. And they tended to reject the technical innovations and management practices advocated by the Bank. The projects rarely achieved the hoped-for rises in beef production, drops in calf mortality, rises in weaning rates and other improvements which should have resulted from better husbandry. And rises in production tended to stem from expansion of extensive-style ranches rather than from intensified production.

The majority of ranchers had other professions, many had urban investments, and most were absentee landowners, even though residency was often understood to be a condition of the sub-loan. The ranchers tended to submit an investment plan for approval to obtain a sub-loan and then to ignore it once they had the credit, and they tended to have good access to existing sources of credit and to consume a disproportionate amount of it. Local project staff tended to spend almost all their time checking and granting requests for credit. Rarely was there enough staff to provide technical assistance or to monitor what was happening on the farms. Bank staff tended to be concerned primarily with the rate of loan disbursement with the result that the ranch impact of projects was poorly supervised. Furthermore, Bank staff tended to over-emphasise the need for the project and then to over-emphasise its achievements at its close, thus inflating the rate of return and making the project appear more successful than it actually was.

From the evidence of another internal Bank evaluation, a 1976 OED study, identical trends existed on 20 agricultural credit projects in Mexico, Uruguay, Pakistan, Morocco and the Philippines. This gives additional confirmation that these are real tendencies in Bank projects and not one-off variations. Thus:

> The greatest gaps between appraisal forecasts and survey results are explained by: expansion in the size of crop farms at rates far greater than anticipated; shortfalls in expected technical improvements, especially from targets implicit in the text of the appraisals; production increases that were everywhere lower than anticipated when measured per cultivated hectare; and the decision by the ranchers to build up herds larger than expected.[28]

Two further patterns emerged from these documents. The first is the way in which projects affected land reform: in several countries ranchers used sub-loans to convince authorities that they were fully exploiting their land and thereby evaded expropriation under agrarian reform laws. The second is the impact of the projects on domestic beef consumption: although most of the projects claimed to aim to raise domestic beef consumption, the Bank pressured countries to liberalise their trade policies in order to boost beef exports, with the result that beef became more scarce and more expensive in the domestic markets – and domestic consumption dropped.

The projects were aimed at medium to large ranchers – a wealthy group in the top 1–2 per cent of the population. But even among this elite a pecking order prevailed and the richest of the ranchers monopolised the sub-loans – as in the case of Ecuador where the largest 39 ranchers accounted for 48.5 per cent of the sub-loans, the 16 largest loans accounted for 26.6 per cent of all loan funds, and the projects ended up addressing the top 0.1 per cent of cattleholders.[29] Projects funded fewer farmers, granted larger sub-loans, and financed larger ranches than expected. In Honduras the first livestock project was to fund 135 ranches but only 78 received funds; the average investment per ranch was 79 per cent greater than expected; and the average ranch was 840 instead of 381 hectares. Ecuador's first project was aimed at 240 ranchers but only 128 received sub-loans; sub-loans were 80 per cent greater than expected. In Colombia's first project 700 farms participated instead of the 1,200 planned and cost per ranch was $33,800 instead of $13,500. In Guatemala there were 232 sub-loans instead of 300 and they were larger than expected. And finally in the Dominican Republic, 153 ranchers were financed instead of the 260 planned and the average sub-loan was $38,321 instead of $22,800.

The audit on this last project explains the bias towards the large farmers:

First, larger farmers tend to be the most knowledgeable about availability of credit funds and more willing and able to accept and cope with the risks involved . . . Second, participating banks tend to concentrate on larger clients because the cost of credit analysis and supervision are lower relative to the potential profit and there are fewer problems with land titles and/or real estate and chattel mortgages. Finally, even the LPD staff tended to look at sub-loan applications of larger farmers more enthusiastically in view of the possibility to commit larger credit amounts with the same effort and the better prospects for successful operations.[30]

But the larger operations were not successful. In fact they were the worst in terms of improving technology and in using land efficiently, a pattern that has been reported elsewhere in Latin America. As the Honduras audit observes:

the divergence from the appraisal design was also caused by the focus of the project on the largest ranchers. Though appraisal and other documents justified this choice on the grounds that the largest were the most efficient, the evaluation suggests that the largest were actually the most extensive and least technically oriented of the project ranches. In addition, the proportion of total property on project ranches in improved pasture decreases consistently as ranch size increases. The same phenomenon was found for value of investment per hectare of land in pasture on project ranches, i.e., a consistent decrease as ranch size increases.[31]

The Bank decided later that this trend in turn was due to who the largest landowners were. The practices that the Bank wanted to introduce relied on attentive management but most of the ranchers were absentee landowners, uncommitted to running efficient farms and with businesses to manage elsewhere: 'the owners seldom live on the farm . . .' (Colombia);[32] 'a large majority did not live on the ranch; half of them spent less than half-time on the ranch; and about half had significant incomes outside ranching. A large minority had urban investments and/or full time urban employment . . .' (Honduras);[33] '. . . most ranchers are absentee and are likely to prefer to keep land in extensive, unimproved holdings, relying on land price appreciation for their return' (Paraguay);[34] '. . . about 80% of the beneficiaries are absentee middle and large landowners' (Bolivia);[35] 'About two-thirds of the farmers have sources of income besides livestock farming . . . 54% of these ranchers were doctors, lawyers, military men, engineers, politicians, economists, agronomists and veterinarians' (Dominican Republic).[36]

In some projects the Bank suggested that if owners were going to absent themselves, they should hire literate and skilled foremen and pay them well. But this rarely happened. In other projects the Bank considered making residency a condition of lending – but never did. Only the Ecuador projects found a partial solution to absentee ownership: 'funds were sometimes included in the loans to build a house on the farm for the owner and his family'[37] – an extraordinary measure given the wealth of the ranchers.

The net effect of lending to the rich, with additional sources of income and little commitment to using their land productively, was threefold. First, the Bank lost at its own game: the Bank's technical suggestions were ignored and efficiency did not increase.

Second, because ranchers were not using the sub-loans as intended by the Bank, they had money with which to expand their landholdings and herds and become even bigger land and cattle owners. And third, as a combined result of the above two points, there was a major project deviation – a Bank term to say that the projects did not turn out as planned.

In Guatemala, the project's main technical objective, the elimination of *esquilmo*, or the deprivation of calves of part of the mother's milk so as to market the rest, failed. *Esquilmo* actually increased and beef production was much lower than expected. In Bolivia, there were no improvements in animal health and a large proportion of the increased beef output was smuggled across the borders into neighbouring countries. In Paraguay, 'increases in beef production and in ranch technology co-efficients [fell] well short of those projected at appraisal'.[38] In the Dominican Republic, 'basic weaknesses of herd management remain[ed] unchanged. Calving rates did not appear to have improved . . . and even deteriorated on beef fattening farms'.[39] In Colombia, the calving rate dropped and 'no noticeable new technical or managerial improvements [were] effectively introduced'.[40] And finally, in Honduras, the ranchers continued the practices that the Bank wanted phased out; they 'sold steers before they reached market weight . . . sold reproducing stock to generate capital . . . milked beef cattle . . . and intended to continue to do so . . . and spent only one third the recommended amount on animal health'.[41] Where productivity did rise, as in Colombia, 'it increased mainly as a consequence of extensive use of additional lands and increased herds'.

And it was invariably less than projected at appraisal.[42] Purchase of land and cattle and the creation of new pasture took place far beyond what appraisal missions had foreseen. The purchase of land was particularly marked in the Dominican Republic. The purchase of cattle occurred in almost all of the projects to such an extent that the price of choice cattle breeds was driven up in many countries. Because of this, many Bank audits query whether the projects significantly increased the size of a country's herd: their main effect may have been to cause the simple transfer of cattle from other parts of the country to the project region as project ranchers gained the finance to buy them.

If the Bank were to be challenged with the statement that the ranchers had taken advantage of its laxness – taken the Bank's money and done as they pleased with it – the Bank would probably murmur something about development being a dynamic process and the need to be flexible. But it does seem that the ranchers never had much intention of doing with the money what the Bank suggested, as in Colombia where, 'there was a tendency for ranch plans to be prepared mainly for the sake of submission to the . . . Loan Approval Committee, and then to be departed from . . .'[43] The Paraguay loans give a particularly vivid picture of the ranchers' lack of interest in anything except the money. The project staff were located in the capital, Asunción, with no vehicles and no travel budget and therefore unable to reach most of the project ranches. The ranchers were willing to fly out staff in order to be appraised and to qualify for a sub-loan. But once they had the credit, unconvinced of the Bank's technical package, they would not fly out the staff to give technical assistance.

But if the ranchers took advantage of the Bank – used its money and ignored its directives – the Bank let them. For example, in the case of Paraguay, the local staff went without transportation for eight years and through three projects with the Bank's knowledge. How can this be explained? A study of these documents seems to suggest that the Bank was not interested in the technical improvements it advocated. In the cases of Brazil and Guatemala, Bank and government officials never actually agreed on *what* the technical package should be. But still the loans went ahead, one to Guatemala and two to Brazil. Later the audit would say of the massive loans to Brazil:

> The Bank attempted to impose a particular approach on
> Brazil without sufficient sensitivity to local conditions,
> ecological, economic and political, while the Government first
> agreed to what the Bank wanted and then altered its position,
> and without adequate explanation. Perhaps, more
> importantly, the Bank and the Government disagreed on
> whether new (foreign) technologies were really fundamentally
> different from those already used in Brazil; how new
> technologies, foreign or domestic, could be tested for
> profitability; and how new technologies, if found beneficial,
> could be diffused throughout the sector. Without such
> agreement, progress was difficult to achieve.[44]

But if the Bank was not interested in the technical improvements its projects were to foster, what was it interested in? From these documents it appears to have been primarily concerned with the smooth disbursement of its loans – which would explain why the technical wrinkles in the Paraguay and Brazil projects (to name just a few) were never ironed out. The evidence for this is twofold. First, at all levels, there was much more pressure to lend money than there was to see that it was being correctly used. From the loan officers in the World Bank who wanted to make their full annual quota of loans, to the Latin American bureaucrats in the Central Banks who wanted to lend to the richest applicants so that the sub-loans could be large and the loan disbursed quickly, the emphasis was on getting the money out.

Most of the audits contain descriptions of how local project staff were so busy appraising ranch plans and approving sub-loans that they had little time to give technical assistance or check up on the use of funds, as in the Dominican Republic, where:

> Although the Livestock Project Division did a commendable job, staff constraints prevented it from fulfilling all functions outlined in the appraisal report . . . provision of technical advice to ranchers and farmers after investment fell short of expectations. It would have been impossible to request the task from LPD, overburdened with its other duties and understaffed. Adequate funds should have been provided in the credit to alleviate budgetary constraints preventing the employment of additional staff.[45]

But as in Paraguay, funds were never provided, although the Bank knew of the problem, because the main task, the disbursement of credit, was proceeding without hitches. Bank staff tended to put considerable pressure on local staff to disburse sub-loans quickly, which meant that local staff had even less time for technical assistance and also that the wrong sort of ranchers tended to be selected. One criterion for borrowing turned out to be the possession of 'urban real estate and non-ranch income . . .'[46] Many other Bank documents, not only those evaluating these 13 Latin American projects, comment on the Bank staff's virtually exclusive preoccupation with the disbursement of loans. The big 1976 OED study of 20 agricultural credit projects in Mexico, Uruguay, Morocco, Pakistan and the Philippines, for example, remarks that 'much higher priority was given to the flow of credit to the farmers than to the impact of the farm investments'.[47]

Such project supervision as there was was of poor quality. The Guatemala audit describes typical supervision:

> 15 different experts . . . were involved in the 16 visits paid to the project. Ten of them visited the project once; another three of them only twice. The 'burden' of continuity was provided by two experts, who paid 3 and 5 visits respectively. In seven cases none of the supervision staff had visited the project before. Only in five cases one of the supervisors had been on the previous mission . . . Thus, field supervision was fragmented, staff continuity, very low.[48]

The most devastating description of the faults of the Bank's project supervision comes from the 1976 OED Agricultural credit study. It claims that fundamentally the Bank does not have a clue as to what its projects actually do:

> The first and lasting impression is one of an enormous amount of work to be done, and of it being done, in haste, by individuals with heavy travel schedules, inadequate time in the office to prepare for travel, and few of them able to pay more than one or two visits on any series of projects to any single country . . . this fact and the consequent lack of familiarity with country and program problems was the single most important criticism voiced by the [representatives] from the five countries . . . only one out of every four individuals made more than one mission on any one series of projects, and only one of seven made more than two . . . 53 out of the 73 individuals never got back on a subsequent mission to look at the programs. The country representatives complained that they hardly ever saw the same person twice, and had to guide each new arrival through the same material . . .
>
> . . . If supervisions were carried out in conjunction with pre-appraisal or appraisal of new projects, the latter functions took precedence in the crowded schedule of the mission . . . [And] four times as many man-weeks were being spent appraising a new project as were spent supervising an old one in any given year . . . It seems clear . . . that for projects without expectations of significant technical change, the supervision system prevailing throughout the study period was

not providing the kind of information needed by the Bank to know what was happening not only in the banks but on the farms . . .

. . . Supervision schedules rarely allow enough time for the extensive field interviewing that even the best of the project staff would need in order to speak confidently about field results first hand. Discussion of impact in supervision reports has been second hand, if it appeared at all . . . The Bank could make no independent judgement as to whether changes on the farms were proceeding as expected . . . Simply put, the Bank did not know what was happening on the farm, let alone how much was attributable to the project.[49]

Research, which was also not central to the main thrust of project work (disbursement), often fell by the wayside too, as in Guatemala:

. . . when too much of its staff's attention was diverted from its major task [lending], the Bank requested that research activities be contracted out. No contract was ever formalised and the research program lapsed.[50]

As this happened in almost every project, the Bank's claim that it is searching for new technologies for Third World agriculture should be treated with scepticism.

Pressure on Bank staff to find new projects meant that often staff embroidered reality to create a project. This gives rise to the second curious pattern that runs through all the projects. In the appraisal reports, the need for the project is exaggerated by describing the situation as worse than it actually is. In the completion report, on the other hand, the achievements of the project are over-estimated. Often this is done by miscalculations of variables such as calving rates but with the mistakes always in the direction that flatters the project and raises its rate of return. The audits usually point this out as in the case of the Dominican Republic where the pre-project scenario is set too low: 'pre-project yields of milk and beef were well above appraisal estimates'.[51] And the post-project scenario is too buoyant:

[The completion report] assumes that production increases will continue at a fast pace but it seems that its provisions are too optimistic . . . Only under very optimistic assumptions, which the text of the completion report itself would seem to rule out, do the audit's calculations reach the [completion report's] estimate of 21%.[52]

The audit concludes that the rate of return is possibly as low as 5–15 per cent. One of the Colombia projects shows a similar pattern:

> Technical parameters have improved on the ranches . . .
> However, the appraisal estimates of their pre-development level were too pessimistic, and of their post-development level somewhat optimistic. Both misestimates [lead] to an over-estimation of the rates of return of the project at appraisal.[53]

And in fact the appraisal reports, the OED staff conclude, consistently over-estimated the projected rate of return (see Tables 8 and 9). In Honduras the Bank staff also exaggerated the ranchers' need for credit to make the project more compelling. The ranchers were starved of credit, said the appraisal report, when in fact they got more than their fair share of it:

> It was also stated at appraisal that the Bank loan would represent the first time that a government-sponsored program in Honduras would make long-term investment credit available to large ranchers . . . The state development bank (BNF), it was said, provided substantial amounts of livestock credit, but restricted its application to small and medium farmers . . . It turns out, however, that many project ranchers had ample access to BNF credit, both before and during their participation in the Bank project. Out of a sample . . . interviewed . . . 88% reported having BNF credits . . . this finding suggests that large ranchers had more than a proportionate share of BNF credit . . .[54]

This pressure to lend has received some Bank scrutiny: the 1976 OED study described pressures 'felt by the persons responsible for the original appraisal draft to describe some projects in the most favourable light – particularly credit projects where . . . nothing definite can really be said at all in advance about how the borrower will actually use his physical resources'.[55]

OED also noted that, 'rather modest values and claims written into the original draft occasionally got embellished in the subsequent review process . . .'[56] But no motivations were given for it.

Table 8 Comparison of Economic Rates of Return from Nine
   Livestock Projects

	Appraisal Forecasts %	Audit Estimate %
Dominican Republic (1 project)	21	5–15
Guatemala (1 project)	13	12
Brazil (1st and 2nd projects)	18–23	8
Paraguay (3rd project)	29	8–10
Honduras (1st project)	18	13
Colombia (2nd project)	22	10
Ecuador (1st and 2nd projects)	27	11–12

Source: PPARs of respective projects

Table 9 Financial Rates of Return: Comparison of Appraisal
   Forecasts with OED Estimates

	Financial Rates of Return (overall investment)	
	Appraisal Forecasts %	OED Survey Estimates %
Livestock		
Mexico (2nd, 3rd and 4th projects)	21–35	13
Uruguay (3rd and 4th projects)	22–30	6
Crops		
Mexico (3rd and 4th projects)	26–37	n.a.
Morocco (2nd project – rainfed cereal farm)	32	5
Pakistan (3rd project – tractor farm)	55	50
Philippines (2nd project – tractor rice farm)	100	50
Philippines (2nd project – tiller rice farm)	65	5

Source: World Bank. 1976. Operations Evaluation Report: Agricultural
   Credit Programs. Vol. II. p. 97.

n.a. The Mexican crop returns were not calculated.

For lack of a better term, the driving force behind the pressure to lend could be called 'institutional momentum': the more you lend, the more important you are. This applies to the Bank as an institution: it wants to remain the largest and moşt influential development agency. It applies to the Director of the Latin America and Caribbean Division: he wants his region to account for the largest share of loans because it adds to his prestige and clout, and therefore gives him better access to senior Bank management. He will be able to demand more staff and a larger budget. And it applies down to the most junior loan officer who knows that if he shows himself to be productive, swiftly appraising new projects and handling old ones, he will get a promotion. Pressure to lend was particularly acute during the McNamara years, when these projects were taking place, as McNamara wanted and got massive yearly increases in Bank lending. But it has always been a major force behind Bank operations.

These 13 projects also worsened land distribution. Ranchers were enabled to use sub-loans to avoid expropriation under land reform movements. This occurred in Colombia, Ecuador and Honduras. In the first Colombia project, sub-loan commitments and disbursements were at their peak at the height of the fear of agrarian reform in 1967 and 1968.[57] In a discussion of both Colombia projects, the 1976 audit says that 'fear of agrarian reform may have induced investments on many ranches for the sole purpose of preventing expropriation . . . investments are believed to have been accelerated because landlords intensified production out of fear that their under utilized land would be expropriated'.[58]

In Ecuador, land invasions peaked in 1968–9 when the first project began disbursing:

the threat of land reform and land invasions made the . . . project more attractive because it seemed to lower the probability of expropriation. Land reform legislation provided for the expropriation of lands which were under utilized, but producers owning under utilized lands were granted a period of delay during which they could demonstrate that their lands were being improved and utilized productively. The existence of a cattle ranching development plan implied a long term commitment to continuing improvements, and the physical investments which were made, such as fencing corrals, other structures and cattle, served as an easily observable indicator that improvements were occurring.[59]

[In Honduras] the threat of invasion and expropriation was an important element in the decision of many sub-borrowers . . . to develop their ranches, or to develop them in the ways that they did. The new law exempted properties that were already being worked, and, particularly pertinent to potential sub-borrowers, properties that had obtained financing to undertake farm development. Pasture was the quickest way to get considerable amounts of land under cultivation [as opposed to crops].[60]

The same phenomenon is reported in the OED study of agricultural credit projects in Mexico, Uruguay, Morocco, Pakistan and the Philippines:

The increase in farm size, clearing of bush, leveling of land and extension of fences and physical infrastructure to further reaches of the borrower's property are in some cases almost certainly in response to the threat which the gathering social reform legislation poses for larger farmers . . . Unutilized property is most vulnerable to legislation written to redistribute land. A cynic could claim that all the Bank has been doing is to help large farmers take evasive action by putting in a minimum of infrastructure to pass legal tests of utilization. Since we are dealing with intelligent producers, it would be astonishing if these considerations did not enter their investment decisions.[61]

A second way that the Bank's activities conflicted with land reform movements was by condoning cattle production on prime agricultural land. Many Latin American agrarian reform laws legislated to confine cattle to pasture and to devote rich, flat and fertile land to crops. In theory, the Bank confirmed this position when in the early 1970s it released a statement that livestock projects should not be sited in areas suited to intensive cultivation or where rural population density was high. However, in practice, this stance made no difference.

In Honduras, in spite of a 1972 law restricting cattle to pasture, the majority of ranches from both projects were sited in populous areas and on land suited to intensive crop cultivation. Thus the projects competed with the thrust of land reform by blocking more rational land *ownership* and more rational land *use*.

> Rural population densities were higher in the areas of concentrated project development, as were organised peasant demands for land. There was a strong statistical association between the countries where project ranches were located and those countries where peasant groups had successfully claimed land under agrarian reform legislation. The intention of the second appraisal mission – to support extensive type improvements only in marginal areas – were not reflected in . . . lending policies. The ranches in the second project like the first, came to be located in those areas of Honduras that were most suited for intensive agriculture.[62]

There was an additional advantage for the ranchers in cattle production. This was that ranching creates few jobs and ranchers therefore did not have to worry about farmhands banding together and demanding their right to land.

Most Latin American land reform movements, including the Honduran, lacked teeth and expropriation was a rare event. However, in this case the ranchers had the Bank squarely behind them: local project staff were lobbying for them.

> [They] supported the cattlemen's association in asking for better treatment of expropriable cattlemen. The project director, who in the past had been executive secretary of the association, was co-operating with the committee set up by the Government to recommend changes to the regulations for the December 1972 legislation. These amendments . . . substantially broadened the class of exceptions.[63]

Not surprisingly, the Bank became identified 'with the forces of rural inequality in the countryside – as supporting the class that was the reform's most organised and vocal adversary'.[64] This is the most explicit case in the documents of the Bank intervening on behalf of ranchers to the extent of securing changes in land reform legislation for them. However, the 1972 Colombia study records that the Bank urged 'the authorities to protect farms covered by its farm credits loans from land reform'.[65]

The Honduras project is also a prime example of unrealistic appraisal followed by an inadequate supervision that focuses on the state of the project rather than the state of the region affected by the project.

From the Bank's point of view, the problem was partly that in some countries uncertainty over the direction the reforms would take caused periods of slow disbursement as ranchers were reluctant to take on loans if expropriation was a possibility, even though the loans were guaranteed by the government. This happened in the Dominican Republic but as the Bank notes approvingly: 'agrarian reform efforts by the government after the election were only hesitantly implemented . . . and many farmers turned back to . . . their livestock operations'.[66]

In Guatemala land issues caused major project deviation. Land disputes and civil unrest in the Pacific region where the project had been focused resulted in sub-borrowers investing the funds primarily in large ranches in Northern Alta Verapaz and the Peten – virgin tropical forest areas only then just recently opened up by roads. These areas are now regions of greatly inequitable land ownership and much violence.

What emerges most vividly from the audits' treatment of land reform is not just the lack of discussion but the tone that pervades them that land reform is a nuisance, interrupting the smooth functioning of the projects. In the Dominican Republic audit, land reform is discussed under the heading 'Weather and other risks'. In the Ecuador audit, Bank staff are reprimanded for not paying enough attention to land reform – a 'potentially disruptive factor in the implementation of the first livestock loan'.[67]

Most of these projects aimed to boost both beef exports and domestic consumption. But the audits fail to trace what happened to the increased production. Analysis seems to stop at the farm gate; another example of how little the Bank knows – or cares to know – about the impact of its projects. However, from other sources it is clear that exports of beef did rise in the late 1960s and early 1970s in Latin America, sometimes spectacularly. On the other hand, per capita beef consumption declined by 13.5 per cent between 1960 and 1974. During that same period Bolivia's per capita consumption fell by 15.4 per cent, Colombia's by 19 per cent, Guatemala's by 12.5 per cent and Paraguay's by 44.7 per cent. It was known by the late 1960s that this drop was occurring and that it was caused by exports: in 1969 the Foreign Agricultural Service of the US Department of Agriculture stated that 'the considerable growth in meat exports in recent years has been at the expense of domestic beef consumption'.[68]

Only the Brazil and Ecuador project documents discuss beef exports and their relationship with domestic consumption. There the discussion hinges on meat prices with the Bank pressuring the two governments to lift price controls so that the price of beef can rise to international levels and thus stimulate production.

Until 1967 Brazil had kept the price of beef low in the domestic market and ensured an abundant domestic supply by intermittently imposing price controls, export prohibitions and export quotas. During the negotiations for the first project, the government promised the Bank that it would remove all price and foreign trade controls on livestock products before the loan was signed. When the government complied, the price of beef shot up higher than expected due to high international prices. In 1970 the price became so high domestically that the government decided to suspend tax incentives for beef exports and to set a quota for the region which supplies meat to Rio de Janeiro and Sao Paulo in order to lower the cost for urban consumers. The Bank was displeased but did not suspend lending. The government assured the Bank that this was a temporary measure until the supply of beef increased.

The appraisal report for the second livestock project, written in 1972, states that 'impressive expansion of beef exports from 30,000m ton to about 200,000m ton . . . between 1966 and 1971 has been achieved at the expense of domestic consumption. An important objective of the Government is to continue the expansion of beef exports but without sacrificing domestic consumption.'[69] Yet elsewhere in the document the Bank continues to press for the permanent lifting of all 'disincentives to investment caused by government policies that [favor] the urban consumer at the expense of producers and exporters', and is clearly willing to go against government policy and to see domestic consumption drop.

Similarly in Ecuador the Bank pressured the government to create greater production incentives by freeing the price of beef. But the Ecuadorians refused. It was politically too hazardous:

> The Bank attempted to obtain a guarantee from the Government of Ecuador that the free movement of cattle and beef to domestic and export markets would be permitted. This guarantee would have ensured that domestic prices for these commodities would fully adjust to export market levels. The Government . . . refused to bind itself by such a guarantee . . . By maintaining . . . controls, the Government of Ecuador places an effective ceiling on prices to producers and thereby reduces the incentives for higher production. This disincentive . . . works particularly strongly against the introduction of capital intensive production techniques such as those which the Bank's livestock projects were designed to promote.[70]

Interestingly, Ecuador is one of only three Latin American countries to experience a rise in beef consumption between 1960 and 1974.

The Ecuador project was audited in 1975 and the Brazil project in 1979, long after the Bank became publicly concerned about the diets of the poor, so these audits are remarkable for their lack of interest in the nutritional impact of the projects.

Land reform in Colombia

> . . . can the Bank influence the course of events regarding the distribution of land, and income from the land, in the sovereign states that are members of the Bank?
>
> World Bank, 1975[71]

The World Bank and Colombia have had a long and intimate relationship dating back to 1949 when Colombia received its first loan from the Bank, one of the earliest the Bank made to the Third World. One of the special features of this relationship is that it is unusually well documented; Colombia was the country of choice when the Bank decided for the first and last time to study the total impact of the Bank on one country. This study came out in 1972 as *Bank Operations in Colombia – An Evaluation* and covers the period 1950–1970. It aroused considerable interest outside the Bank; for example Keith Griffin wrote about it in his book *Land Concentration and Rural Poverty*:

> Ex post evaluations of aid programmes are rare, and thus it is impossible to refute the claim that failures are exceptional and

> success the rule. The World Bank, however, is known to have
> assessed its operations in Colombia: rumour has it that the
> results were unflattering. In any case the report was not
> released . . .[72]

It has still not been released, but along with several other
documents written on Colombia, it has, since then, been leaked.
They provide details of the Bank's role in Colombian agriculture
and of seven Bank agricultural projects in Colombia. From this
information, it emerges that Bank projects worsened land tenure
and, by funding land settlements in remote areas, reinforced the
Colombian government's policy of substituting land settlement
for genuine land reform.

Land ownership in Colombia is concentrated in the hands of
relatively few people. The best figures on land tenure in Colombia
date from 1960 but they are generally thought to apply today.
They show that 1.2 per cent of the farms occupy 45 per cent of the
land and that 5.7 per cent of the farms occupy 70 per cent of the
farmland.[73] More recent statistics show that, if there has been a
change in land tenure since 1960, it has probably been for the
worse: between 1960 and 1971 the number of small farms (under
10 hectares) decreased and the number of large farms (over 200
hectares) increased.[74]

Concentrated land ownership has been long recognised even by
conservative Colombians as a problem, primarily because of its
association with backwardness in agriculture, and as long ago as
1936 the Colombian government passed a law allowing some land
reform. However, this law was ineffectual. The main initiative on
land reform in Colombia had to wait until 1961 when Law 135 was
passed and INCORA, the National Institute of Colonisation and
Agrarian Reform, was set up, partly in response to pressures from
the United States under the Alliance for Progress. The Alliance for
Progress was one of the reactions by the United States to the
Cuban revolution: to forestall more revolutions, the US wanted
Latin American governments, in return for financial aid, to improve
the conditions of their people and, specifically, to improve rural
living standards by 'effective transformation of land tenure and
use'.[75]

However, the Alliance was very vague about how this reform
should be carried out and at what pace. It was only certain that it

did not want a total reform, like Cuba's, which would completely alter all existing social, political and economic structures. Feder points out that this vagueness was the Alliance's downfall: 'it [was] left up to existing governments to break up *latifundios* for the benefit of the peasants', which, understandably enough, they were loath to do as, 'in most cases the governments owed their very existence to the *latifundio*-owning class'.[76]

Lack of political will meant that throughout Latin America land reform proceeded at snail's pace during the early 1960s, and had virtually come to a standstill by the mid-1960s. Colombia's land reform law was typical of the land reform laws enacted all over Latin America: it was cumbersome, weak and full of loopholes which favoured the landowners. It made genuine land reform impossible, if by land reform is meant 'giving the landless and nearly landless rights to good farm lands now held in large estates'.[77]

The Colombian law decrees that landless peasants should be settled first on publicly owned land, a move which should correctly be called colonisation and not land reform. After that, private land can be expropriated and peasants settled on it, but only in this order: first, if it is unused, then if it is inadequately used, then if it is cultivated by sharecroppers and small tenants, and then if it is land that the owners have voluntarily given to INCORA. Only as a last resort can peasants settle on land that is being put to good use and the law does not define what constitutes 'good use'.

There is no time limit in Law 135, so that if land is not being well managed and expropriation is looming, the owner has the right and an undefined amount of time to begin to manage the land by renting out part of it or by putting cattle on it – as occurred in the livestock projects described in the previous section, including the two Colombian livestock projects. The Colombian law refers only to 'land' and not 'farms', thus whole farms are not expropriable but only that part of them that is unused or inadequately used and this is usually the poorest land. The Colombian law also allows owners to keep at least 100 hectares, regardless of whether the land is well used or not. Feder reports that, 'In fact, the owner of poor farmland can request an additional 100 hectares – an example of equity in reverse.'[78] Importantly, Law 135 does not make concentrated land ownership or *latifundio* illegal.

Finally, the ability of INCORA to focus its efforts on land reform was deliberately curtailed by the Colombian government when it shifted on to INCORA many of the tasks of the Ministry of Agriculture: market organisation, road construction, co-operatives, land improvement, irrigation and drainage, livestock and crop development programmes, and credit and technical assistance not only for land reform beneficiaries but for other farmers as well.[79]

Predictably, the result of Law 135 and of INCORA's efforts was that a small amount of land settlement occurred but almost no expropriations of private estates. Between 1961 and 1968, INCORA's most dynamic period, only 3,500 out of a target of 175,000 families benefited from the reform and expropriation accounted for only 1.8 per cent of the land handled by INCORA; the vast majority of the land INCORA dealt with was public. At this rate, Feder estimated in 1971, it would take 1,300 years to settle the number of landless peasants that there had been in the 1960s and centuries more if population growth were taken into account.[80]

INCORA concentrated on land settlement projects and, to a lesser extent, assistance to areas of spontaneous colonisation, neither of which were in the central fertile regions of Colombia. This emphasis on colonisation, as opposed to redistribution, occurred all over Latin America. In Ecuador, for example, after 12 years of land reform only 12–15 per cent of the land distribution planned had taken place and 73 per cent of that 'distribution' had taken the form of colonisation schemes.[81]

Colonisation schemes have emerged as the way in which governments avoid expropriating fertile land held in big estates. A joint report of the FAO and the ILO on the progress of land reform between 1968 and 1974 stated that:

> Efforts have been made to persuade governments not to divert from the real problem of the needed structural changes through settlement projects under the pretext of a need to extend the agricultural frontier.[82]

Feder has called land settlement schemes 'anti-land reform measures'; furthermore they are expensive and usually unsuccessful:

> Colonisation schemes are always extremely costly . . . But the high costs of these schemes, which benefit the construction firms or the cement industry much more than the peasants,

have never been a deterrent to planning new ones. This demonstrates that costs do not matter when the preservation of the status quo is involved. Scarcity of resources is alleged only when it comes to effective programs to assist the peasants. Nor is it a deterrent that most colonisation schemes have been dismal failures for the peasants . . .[83]

Even the Bank, in its *Land Reform Sector Policy Paper* in 1975, said that:

There are severe limitations on settlement as a means of reaching large numbers of landless people or relieving pressures on the land . . . The capital requirement of more than $5,000 per family limits the prospects of this approach. Clearly, the whole approach to capital-intensive settlement requires re-examination considering the magnitude of the problem . . .[84]

However, in spite of this consensus that colonisation schemes are a costly, inappropriate and inadequate response to the needs of landless peasants, and in spite of the agricultural problems that tend to arise due to poor soils (if the soils were not poor, the rich would own the land already), the World Bank has made settlement schemes a major component of its agricultural strategy in Colombia and Latin America in general. At present the World Bank is funding large colonisation projects in Brazil and Peru, and a scheme for the jungle area of Western Ecuador was under consideration in 1980.

Between 1949 and 1983 Colombia's agricultural sector changed in a way that has been repeated all over the Third World. On the one hand, small farmers lost their land and the per capita production of food for domestic consumption, carried out by small farmers, declined. On the other hand, large commercial farmers expanded their landholdings and the production of export crops grew. This pattern occurred because of population growth, because there was no land reform, and as the 1972 Bank document explains, 'because of the availability of credit, supporting services and new technology, all of which has tended to favour the larger farmers and inadvertently work to the disadvantage of the small farmers'.[85] Colombia has retained its traditional agricultural structure: cattle and other export crops (with the exception of coffee) occupy the flat land in the mountains and the wide river valleys, and domestic food production is restricted to the steep sides of the hills and mountains. Griffin estimates that in Colombia, 'nearly four times as much land is devoted to extensive grazing of cattle as is devoted to crops'.[86]

Relatively new features in Colombian agriculture are exports of flowers, which the Bank calls 'a success story' ('they are grown in areas adjacent to Bogota, taking advantage of the year round favourable climate, and shipped by air to world markets'), and exports of marijuana.[87] However, the main impact of these new exports has been to create additional wealth for the already wealthy and, like the expansion of the more traditional exports, to exacerbate conditions in the rural areas.

By 1983 the Bank had made 14 loans to Colombia's agricultural sector amounting to $280.6 million. This is out of a total of 28 loans and $1585.7 million committed to Colombia since 1949. Four large Bank missions in 1949, 1955, 1956 and 1970 looked into the problems of Colombia's agricultural sector. The Bank's strategy, if it can be said to have had one, seems to have been to deplore the inequality in the countryside, to emphasise increased productivity through its projects, and to turn a blind eye when the wealthy received the majority of loan benefits but did not increase their productivity. With respect to land reform, the World Bank took a negative stance: asking the government not to allow expropriation of land from ranches receiving Bank sub-loans, promoting colonisation schemes, paying little attention to tenancy arrangements, and providing minimal supervision of projects so that the largest ranchers received the majority of project benefits.

Over the years the Bank has maintained a steady concern about the technical problems holding back Colombian agriculture – the lack of soil conservation, irrigation, credit and mechanisation. In each of its big studies, it has also pointed out the concentrated land ownership, but not always from the same perspective. In the 1950s and 1960s unequal ownership of land was seen as an obstacle to raising productivity and production, while in the 1970s and onwards the Bank documents tend to discuss it more in terms of equity and fairness. In practice, however, the Bank's approach to the problem of land ownership has remained consistently laissez-faire and neglectful.

The 1950 report described the unequal distribution of land as the single most important factor holding productivity down, stating urgently that some way had to be found 'of inducing owners of arable land either to put it to its most economic use, or to dispose of it to others who will'.[88] The Bank recommended two courses of action. First, the Bank wanted a system of taxation which would penalise poor use of good land. It proposed that the best farm lands be revalued for tax purposes to reflect their true value, a proposal the Colombians rejected. Second, the Bank wanted to see an expansion of the work of the Institute for Parcelisation and Colonisation which had been set up in 1948 to assist families to settle either on public land or on parcels of large farms that the Institute was to buy and subdivide.

But the Bank did not pursue these solutions with any vigour. One reason was that throughout the 1950s the Bank believed that the fundamental problem was not a maldistribution of land but rather a maldistribution of people. The 1950 report claimed that:

> In order for additional goods and services of all kinds to be produced in Colombia, it is necessary that a smaller percentage of the population be engaged in agriculture and that more people be engaged in the production of other things. This means, in turn, that the productivity of each agricultural worker must be very much greater than prevails today.[89]

Dr Lauchlin Currie, head of the 1949 mission, certainly promoted this position. Currie, an enthusiastic advocate of industrialisation, worked closely with the Bank for several decades and was advisor to many Colombian governments. His position on agriculture reached its apogee in 1961 when he published an economic formula for Colombia: Operación Colombia. The formula, which received wide publicity at a time of national debate over land reform, said that:

> Colombia's real rural problem was an excess rural population. . . . This excess should be transferred, forcibly if need be, to the large cities and employed in public works in order to create increased consumer demand, which in turn would be met by increased industrialisation. Colombian agriculture would, meanwhile, be intensively mechanised, and the remaining rural population would be employed by these large, mechanised farming operations.[90]

The plan was never implemented, primarily because it would have been impractical and hugely expensive. However, the idea that people were in the wrong place and not land in the wrong hands, was inherent in the justifications for colonisation schemes. The next big Bank report on Colombian agriculture, in 1956, also suggested tax measures, this time a presumptive income tax, to increase land use in the big estates. This proposal was never effectively implemented.

In terms of agricultural projects the Bank was largely inactive during this period, apart from two loans for agricultural machinery in 1949 and 1954. For in spite of the ample attention paid to Colombian agriculture in reports, the Bank's main strategy at that time was the building of infrastructure for industrialisation. The Bank made three loans for agriculture in 1966, 1967 and 1969; two were for ranchers and one for the settlement of landless peasants. Then in 1970 a Bank mission studied the agricultural sector and faced, 'for perhaps the first time since 1949, the problem of rural poverty'.[91]

It also had to face the fact that taxation measures were not having their desired effect of increasing use of the land held in the large estates. Its response was to reprimand the Colombians for not carrying out more land distribution – this had a hollow ring, given the impact of the Bank's own projects.[92]

The next major Bank comment on Colombian agriculture is in the big internal OED document produced in 1972. It is emphatic that land redistribution is vital for Colombia and is critical of the Bank's performance with respect to land reform over the decades 1950–1970.

> The most significant shortcoming of the Bank policy in the agricultural field is to be found, not in the projects it could have financed and did not, nor in the limitations of the projects which it did finance, but in the very reticent attitude which it generally adopted towards land reform. This attitude may partially explain the lack of any significant progress in this field, perhaps by having created what could be considered a self-reinforcing situation whereby some Colombian policy makers have argued that land reform is not an advisable course as evidenced by the lack of interest expressed in it by the Bank, and some Bank staff would have argued that this

issue is not worth raising because it would not receive any effective political support. This is not to imply that the Bank has either willingly or actively obstructed land reform, but its clearly sceptical outlook, in principle, on this issue appears to some extent to have been used by powerful domestic interests groups opposed to land redistribution.[93]

It also stresses that colonisation is not an answer to the problem, and it advises that the Bank should either clearly support land reform or, 'if it is determined that land redistribution is not critical', then explicitly formulate alternative solutions.

The Bank opted for the alternatives – colonisation schemes and integrated rural development projects. The discussion of agriculture in the Bank's 1981 economic report on Colombia is as if the 1972 document had never existed – there is no mention of land reform:

> The primary objectives of investments in the agricultural sector are to expand supplies of basic foodstuffs . . . to diversify exports so as to lessen the country's dependence on coffee exports, and to improve the welfare of small farmers and landless rural workers . . . Investments in colonization, irrigation, land improvement and increased agricultural research and extension, are expected to raise agricultural productivity, particularly that of small farmers . . .[94]

The Bank has backed itself into a corner. By lending to an agricultural sector which desperately needs but undertakes no land reform, and being unable to lend to the larger farmers because of distributional concerns, the Bank is constrained to lend for integrated rural development projects or settlement schemes. The first, if they are in established agricultural areas, tend to be unsuccessful at increasing productivity and to worsen income distribution. The second tend to be environmentally and agriculturally unsound and also worsen land and income distribution. The Bank was concerned with two major settlement schemes in Colombia. One was the Caqueta land colonisation project. The first loan for Caqueta was signed in May 1971. Caqueta was one of the first integrated rural development projects – providing roads, farm development, research centres, primary schools, health centres, tree nurseries and forest reserves. The aim was to support the spontaneous settlement of smallholders in the Colombian Amazon who, by and large, were already in the jungle trying to eke out a living by clearing trees and growing food. Most had been driven from the Andean highlands by civil conflict (La Violencia) and by the inequitable land ownership. Although the project had many components, the Bank's contribution was to go almost entirely for roads and cattle: $3.73 million for roads, $3.77 million for cattle, and only $0.41 million for health and education and $0.14 million for administration.

The project was over-ambitious at appraisal and had to be scaled down. Fewer roads were built than planned, although they cost 210 per cent more than expected due to inaccurate appraisal and technical problems, foremost among which was a nine-month rainy season during which work had to be suspended. Furthermore, the government failed to provide funds for road maintenance and many subsequently broke up. Only 60 instead of 90 schools were built. And only 1,700 farmers instead of the planned 4,500 received credit.

The crucial technical assistance programme, 'for which no explicit allowance had been made',[95] was completely inadequate: when the second Caqueta project was appraised, it was noted that an outstanding problem of Caqueta 1 was the 'lack of technical assistance to farmers'.[96] One of the difficulties was that the 'Loan supervisors devoted most of their time to loan control rather than technical assistance'.[97] The research programme took several years to become operational and in 1978 had not yet had an impact on regional technology.

Undoubtedly the two most important issues surrounding this project and its follow-up projects are, first, land distribution and, second, the project's ecological impact, an issue that critics of the Bank have tended to neglect, perhaps because of a misguided notion that concern about the environment is a luxury the Third World cannot afford. When the Bank appraised this project it claimed that Caqueta was virgin territory – although the area had been opened up by the rubber boom at the turn of the century, was later the site of military activity due to border conflicts with Peru, and was also the site of unsuccessful government colonisation schemes in the 1950s and early 1960s, some of which received USAID money.

This was a fundamental appraisal error on the Bank's part. For the land was not at all virgin: land tenure patterns were well established and were 'already highly concentrated, replicating the land distribution of the older interior regions of the country'.[98] Census data from 1961 and 1971 showed that the largest 10 per cent of landholdings accounted for 57 per cent of the area, while the smallest 50 per cent accounted for 10 per cent of the area, with 54 per cent of holdings smaller than 50 hectares. The audit says that the Bank did not know any of this until it began preparing for a second Caqueta loan. Then it became clear that under the first project credit had gone to medium-sized landowners and not smallholders: no credit had gone to farmers with less than 50 hectares, 63 per cent of loan funds had gone to farmers with between 50 and 160 hectares, and 37 per cent went to farmers with more than 160 hectares (average farm size in this category being 257 hectares). From the data in the audit, it also appears that the Bank was lending primarily to wealthier migrants who could buy out the earlier colonists who had cleared the land; 63 per cent of the loans under Caqueta 1 went to farmers who had obtained their land by purchase rather than the claim of public lands which is what the first colonists would have tried to do. The original settlers were usually driven deeper into the jungle:

> The increase of farm land was not only achieved by clearing more forest but also by purchasing farm land cleared by pioneering settlers who moved on as the frontier of development advanced. This process of enlarging farms by purchase was accelerated by the soaring cattle prices. Although this development is not yet critical for the social structure of the area, INCORA is watching this process carefully and may have to intervene to avoid serious distortions in the equity of land ownership in the area.[99]

It is hard to imagine how INCORA, one of the weakest, poorest and least politically powerful government agencies, could closely monitor or intervene effectively in this situation. But how did it happen that the Bank, intending to lend to squatters, lent to medium-sized farmers instead? Firstly, a land title was a condition for receiving credit, but according to the audit, the 'land titling system favour[ed] those with greater personal resources, both financial and physical . . .'[100] And secondly, INCORA, powerless and under-funded, 'had difficulties in building up an adequate staff . . . for land titling.'[101] What staff it did have concentrated primarily on sub-loan disbursements, to the neglect of technical assistance.

The ecological impact of colonisation in tropical forest is at the heart of questions about this project. Can the fragile Amazon jungle support colonists? Experience from the Brazilian Amazon suggests that it cannot. There clearing forests for livestock exhausted soils and created hard-baked deserts. The Bank and the Colombian government knew this but both argued that without the project environmental damage would be worse as the settlement would be less controlled and rational. This is a dubious argument since the project would have speeded up the influx of people into Caqueta and beyond through the construction of roads, and since the measures taken by the project to protect the environment failed. The project claimed its intention to demarcate forest reserves, 'To provide for sustained timber production and also to fulfil ecological functions.'[102] But forestry does not appear on the table of projected costs and no Bank funding was allocated for it.

The environmental impact of the project has been grave. The colonists have removed almost all trees along river banks, leading to erosion and changes in the rivers:

> Rivers which once provided deep channels throughout the year and which were capable of navigation by paddle have increased their width several times and, in the process, become more shallow and filled with shifting sandbars. Navigation of large boats is now impossible in many parts . . . Caqueta has lost important transportation arteries as the rivers have deteriorated – and erosion has also eliminated many hectares of the area's most valuable soils.[103]

In spite of the environmental damage caused by the first project, the Bank decided to leave protective measures in the second project up to Colombian agencies – even though the Bank knew that these agencies would not be able to protect the environment as they are weak, poorly funded and staffed, and by the nature of their work, up against powerful vested interests.

The Bank's evaluation of the first project stated that,

> Laws have existed for some time requiring that colonists maintain forests for 50 meters from the river bank . . . These

laws simply are not respected, nor enforced and there appears to be no viable method to achieve enforcement without the use of a police power which does not exist in the zone. In appraising the second project the Bank considered developing a program to encourage tree establishment along the river banks, but decided that this work could be left to the government's own initiative. Little has been done to date.[104]

Basically, the ecological problem in Caqueta can be attributed to two things: political priorities and land tenure. For the Bank and the Colombian government prefer to permit ecological damage, with its harmful impact on natural resources, productivity and the quality of life, rather than to redistribute the ample good agricultural land owned by the wealthy to the rural poor. The following quote from the Bank evaluation of the first project, which really is nothing less than tragic, shows this clearly. It also shows the strain that peasants are forced by land tenure patterns to place on marginal environments, and in turn, the terrible toll that environmental collapse takes on peasants:

> The Bank was also concerned about appropriate forest use and the general ecological effect of widescale deforestation in this area of the Amazon . . . Although existing laws require recipients of more than 50 hectares of public lands to keep 20% under forest and allow Government to maintain 10% of the area as a protective zone, it has been impossible to enforce farmers' obligation. The Bank and INCORA attempted to set aside a forest reserve of 16,000 hectares during the second project to retain a significant area of forest cover . . . The effort was a failure; although an area of marginal development potential removed from current settlement was selected, political activists decided there must be something special about the area if an effort was being made to exclude colonists. The activists forced the forest guards out of the area and brought colonists into the reserve. INCORA and the Bank decided to give up the idea of a forest reserve rather than initiate the social conflict which might have occurred had an effort been made to recover the area invaded. No other zone of appropriate size for a forest reserve is available.
>
> Another ecological problem exists in the Andean cordillera. Although not located within (the project area), the cordillera

forms the catchment of most rivers flowing through the project area and accordingly developments there can strongly influence project activities. Many peasants accustomed to farming on the slopes in the highlands, migrated towards Caqueta in hopes of colonizing land. Discouraged by conditions in the tropical forest, they chose to remain at higher altitudes and established small farms on steeply sloping mountainsides. After deforestation and the planting of crops, or pasture formation, erosion has increased and threatens to devastate large areas. Rainfall now runs off the cordillera more rapidly, causing rivers in the project area to flood and erode during the rainy season and to run dry the rest of the year. Some claim that the weather itself is changing in the area, with less rainfall occurring . . . Efforts have been made to reduce erosion on the cordillera slopes, but the problem is extremely sensitive socially and politically. The only real solution is to move people out of the zone, prohibiting farming, and to reforest on a broad basis. There is no land, however, on which to place the inhabitants who would be displaced and pressures for land in other parts of Colombia would make new invasions by other peasants almost a certainty. The Government is considering a reforestation program to pay peasants for planting trees . . . If some radical reduction in erosion . . . is not brought about . . . it appears that damage in the project area may be great.[105]

Despite all this, the project completion report, prepared by the Bank staff responsible for the project, claims that,

The Caqueta Land Colonization Project is demonstrating, probably for the first time in South America, that a squatter can be assisted to settle permanently and establish a farm providing a reasonable living for himself and his family. The project has already shown the feasibility of the productive land use in the Amazon basin.[106]

This is an extraordinarily self-congratulatory claim, particularly as this project *did not* assist squatters and as Caqueta *is* being devastated like areas of the Brazilian Amazon. And in spite of the many serious unsolved problems with the first project, the second Caqueta project (for $19.5 million) became effective in 1976. It provides primarily for livestock purchase and road construction, but also for the construction of primary schools and health centres.

In 1979 the Bank began appraising another land settlement project. This was called El Retorno and was in the Orinoco-Amazon river basin of Colombia. The stated objective was to improve the income and social prospects of 1,500 settler families, to develop appropriate uses for tropical forest areas, to slow migration to other frontier areas and to minimise ecological damage. The project was to do this by providing credit for livestock and other farm investments; technical assistance, land titling and training, monitoring and evaluation; key roads, a ferry and internal feeder roads; health and education facilities and malaria control; tree nurseries and a research centre. The Bank was to lend $8.2 million primarily for roads and cattle; the total project was to cost $35.4 million.

When the El Retorno project was being prepared, it came to the attention of World Bank's Office of Environmental Affairs, who thought that it resembled the Caqueta projects in being economically and environmentally unsound. As in Caqueta, it seemed that the land titling system would result in fewer and richer beneficiaries, and it looked unlikely to come up with new uses for tropical soils as by funding it was primarily a livestock credit loan. The road building appeared more likely to hasten rather than slow migration to other frontiers, and ecological damage would probably be as difficult to prevent as it had been in Caqueta. When an early draft of the appraisal report came out, the Bank environmentalists criticised the project item by item. Two points in particular made the environmentalists suspicious that in spite of the document's progressive wording about new technology for tropical forests and the protection of the environment, the project was just an old-style livestock credit project masquerading as an innovative rural development project.

The research, on which the success of the project was supposedly based, was to receive only $500,000 over five years and this sum was meant to include environmental monitoring and satellite imagery. Could this possibly turn up new technology? Had the Caqueta research, similar in aim, come up with anything? And was INDERENA, the natural resource agency chosen to do the work, strong enough? INCORA had dismissed it the year before from

Caqueta because it 'remained unsatisfactory as a consequence of deficiencies in its technical, administrative and managerial capacity'.[107]

Even worse, the forest budget was only $180,000, which was to provide salaries for two foresters, establish a tree nursery, provide technical assistance to settlers to protect steep slopes and river banks, ensure that 30 per cent of the area remained under forest, implement fire control methods and start training programmes for settlers on the importance of forests. Furthermore, the project was actually predicated on the destruction of forest: 600,000 hectares of the 800,000 project area was a legally designated Amazon forest reserve. The project's going ahead depended on INDERENA transferring this land into INCORA's jurisdiction.

There was also a further concern. The project area surrounded three Indian reserves and there were Indians living in the eastern part of the project area. The anthropologist working with the Bank appraisal team reported 'open-conflict and tension between Indians and non-Indians due to encroachment of colonists on Indian land'.[108] She concluded that little could be done to prevent this, that the Indians might be better off if they were to move away from the reserves deeper into the jungle and that, 'it is unlikely that the Indians [on the three reserves] will survive in the rapidly changing socio-economic environment'.[109] Ultimately, the project's success depended on the government giving INCORA strong support, on accelerated titling and on the development of new technology for tropical forest soils – all of which sounded unlikely given the text of the appraisal report and the Caqueta experience.

Because of the environmentalists' criticisms, the Bank's agriculturalists revoked their approval of the project which was essential if the project was to proceed on towards the loan committee. Enraged, the Chief of the Region claimed on procedural grounds that the agriculturalists' move was invalid (approval had been withdrawn too late) and that the project would proceed to the next stage of appraisal. This was in late August 1979. Then silence descended over the project, until a staff member, who was newly assigned to the project, returned from Colombia and reported that sections of the government were opposed to the project on the grounds that it was unsound. The Bank, the official wrote in a memo, should push the project no further.

This is a revealing memo for at least two reasons. First, it shows how reluctant the Bank is to halt a project, no matter how unsound it is, once it has reached the appraisal stage because of the time and money invested in it already. And second, it shows that a project can be imposed on an unwilling country with very few Bank staff knowing of it. Certainly the Bank environmentalists and agriculturalists had no idea when they were criticising the project that they were echoing their Colombian counterparts. The text of the memorandum is as follows:

[We] set out initially to determine the progress in complying with conditions precedent to negotiations and Board presentation of the proposed loan. We confirmed . . . that no progress had been made on the two principal issues – transferring 600,000 hectares of land from INDERENA to INCORA and appropriating sufficient funds for the project . . . In the course of further digging, however, it became evident that there was a substantial opposition to the project which was likely to stall further action indefinitely.

INDERENA . . . continues to refuse to transfer the lands . . . The basis for this view is a lengthy unreleased study by INDERENA's technical staff which concludes categorically that it will not aid in encouraging further colonization which will result in further destruction of the delicate ecological balance of the region. DNP (the national planning office), for its part, had similar doubts about the project and . . . also expressed scepticism about the economic impact of the El Retorno project and explained that its technicians felt that the with project situation was optimistic while the without situation was unduly pessimistic.

DNP was responsive to arguments of the Bank that the colonos were already there, that the environmental destruction would be far worse without the project and that a great deal of Bank effort had been expended on the basis of Government interest and request for a Bank loan . . .

Reservations . . . are not limited to DNP and INDERENA. A Dutch technical assistance team . . . studying the soils . . . has expressed some concern about the potential of the area based largely on their findings that the soils are some of the poorest in the region . . . Under such circumstances, it seemed apparent to the Resident Mission, as well as us, that pushing this project as it stood at the highest level of Government was not an appropriate course of action.[110]

The memo goes on to discuss turning El Retorno into a small pilot project with a view to presenting the loan to the Board before July 1980. The memo says that Bank's work doesn't have to be wasted: 'I do not believe that a full scale re-appraisal will be necessary since large portions of the previous appraisal work and report would appear to be salvageable and useful.'[111]

But El Retorno was never resuscitated and the project never came up in front of the Board.

This is one of the few examples of successful opposition to a project by the small environmentalist group in the Bank. However, it is doubtful if the environmentalists could have stopped it on their own. The support of the agriculturalists and the reluctance of sectors of the Colombian government to accept this project were vital.

9. Rhetoric and reality

Political bias

In its statutes the Bank is debarred from taking political considerations into account in its lending policies. This caused problems
from early on. But, as a British Foreign Office official noted in a
memorandum in 1946, 'It will never be difficult to discover tenable
economic reasons for turning down an application, and I do not
think that political considerations, as such, need ever emerge into
the open. If they did we should have to resist the attempt.'[1]

In its publications the Bank repeatedly assures its readers that it
is politically neutral and disinterestedly concerned with matters of
technical efficiency. Thus its publication *Questions and Answers*
(1976) says:

> Under its Articles, the Bank cannot be guided in its
> decisions by political considerations; they must be based on
> economic criteria alone. The Bank is further required not to
> interfere in the domestic politics of member countries . . .
> Its political impartiality gives the Bank the maximum degree
> of operational flexibility; its contribution to the world
> development effort is not compromised by the intrusion of
> political considerations (p. 7) . . . The Bank's Articles of
> Agreement provide that economic considerations alone are
> relevant to its lending decisions. The Bank is expressedly
> precluded from taking the political character of the
> prospective borrower into account (p. 13).

Sometimes its claims of objectivity are given peculiar twists. Thus
Clausen, President since 1981, noted in his introduction to the
Bank's report on Sub-Saharan Africa that its major recommendation
is for 'greater reliance on the private sector'. But, he says, 'this is
not a recommendation which derives from any preconceived

philosophy of ownership. It derives from considerations of efficiency'.[2] Again, asked at a press conference at the 1983 annual meetings about a report that fishing unions in Peru were accusing the Bank of making its lending conditional on forced divestment of public enterprise, Clausen said the Bank's thrust was on efficiency, rather than there being any question of saying 'to heck with public ownership'; 'the Bank is not a political organisation, the only altar we worship at is pragmatic economics'. The problem is of course that not everybody would accept the bank's equation of efficiency with private ownership and reliance on market forces, however sincere its staff may be in their beliefs. But Clausen is merely following in a hallowed Bank tradition. One of his predecessors, Eugene Black, said to the Board of Governors in 1957: 'What government does not already have its hands full without reaching out into new fields? What government has so much foreign exchange that it can afford to bar a responsible foreign investor? There is no ideological argument here. Just common sense.'[3]

The Bank's reputation for political impartiality, shaky though it may be, is often seen as one of its greatest assets as an instrument of Western, especially US, foreign policy. But the Reagan administration was initially hostile to the multilateral institutions, and is still unwilling to increase its funding of them. Its hostility was based partly on the peculiar notion that the Bank promoted 'socialism' at the expense of the private sector. Regan, the Treasury Secretary, in his 1983 speech to the Board of Governors, which was devoid of any obvious attempt to please the assembled governors, said the Bank 'could play a vital role in acting as a financial catalyst in the development process', but

> this catalytic role must be firmly focused on the importance
> of stimulating private investment. That is why we continue
> to have serious reservations about the appropriateness of
> lending scarce Bank or IDA resources for projects, such as
> energy development and production projects, which are
> clearly capable of attracting alternative financing.

In 1981, soon after Reagan took office, the US Treasury was reported in the *Boston Globe* as having 'quietly commissioned a staff study to determine whether World Bank lending has encouraged socialist government at the expense of private enterprise'.

The study was to be directed by the Under Secretary for Monetary Affairs, Beryl Sprinkel, and although it would also deal with some other agencies, including the IMF, its focus would

> be heavily on the World Bank, where Sprinkel believes there is at least 'some truth' to charges that it has 'overstepped proper bounds' . . . 'We're a major force in the World Bank' [Sprinkel said] . . . 'and we expect to work to encourage those kinds of developments that we think are proper, and that includes strengthening the private sector of less developed nations' economies as well as our own.'[4]

The Treasury Report, when it came out in 1982, was nevertheless almost wholly favourable to the Bank. It stated that its conclusions were based on 'the Administration's basic policy preferences and priorities'. It argued that the appearance of political impartiality was an asset:

> While bilateral aid . . . better serves US short-term political interests, multilateral assistance can provide a useful complement. For example in Egypt where political interests inhibit US ability to promote economic policy changes, economic policy reforms have been fostered, in part, through the IBRD . . . *Because of the recipients' perception of the impartiality of the MDBS* . . . [the multilateral development banks, including the World Bank] are better placed to advise LDCs of the benefits of an international system based on trade and capital flows and to elicit market directed changes in recipients' economic policies.[5]

The Report also says, in language very similar to that of Regan's speech: 'The catalytic role the MDBS can play in promoting the prudent economic policies necessary to facilitate private financial flows is expected to remain highly important . . .' (p. 1).

The US Treasury Report addressed itself, in addition, to criticisms of the far right, who do not dispute that the World Bank helps the banks and private business, but whose opposition to it is based, like Professor Peter Bauer's in Britain, on a general opposition to any form of public subsidy for private enterprise. Jude Wanniski, writing in the *Wall Street Journal*, put the right-wing case thus: 'For several decades, US foreign policy has been wagged by [the] tail of global debt. *The IMF and the World Bank are run by and for the money-center banks*, the aim being the aversion of international financial collapse and their own bankruptcies'.[6] In answer to this type of criticism, the Treasury Report says, first, that this is not a 'misguided objective':

> To the contrary, and in large part because of the
> US initiative, the IMF and the World Bank were created
> specifically to prevent the recurrence of the economic havoc
> of the 1930s. These institutions enable developing countries
> to weather temporary balance of payments crises and to
> pursue their goals of economic and social development,
> thereby helping to perpetuate a free and open international
> economic order. That the money center banks also benefit
> from a healthy international economic system does not in
> any way imply the Bank and the Fund are their creatures
> (p. 157).

The argument, de-coded, is that in the 1930s, because market forces were allowed to operate, there were widespread defaults. And anyway, the Report argues, the 'sole purpose' of the World Bank is not to '"bail out"' the banks (p. 158), because its lending is too small and is mainly for projects.

The aversion to public subsidies as such obviously affects the Reagan administration. But much of the criticism of the World Bank in the early 1980s, especially in the Reagan administration and the US Congress, arose from the fact that many people took the rhetoric of the McNamara period at face value. During McNamara's presidency, from 1968 to 1981, the World Bank presented a new rather radical face to the world. Whether because, as some maintain, McNamara had a genuine moral conversion and regarded his time in the World Bank as expiation for his crimes in Vietnam, or because, having failed in his military endeavours, he hoped to do better by economic means, the McNamara period was marked by a totally different rhetoric. McNamara's speeches became dominated by eloquent allusions to the poverty and human degradation suffered by the peoples of the Third World and the Bank became, at least in its rhetoric, devoted to the cause of the 'poorest of the poor'. In practice it is doubtful how much change there was from previous, and current, reality (see below). And to accuse the Bank of promoting socialism, as some of its wilder critics in the United States did, was a gross distortion of reality. As McNamara reputedly said, in private discussions with senior World Bank officials, the Bank 'had got to find a capitalist alternative to China', since everybody knew that China had been more successful than capitalist underdeveloped countries in eliminating hunger and providing basic health and education services.

Clausen, though clinging to the Bank's misleading cloak of political impartiality, has changed the rhetoric. No doubt this is to a great extent in response to the Bank's increasingly desperate quest for congressional support. According to one Bank official, the Bank's 'poverty orientation' (or lack of it) has not changed; its public image has changed: McNamara thought he could wring the hearts of the US Congress; Clausen is trying another tack. No doubt also the Bank's changed image accords better with Clausen's personal inclinations, and with reality. In any case Clausen has been more open than his predecessors about the Bank's role in promoting the interests of the private sector and the banks. Thus in an interview in the *Financial Times* he is reported as saying: '"One of my main management objectives is to make the perception of what the Bank does closer to what it actually does"'; that the Bank had always done many of the things which its (right-wing) critics now urged; that:

> People in the Congress say the Bank lends to socialist
> countries, that it keeps less than superb governments in
> power, that it hands out 'welfare' and wastes money. They
> are wrong . . . But even my perception of the Bank was
> wrong before I saw it from the inside. It is a much more
> conservative, efficiency-oriented and soundly-financed institu-
> tion than I ever thought before I got there.

Pursuing a balancing act between displeasing his right-wing and his left-wing critics, Clausen nevertheless adds: '"We are a non-political institution and we are happy to lend to socialist countries and public enterprises."'[7]

When Clausen was asked at a press conference in Washington in September 1983 before the annual meetings what he saw as the Bank's new role, he said, echoing the language used by Regan and the US Treasury Report, that the important question was 'How can we adapt ourselves so as to be more of a catalyst for private sector flows.' The Bank's plug for IDA replenishment, in a briefing for the press at the 1983 annual meetings, was unabashedly aimed at the right. Failure to replenish IDA on a significant scale, it said, would, in the case of India,

> jeopardise the World Bank's ability to continue urging the government to reduce controls, encourage foreign competition in the domestic sector and place greater emphasis on the private sector – policy initiatives that are currently showing success and hold great promise . . . China . . . too has undertaken a fundamental reorientation of its development strategy. That strategy involves the introduction and increased use of incentives and market mechanisms into its system of economic management and greater openness to international commerce. While China has co-operated with the World Bank in discussing policy changes, the provision of IDA credits is needed to ensure that China is able to carry through reforms . . .[8]

The clearest evidence that the Bank is not, in fact, politically impartial is of course to be found in its treatment of the governments it lends to, or does not lend to. The Bank has, as it frequently says, a 'broad international membership'. But some countries are not members and some are unable to borrow from the Bank; nearly all of these are left-wing. The Soviet Union, although it took part in the Bretton Woods negotiations, did not join. Poland and Czechoslovakia joined initially but later withdrew. Cuba withdrew from the Bank after its revolution. Angola and Mozambique did not join when they became independent from Portugal. China replaced Taiwan as a member only in 1980. Countries which have had left-wing, or merely populist or reformist, governments from which World Bank lending has been withdrawn at one time or another include Chile (see p. 118), Vietnam, Nicaragua, Grenada, Algeria, Peru, Brazil, Egypt, Jamaica (see p. 117) to name a few.

The Bank does not apparently have problems with right-wing governments. In the late 1960s it was still lending to South Africa and Salazar's Portugal; in 1966 the Bank indeed engaged in legal arguments with the United Nations to defend its right to lend to those countries on the grounds, the Bank said, of its duty to disregard political considerations.[9] The Bank co-operated with the US administration's desires that it should provide a multilateral cover for lending to Saigon shortly before its liberation, and it is currently, under similar prompting, negotiating to lend to El Salvador. Like the IMF, the Bank is prepared to be lenient towards corrupt, inefficient and frequently brutal right-wing governments that are of economic and strategic importance to the West.

Asked in 1981 whether the Bank had ever stopped lending to a right-wing government, Bank officials said: 'Zaire'. But the gesture was short-lived. In 1983, IDA approved loans to Zaire amounting to $88 million.[10] It would require none of the usual manipulations of language for the Bank to declare that Chile is currently uncreditworthy (see above). But, in 1983, Chile received approval for a loan of $128 million. The Bank's main criticism of the recent economic policies of the Pinochet government is 'maintenance of an over-valued exchange rate', which is the stock monetarist response to those who say that monetarist policies in Chile have failed. In its 1983 *World Development Report*, the Bank says: 'Chile started with widespread distortions [in 1973] and made major changes over a remarkably short period; adjustment was followed by rapid growth in GNP and considerable success in controlling inflation. However, distortions have subsequently re-emerged in certain key areas' (p. 65). And as in the case of the IMF, it was clear that the earlier phases of the Pinochet government's policies came close to the World Bank's ideal (see above, p. 118). Egypt, a country vital to US strategy in the Middle East, 'suddenly', according to a Bank official, 'started getting World Bank money when, by any standards of "performance"', its economy was in a mess; it didn't meet supposedly the most important criterion for lending, that of having 'a coherent plan or programme'; Bank management apparently justified this decision by saying, 'Well, they need our help to get one.'[11] Similarly, Bank officials say that lending to Turkey started at a stage when, by all the usual standards, the country was not creditworthy. And there is no very convincing case to be made, in terms of economic management, why 'Four countries that have suffered military takeovers or the imposition of martial law since the early 1970s (Uruguay, Chile, the Philippines and Argentina) received a sevenfold increase in World Bank lending by 1979, while other Bank lending increased only three-fold'.[12]

The Bank's bias against left-wing governments revealed itself early. Poland and Czechoslovakia withdrew, in 1950 and 1954 respectively, when it became clear that they would not get any money from the Bank. Both had apparently serious negotiations for loans from the Bank. In the Polish case, the loan was not presented to the Board when the US executive director made known that he would veto it. In one of the earliest of many similar rationalisations, the Bank commented:

> The Bank is fully cognizant of the injunction in its Articles of Agreement that its decisions shall be based only on economic considerations. Political tensions and uncertainties in or among its member countries, however, have a direct effect on economic and financial conditions in those countries and upon their credit position.[13]

Mason and Asher comment on Czechoslovakia's experience as follows: 'As is usual in such cases, the argument was not simply a legal one and was complicated by grievances Czechoslovakia and the United States had against each other, grievances which may belong in a history of the cold war but need not be analyzed here.'[14]

These events foreshadowed numerous similar interventions by the government of the United States attempting, usually with success, to stop the World Bank lending to left-wing governments. On some of these occasions the Bank would no doubt have stopped lending in any case. There are also cases of the Bank refusing to lend to leftist governments in which there may have been no overt US pressures. During the period of the Alliance for Progress, World Bank officials at times appeared to adopt positions to the right of their counterparts in the US Agency for International Development (AID).[15] It is not easy to find out how willingly the Bank complied with US desires that it should not lend to Nicaragua, Grenada, Chile under Allende and other countries. Especially during the McNamara period the Bank might have been expected to take the 'enlightened' view that it was in the interest of the West to keep open channels of communication, and the possibility of influence, in countries with left-wing governments. This perhaps explained the Bank's presence in the early years after the Nicaraguan revolution (see below). In the case of Chile, at least some members of the Bank's staff claim that, like the Swedish and other Executive Directors, they wanted the Bank to continue lending to Allende; but in fact the loans which they were negotiating did not go to the

Board until after Allende was murdered. Bank lending to Vietnam was stopped by McNamara (see below, pp. 226–7).

Perhaps the clearest case of the allocation of Bank lending being influenced by McNamara's reformism is the case of Tanzania. It seems that McNamara had a 'soft spot' for Tanzania and saw Tanzania as a non-socialist alternative for the Third World. Tanzania is often cited by Bank officials as an example of Bank collaboration with a left-wing government. The bulk of the Bank's lending to Tanzania actually came in the 10 years after Nyerere announced a leftward turn in the Arusha declaration in 1967. By 1981 more than half of Tanzania's external debt, or $1.2 billion, was owed to the World Bank. Tanzania had also received a great deal of money in grant form from bilateral donors and became, in spite of all the talk of 'self reliance', one of the major recipients of aid in Africa.

But the actual history of the Bank's relationship with Tanzania was a sorry one.

The Bank, which had been partly responsible for many of the policies, especially in agriculture, adopted by the Tanzanian government during the 1970s, then turned bitterly against the government when these policies, combined with external economic forces, produced disaster. Initially it seems that the emphasis put by Nyerere on rural development and equitable income distribution did appeal to McNamara and some of his advisers; McNamara made at least half a dozen visits to Tanzania during the 1970s. An official close to him claimed that:

> Both McNamara and Julius Nyerere saw the essential
> importance of small-scale farming. I remember one Cabinet
> meeting we attended where Julius was in the chair. He said
> there wasn't any future in extensive farming, it had to be
> done by peasants intensively. When that happened, that
> would be the day when there was a real increase in
> production. And then McNamara chipped in by saying
> that's how the poor will increase their productivity and get
> richer, not by wealth trickling down from above.[16]

This is, in fact, an enunciation of the 'poverty orientation' of the McNamara period (see below), and it is doubtful how much the Bank officials operating in Tanzania shared McNamara's views. But a point at which the interests of the World Bank and those of the Tanzanian state did coincide was in villagisation, which involved the concentration of 13 million people between 1969 and 1976 into village settlements. The Bank was apparently behind Nyerere's support for the idea in his inaugural speech in 1962. The Tanzanian government justified it on the grounds of the need to group people together to provide water, education and health services. But the Bank's interest in villagisation was based more on the potential it was supposed to offer for increasing agricultural output. The programme made it easier to control the peasantry and to dictate how, when and where they should produce their food and export crops. Indeed the compulsory final stage of villagisation from 1973 to 1976 when most people were moved was accompanied by rules on cultivation that recalled the agricultural ordinances of the colonial period. These decisions were taken by the government, but the philosophy behind them was reinforced by the backing of the Bank. In the 1976 Village Management Programme the World Bank took the opportunity to extend the state's authority over the villages. The original proposal was for a project to train locally selected representatives of village councils in basic administrative techniques but the Bank turned it into a retraining programme for extension workers and secondary school leavers to manage villagers, rather than to represent villagers.[17]

The costs of villagisation were considerable. They are difficult to quantify because they coincided with the Sahelian drought of 1973 to 1975. But 940,000 tons of cereals had to be imported in 1974 and 1975 through food aid and Tanzania's reserves and cotton and cashew nut production also declined sharply.[18] This was the first clear economic crisis in Tanzania since independence. The Bank had always had reservations about the socialist rhetoric associated with villagisation but it was also well aware that the amount of collective agriculture actually taking place was very limited. Moreover, after 1973 the ideal of communal agriculture was abandoned and 'ujamaa' villages became 'development' villages. The Bank nevertheless decided to be wise after the event, and it swung against villagisation. An April 1974 World Bank report maintained that villagisation rather than drought was responsible for the food shortages because of the general disruption, the emphasis on social services, and the displacement of 'progressive' farmers. It argued strongly that there should be less spending on social services, higher producer prices and an end to the communal villages policy. The quid pro quo for the Tanzanians was a major aid programme to increase food production.[19] In February 1975, the *Guardian* reported that the Bank had threatened to cut off lending unless the government suspended its 'ujamaa programme', but by then the process of villagisation was virtually complete.

At the same time as the Bank put out its report in 1974, the government approved an adjustment package which included increases in producer prices (particularly for food crops) and cutbacks in public investment and services except in primary education, agricultural extension and rural health.[20] The Bank, in turn, provided aid for the National Maize Programme, also backed by USAID. Subsidised fertilisers, hybrid seeds and other inputs were supplied to farmers and eventually extended to cover two-thirds of the country. But returns have been poor as Tanzanian farmers have been unhappy about relying exclusively on less hardy hybrid maize.

The World Bank also channelled aid into food and cash crop production through regional integrated development programmes (RIDEPS) which boosted inputs, credit, extension services and other assistance in particular regions. The World Bank set up the first RIDEP in Kigoma in 1975 and became responsible for another four later on; bilateral donors including Sweden and Canada were responsible for RIDEPS in Tanzania's remaining 15 regions. However, a World Bank report on the agricultural sector in 1982 severely criticised the RIDEPS and argued that Tanzania lacked the managerial and institutional resources to run them effectively. This argument is supported by well-documented reports of the almost random dumping of expensive fertiliser in villages and of excessively stringent cotton bye-laws in the first World Bank sponsored RIDEP in Kigoma.[21] Once again the wisdom of the Bank has been based on hindsight.

By 1977, the Tanzania economy had pulled out of its balance of payments crisis thanks to an end to the drought, the government's adjustment programme, the short-lived boom in commodity prices especially coffee, and financial support from the IMF and the World Bank. Sufficient foreign exchange reserves had accumulated to cover five months' imports and under pressure from the IMF and the World Bank (particularly from the Bank which was more closely involved in Tanzania and therefore had more leverage) the government liberalised its import controls. Inessential consumer goods flooded into the country and by the end of 1978 the reserves only covered 10 days' imports. The break-up of the East African Community, the Ugandan war and the collapse in international terms of trade made things worse. By 1979, Tanzania was forced into the negotiation of a high conditionality borrowing from the IMF. Although the World Bank was not responsible for the global pressures on Tanzania's balance of payments, it had pressured Tanzania into surrendering the reserves that ensured the availability of essential imports and it had further increased Tanzania's vulnerability by urging it to borrow more.[22]

Tanzania is now locked into its worst economic crisis since the 1930s. Foreign exchange reserves are non-existent. Essential imports such as spare parts are not coming into the country and industrial and agricultural production is steadily declining. Peasants are reverting to subsistence food production and neglecting their export crops. If farmers have spare food, they can sell it on the black market for high prices which allows them to compete for scarce consumer goods. Over 200 development projects had to be shelved in the 1982 Budget. The World Bank is taking a tough line and wants to see substantial policy changes and an agreement with the IMF before it will commit funds for a structural adjustment loan.

Although the catastrophic decline in Tanzania's terms of trade has undoubtedly been a major cause of the Tanzanian crisis, for the Bank terms of trade were less important than poor producer prices caused by an over-valued exchange rate. In the Bank's report *Accelerated Development in Sub-Saharan Africa*, Tanzania and Ghana were singled out as examples of how an over-valued exchange rate had damaged the output of export crops. There is some truth in this. African exchange rates have appreciated against the SDR by about 45 per cent over the last decade and Tanzania is no exception. As a result farmers get less local currency for their crops than they should and the problem is compounded by the high overheads of the crop marketing authorities. But Tanzanian peasants are as concerned about the availability of consumer goods as they are about prices and the import cuts have meant that there is little for them to buy.[23]

Tanzania has substantially increased producer prices for export crops since the late 1970s and has devalued the shilling several times. But it has not gone far enough for the Bank. The project document for an interim $50 million export rehabilitation loan in 1981 admitted that Tanzania had been badly affected by poor terms of trade and the Ugandan war and that its adjustment programme had cut imports, frozen wages, and concentrated expenditure on the productive sector. But it argued: 'Aside from the devaluation [of 10 per cent], little scope was given to market forces and Tanzania made no basic changes in its system of administered prices and government controls. Indeed the government introduced more controls and administered prices after the crisis.'

Once again the World Bank was being wise after the event. At least part of the pricing problem was the Marketing Development Bureau of the Ministry of Agriculture, a body largely staffed by expatriates and funded by the Bank. The MDB was responsible in the late 1970s for erratic cross-pricing which resulted in excessive production of beans and pulses and in accelerating the decline in the output of cashew nuts through a very low producer price. The MDB has also been blamed for inadequate monitoring of crop parastatals and for attempting to block the decentralisation of storage and the reform of the National Milling Corporation in 1980 when it was discovered that huge losses were being incurred. It has also been alleged that the MDB went so far as to clear its reports with Washington before submitting them to the Ministry of Agriculture.[24]

Early in 1982 an attempt to solve the differences between the Bank and Tanzania was made by setting up a three-person advisory group to prepare a mutually acceptable structural adjustment programme. The salaries and expenses of the liberal Western economists on the advisory group and its back-up secretariat were covered by a World Bank technical assistance loan. The idea of the advisory group was personally sponsored by McNamara and was a last concession to Tanzania's previously favoured status. A Structural Adjustment Programme, based on their recommendations, was published in June 1982. Many of the proposed reforms are underway. Regional co-operatives became operational in 1984. Private Asian farmers have had large blocks of land assigned to them and the multinational Lonrho is returning to its tea estates and other agricultural interests. Pan-territorial pricing has been modified. There was a further 20 per cent devaluation in 1983 and the government is prepared to accept further phased devaluations.

But apparently the Tanzanians have not gone far enough to get the loans they are negotiating for, from the World Bank, the IMF and bilateral donors. The IMF wants an immediate 50 per cent devaluation. A more fundamental liberalisation of the economy is being demanded. The World Bank is no longer soft on Tanzania. Indeed, shortly after Clausen took over from McNamara, disbursements to Tanzania were cut off for five months after it fell $1.3 million behind on debt servicing, a small amount that a more favoured country might have had covered by additional programme assistance.

It is clear that important sections of the Bank's staff were never fully behind the reformist positions of the Tanzanian government or in sympathy with McNamara's support for them. As Cheryl Payer puts it:

> Which World Bank are we to take seriously? The one which promotes and funds rural integrated development programmes, or the one which condemns them as failures?[25]

The Bank also cites its lending to countries such as Hungary and China as evidence of its political impartiality. China became a member of the Bank only after Nixon's famous visit, its 'opening up' to the West, and US recognition of its usefulness as an ally against the Soviet Union. Hungary is also a country opening up to the West, singled out by US Vice-President Bush in Vienna in 1983 as a country pursuing market-orientated policies which should be rewarded with an increase in 'Western aid', and favoured with a visit from Thatcher in 1984.

Some observers have commented that the Bank is 'happier' with established left-wing governments than it is with transitional ones. Happy or not, it has few opportunities for de-stabilisation in the former; threats to discontinue lending are unlikely to cause many tremors in China or Hungary. The Bank might as well, therefore, lend to them, in the hope that by doing so it can add a little weight to the tendencies within those countries towards greater openness to the West and adoption of its economic policy models. But in countries such as Nicaragua and Grenada and even Chile, a boycott by Western financial agencies can add to their immediate financial problems, and is therefore frequently resorted to.

Algeria is now claimed as 'an example of co-operation between a socialist government and the World Bank'.[26] Since 1973, Algeria has received so much money from the Bank that it is one of the 21 countries for which 'cumulative lending operations' exceed \$1 billion. Now that Algeria is flush with oil funds and a prime target for the sales drives of Western corporations and banks, it hardly needs the money, and in fact one of the Bank's biggest problems in Algeria is getting the government to use the money it has committed. But there was a time when Algeria's needs were rather desperate. During that time, in fact for the first ten years after Algeria became independent from France, the Bank refused to lend to Algeria. The long war for independence had wrought considerable damage. The French *colons* had abandoned their land and businesses, sometimes destroying what they could not take with them; Algerians had occupied only the least skilled jobs and lowest administrative posts; agriculture had been disrupted by the French policy of moving thousands of peasants into 'protected' villages.

The Bank's refusals to lend were clothed in technical language. It sent numerous missions to Algeria between 1962 and 1972, consuming much of the time of many Algerian officials. The government asked the Bank to finance an irrigation project, making use of the water accumulated behind a dam built by the French. The Bank refused. If the costs of building the dam were included, it said, the financial returns were inadequate. But, said the Algerians, the dam had already been built, so its existence could have been treated in the way that one might treat, say, the existence of a lake.

On another occasion the Algerian government asked the Bank to finance a fertiliser plant. The Bank said the market was too small. The Algerians arranged contracts with neighbouring states to purchase the products. The Bank said, hold on, you've gone too far: we haven't agreed to finance the plant yet. Similarly the Bank's refusal to finance the state oil and natural gas industry was 'well enveloped' in requests for information which the Algerians could not, or did not wish to, supply.

Algerian officials say that the Bank's actual purpose was to cause the failure of their socialist experiment and assertion of economic independence. The Bank, as has been said, does not lend to countries which nationalise foreign assets without 'fair' compensation. In the case of Algeria it was made clear, at least to senior officials, that the problem was compensation to the French *colons* and, in the early seventies, for French oil interests. The early French settlers had, by and large, acquired their land by the forcible eviction of its original owners. The Bank was thus insisting that Algerians pay for land which was first stolen and then abandoned. As for the oil, the Algerians agreed on the principle of compensation; the problem was how much they should pay.

The Bank made other objections. It was of course unwilling to finance industrial projects in the state sector. The first Bank missions to discuss a loan to the Algerian Development Bank for small enterprises wanted, according to the Algerian officials involved, these enterprises to be in the private sector; the loan was not signed until 1975, after many hard rounds of negotiations, when the Bank finally agreed that the loans could be made to local public authorities. But the Bank has not given up trying: in recent negotiations for a fisheries loan, the Bank favoured loans to the private fishing sector for importing boats, rather than the construction by the government of boat-building capacity in Algeria. The Bank's reports also advised against the setting up of heavy industries. According to Algerian officials, one of the Bank's arguments was that such industries would compete with those of the already industrialised countries which were capable of supplying the needs of Algeria; Algeria should therefore stick to food-processing, textiles, 'biro pens', or whatever, in line with its comparative advantage: 'the most bare-faced liberalism', as one Algerian put it.

By 1973 the situation had changed enough for the Bank to make its first loan to Algeria since independence. But there was no change in the projects submitted to the Bank. Some of the changes took place in the Bank itself. As a representative of the Algerian FLN put it in 1981, the McNamara era in the Bank represented an abandonment of gun-boat diplomacy in favour of 'intelligent conciliation'; he expected a return to hostilities under Clausen and Reagan. By 1973, Algeria had become prominent in the Group of 77 and in OPEC. McNamara, reproached by Algerian negotiators for the Bank's refusal to lend to Chile under Allende, replied that the Bank did not like lending to revolutions which failed; thus flatteringly implying that Algeria's would succeed.

But it is also likely that the World Bank would have started lending to Algeria by 1973 without McNamara. After all, McNamara became President in 1968 and 'naturally', said the Algerians, supported French claims for compensation. By 1973, however, the Bank had apparently 'succeeded in convincing itself' that Algeria was proceeding with compensation. Also it took time to convince the Bank that 'we were not really red; only a little pink'. The nature of the Algerian political system had become clearer by the 1970s. *Autogestion*, the Algerian form of workers' control, had lost much of its revolutionary content; control was largely in the hands of the state, which was not itself controlled by the workers. State ownership of the means of production is extensive in Algeria; Alan H. Gelb wrote in a 1981 World Bank Staff Working Paper: 'A considerable effort needs to be made to channel resources to private sector agriculture and manufacturing, assuming that the road ahead is not to be that of a state-owned economy.' The Bank was also probably more willing in the 1970s to approve of Algeria's relatively high expenditures on education and social services, and in fact suggested more expenditures on housing in particular. But even in earlier periods the World Bank claimed not to be opposed to social expenditures as such; it was, and is, opposed to them when they jeopardise financial equilibrium, repayment of debts, and so on; in Algeria they did not, thanks to oil and natural gas.

There were other reasons for the Bank to become involved in Algeria. After independence some Algerians had argued for what was seen as the Chinese model of labour-intensive industrial development, partly because it implied less dependence on foreign capital and technology; others favoured concentrating on heavy industry based on capital-intensive methods. After Boumedienne took power in 1965, the latter prevailed. Algerians therefore went abroad for capital equipment and credit. They met with hostility from official agencies such as the World Bank and the US EximBank. But private suppliers took advantage of Algeria's willingness to invest massively in the latest technology and the continuing dependence on imports of technology and spare parts which this created. Algeria was able to finance its industrialisation with suppliers' credits and increasingly its oil and natural gas revenues which, unlike other oil-exporting countries, it has invested entirely in its own development. In 1971 it also borrowed for the first time on the eurodollar market; by 1978 its foreign debt amounted to 20 per cent of the value of its exports. In these circumstances, the Algerians thought, the World Bank could be expected to wish to exercise some control.

Foreign lending to Algeria also made possible a higher rate of extraction of oil and natural gas. Although the World Bank refused to lend to Sonatrach, the state oil company, for exploration, it did lend for the improvement of port facilities. The Algerians themselves now intend to reduce their foreign borrowing and also the rate of depletion of their oil and natural gas. They may, curiously, find themselves urged by the World Bank to borrow more. Algeria has in fact delayed spending some World Bank loans and cancelled others; a Bank mission was sent to Algeria in 1981 with the specific intention of urging Algeria to spend the considerable portion of Bank loans which had not yet been disbursed. Some Algerian officials blamed their non-utilisation of Bank loans on the fact that they are generally available for the import content of projects only, and that the Bank has been unwilling to offer any preferences to local suppliers.

As always, once the World Bank is involved in a country, its interest extends beyond the question of projects and their financial viability. Few senior Algerian officials went so far as the Minister of Finance, M. Yala, who at a meeting with Bank officials in Washington in October 1981, according to *El Moudjahid*, 'particularly wished . . . to underline the exemplary character of [the Bank's] intervention, which has taken place with strict respect for our development options'. Most said the Bank did try to influence policies. But they insisted that the Algerian government could not be pushed around like other governments because Algeria had no severe financial problems, because Bank loans were a small fraction of total investment, and because the government knew what it was doing. Other officials nevertheless pointed out that the influence of the Bank was 'insidious', that it could make its views felt by 'small interstices', or even that those who called in the Bank did so for their own personal interests. In any case negotiations with the Bank were 'hard', even 'atrocious'.

It was rather generally agreed that the state sector in Algeria is inefficient and in that sense, at least, there was said to be 'convergence of views'. Since Algeria is currently engaged in a process of 'restructuration' of the public sector, there is greater opportunity for the Bank's views to be heard. The Ministry of Finance asked for, and got, a report by the World Bank on the relationshhp between Algerian banks and state enterprises; the report proposed greater control of the latter by the former and that the banks should charge higher interest rates. Although Bank officials are careful not to express their preference for the private sector too openly, they may favour it in the context of projects, or by implication in their persistent criticisms of the inefficiency of the state sector, coupled with suggestions that the private sector 'can help'. They are less reticent in arguing for 'at least' greater autonomy for individual sectors and enterprises and more decentralisation. But, though many may agree with these principles, they are not neutral questions, empty of political content; much depends on how decentralisation is carried out. For the Bank, financial autonomy implies profitability at the level of individual enterprises and services and, frequently, increases in tariffs and prices so that subsidies can be reduced (and Bank loans repaid). Thus small peasants are expected to pay prices for water that cover the full costs of irrigation works; the prices of transport, electricity and bread are expected to go up; and in general, people's access to goods and services must be rationed, not by what the economy as a whole is capable of supplying, but by the individual's capacity to pay.

Similarly with the question of agriculture. The World Bank was undoubtedly correct in arguing that agriculture in Algeria had been badly neglected. But for Bank officials to say, as they do, that 'inefficiency' in agriculture is the result of 'state ownership' is another matter. The Bank's involvement in agriculture in Algeria is considerable. Its involvement is not merely technical. It has financed studies on agricultural extension, on credit, which means credit to the private sector, on regulating nomadic grazing lands, on the 'integrated development' of a mountainous area; and it is negotiating a loan for studies on the 'restructuration' of self-managed farms at Sidi bel Abbès. When the FLN Central Committee was debating whether self-managed farms should become state farms, continue under self-management, or be privatised, a World Bank official wrote a memorandum spelling out the consequences of each option. In 1980 the Bank produced a sector report on agriculture with the close co-operation of Algerian officials; it proposed the liberalisation of internal trade in agricultural products, an increase in producer prices, more credit to the private sector, and reorganisation of the self-managed sector with greater financial incentives for the workers. Internal agricultural trade was in fact liberalised; this was said to be the result of a 'coincidence of views'. The Bank's conditions for lending for the Sidi bel Abbès project were said to be the product of extensive discussions between Algerian and Bank officials; they included proposals that workers' wages should be adjusted, upwards or downwards, according to levels of production, that much stricter provision should be made for the payment of debts, and so on. Whatever the effectiveness of Bank intervention, its involvement, particularly on the question of self-management, went to the heart of important political questions.

The World Bank may not have greatly changed the balance of forces in Algeria. But there is no doubt that that is, in part, its intention and that it has found Algerian politicians and officials ready to co-operate with it. The ideological nature of its intervention in Algeria, even though it has been able to operate in an economy with predominant public ownership and even though it no doubt treads more delicately than in other more vulnerable countries, remains clear.

The case of Nicaragua provides an even clearer example of the Bank intervening, or attempting to intervene, in the policies of a country with political objectives, but ceasing to lend when its efforts appeared to have little chance of succeeding.[27] In the period immediately after the Sandinista victory, the Bank did lend considerable sums to the Sandinista government. But the relationship between Nicaragua and the World Bank has mirrored closely the relationship between Nicaragua and the United States: as the US stepped up its moves to destabilise Nicaragua, the Bank assumed increasingly harsh stances towards the Sandinistas, eventually ceasing to lend to Nicaragua in early 1982. The Bank claims that economic reasons prevent it from lending to Nicaragua, but internal Bank documents show that pressure from the US and the

Bank's own political bias are the real reasons.[28] Similarly, in Chile in 1970–73, although no Bank documents have surfaced to prove that the US stopped the Bank from lending to Allende and the Bank has always denied it vigorously, a recent US Treasury Department report describes this incident as a successful case of US pressure making a multilateral development bank work for US foreign policy goals.[29]

It is impossible to say to what extent the US leans on the Bank to isolate left-wing countries and to what extent the Bank takes it upon itself. However, it is known that the Bank's withdrawal of loans to Nicaragua is one part of an overall US strategy to politicise the main international finance institutions into backing US policy in Central America. The strategy includes pressures to lend to Guatemala and El Salvador. Although the US controls the largest block of votes in each international institution (19 per cent in the IMF, 21 per cent in the Bank and 35 per cent in the IDB), it cannot block money for Nicaragua outright, or allocate loans to Guatemala and El Salvador without forming alliances with other right-wing countries, and without running into stiff resistance from Canada and the more liberal Latin American and European countries. (The exception is in one section of the IDB, the Fund for Special Operations, where the US vote can block loans as they have to pass by a two-thirds majority. Bitter arguments erupted there in 1983 when the US delegate repeatedly vetoed loans to Nicaragua, with Canadian, Latin American and European delegates accusing him of shamelessly bringing politics into the IDB.)

After the Sandinistas' victory in July 1979, relations between Nicaragua and the World Bank were relatively amicable. The Bank lent Nicaragua $20 million for agricultural and industrial rehabilitation in December 1979, was unusually understanding about the chaos of that period, and excused the Nicaraguans from having to submit a formal project proposal. Three other IBRD loans were made before lending ceased: a $3.70 million loan for Managua's water supply in April 1981, a $30 million loan for industrial rehabilitation in June 1981, and a $16 million loan for municipal development in January 1982. In addition, the IDA made a credit of $37 million available to *Finapri*, the Nicaraguan agency in charge of all pre-investment work on projects.

In October 1981, the first Country Economic Memorandum on Nicaragua came out inside the Bank. A confidential, grey-cover document, it was complimentary to the Sandinistas, recognised the economic devastation caused by the war and appeared to accept the Sandinistas' commitment to a mixed economy. The Nicaraguans thought it fair, but inside the Bank and the IMF it was considered by most staff to be too optimistic. The prime concern of the document was that the Sandinistas should define a framework within which the private sector could operate with confidence. It recommended that the government check its expansionary policies; direct public and private investment towards projects that generate or save foreign exchange (if necessary, delaying social projects to do so); encourage the private sector; implement an export promotion strategy; acquire large amounts of external financing; and improve the efficiency of state enterprises. The Bank discussed these recommendations with the government and reported that the government was in 'general agreement'. The document concluded:

> These intentions are encouraging. If the government is successful in implementing these measures . . . Nicaragua will indeed be able to reconstruct its economy as well as continue to enhance the social situation of its citizens.[30]

But this benign Bank document was the quiet before the storm. It had been written by staff members and consultants sympathetic to the Sandinistas, including a Salvadoran who had been forced to leave his country. These officials refused to produce a Country Program Paper acceptable to senior management, and at least two of them subsequently were forced to move to different departments in the Bank. In December 1981, a Bank mission to Nicaragua, composed of different staff members, told the Sandinistas that if they did not reassure the private sector, the Bank would cut off lending. In January 1982, the then US Secretary of State Alexander Haig insisted that the US vote against the Bank's proposed municipal development loan, in spite of the fact that the US Treasury Department, the Latin American bureau of the State Department and the US Executive Director at the Bank all recommended voting for it; the US was the only country to vote against it.[31] And then in February a Country Program Paper (CPP) on Nicaragua, prepared by a South Asian Bank official, was circulated at the highest levels in the Bank; an early draft of it was nevertheless leaked to the press.

The CPP reflected the Reagan administration's concerns on Nicaragua. Thus it says:

> The Sandinista movement has always been strongly
> nationalist and anti-American . . . The US is concerned about
> the large army that has been built up with the help of
> Cuban advisors and claims that Nicaragua is helping the
> revolutionary movement in El Salvador. The Reagan
> administration is unhappy about the Marxist/Leninist bent
> and anti-US posture of the Sandinista leadership.[32]

To balance this US viewpoint, the CPP adds that: The Nicaraguan authorities argue that the US, Guatemalan, and Honduran governments have condoned the organisation of anti-Sandinista groups, and even commando training camps, in their territories.[33]

The document has a notably unsympathetic approach to the 'burgeoning' public sector. For example, it describes how the Ministry of Agriculture has expanded greatly and now administers almost one-quarter of cultivated land, without mentioning that this land belonged to, and was abandoned by, Somoza and his family. Similarly, the CPP describes the publicly owned construction industry as a 'major bottleneck', again without mentioning that it too was almost entirely owned by Somoza and that it was scuttled at his command as he left the country.[34] In contrast to this hostility to the public sector, the CPP sympathises with the private sector's lack of faith in the Sandinistas and never mentions 'decapitalisation' on the part of the private sector (see below). The attitude of the Bank to the two sectors is summed up in this quote:

> the Government has so alienated the business community
> that even in the unlikely event of a shift to a pro-business
> policy it would take a year or more to produce investment
> results. Furthermore, the *unknown but probably* poor
> efficiency of the state industries augurs ill for such increased
> exports from that quarter.[35] (original emphasis)

The CPP states that Nicaragua is a high risk country, unlikely to receive adequate amounts of external financing for its needs. It does not mention that the decision of aid agencies like USAID, which discontinued aid in late 1980, and the World Bank not to lend to Nicaragua immediately sets up a destabilising and vicious circle in which private banks are less willing to lend, and so on in a downward spiral.

The CPP, finally, discusses alternative strategies towards Nicaragua. Hard decisions have to be made, it says, because the Sandinistas have not responded to the Bank's recommendation that 'clear and consistent rules of the game for the private sector' be laid down.[36] The first alternative, according to the CPP, is to:

> offer major direct and indirect assistance (i.e., through encouraging recourse to the IMF) . . . Measures to be taken would have to include (i) revitalising the private sector through an effective system of guarantees and longer term incentives and, in particular, a clear delineation of its area of responsibility in accordance with clearly established adequate 'rules of the game', (ii) strengthening and improving substantially the efficiency of the public sector . . . (iii) reconciling the much needed Government austerity plan with its minimum development targets . . . (iv) controlling inflation . . . including . . . establishing a realistic exchange rate . . . On the part of the Bank, this alternative will require a willingness to commit substantial funds . . . a commitment of considerable staff resources and high institutional exposure.[37]

But the CPP rejects this option:

> This, however, is a high risk approach; even in the unlikely event of Nicaragua's leadership adopting appropriate economic policies designed to attract private sector investments, these may not be sufficient to induce the private sector to invest in the absence of greater political rights. *In addition, the increasing constraints and political limitations on the Bank may render this alternative unfeasible.*[38]

The second alternative is to stop lending altogether,

> until the government has taken the difficult actions (both political and economic) to resolve the pending economic crisis. However, complete withdrawal of Bank support would have a negative effect on a situation which, while extremely serious, is still in flux. The Bank might also be accused of an inability and/or unwillingness to support a

'progressive' Government in Central America and of not understanding its post-revolutionary difficulties.[39]

The third option, which the CPP elects to follow, is to lend for high priority projects in strategic sectors,

> provided the Government continues to improve demand management, pay its debts, and maintains not only a close dialogue with the Bank but gives some indication that it plans to follow our policy advice.[40]

It recommends that lending for water, roads and education be suspended. In agriculture it recommends lending to private livestock ranchers, and also suggests possible projects in the energy and industrial sectors.

In Nicaragua there was a mixed reaction to the CPP of surprise, outrage and, from the more worldly wise, shrugs of 'what do you expect from the World Bank'. A top Bank official hastened to reassure the Nicaraguan Minister of Finance that it was only a draft and not official. Over the following months, however, the Bank took an even harsher stance than the one proposed in the CPP: it cut off lending altogether. Nicaragua has received no new commitments from the Bank since early 1982. For the fiscal year 1983, the Bank included four Nicaraguan projects on its Monthly Operational Summary: a $30 million loan for the expansion of Managua's water system, a $15 million loan for agricultural credit, a $10 million loan for an energy project, and a $4 million loan for the rehabilitation of coconut plantations. But all of these projects were frozen; the Monthly Operations Summary reported that for each project, 'further processing depends on agreement being reached with Government on actions needed to resolve current economic problems.'[41] Early in 1984, negotiations were resumed. There was speculation within the Bank that this was motivated by a desire to disarm the expected criticism of a resumption of Bank lending to El Salvador, or alternatively in order to 'protect the Bank's portfolio' in Nicaragua. It is not clear whether it will in fact lead to a resumption of lending, or whether, as in the case of Chile, negotiations have resumed in response to political considerations, and so that the loans could in theory be ready to submit to the Board after the Sandinistas had been overthrown by military force.

What both the US and the World Bank claim to want from the Sandinistas are clear 'rules of the game' for the private sector. This is a theme of the CPP and officials of the US Treasury Department repeat it when they explain why the US does not approve funds for Nicaragua. Both institutions say, often in identical words, that the problem is economic and not political: 'funds risk being wasted' unless the Sandinistas 'revitalise the private sector' and 'improve the efficiency of the public sector'.[42] Treasury officials specify further that they would like the Sandinistas to remove price controls and subsidies, to devalue their currency and in general to make Nicaraguan institutions more responsive to market forces.[43] Underlying all these concerns about the private sector is a conviction that the Sandinistas are not committed to a mixed economy.

A senior Bank official also claimed that 'some of the best technocrats' had left the government, including Alfredo Cesar, President of the Central Bank, which 'made our own dialogue at technical level very difficult; there are no counterparts on the same wave-length of technical analysis'.[44] This official failed to mention that the Bank's own attitude, as revealed in the leaked CPP, clearly strengthened the position of those in the Nicaraguan government who had always believed that negotiation with the Bank was fruitless; another Bank official complained that, after the CPP, 'doors closed in our faces'. A related bone of contention between the Bank and the Sandinistas is that at present the Sandinistas have no medium-term economic plan. Bank officials say that the Bank cannot lend to a country without a plan. The Sandinistas say, 'why have a plan if the country is on the brink of being invaded and we are forced to re-evaluate our situation from day to day?' They add that most countries have plans but do not stick to them, rendering them meaningless.

But do the reasons that the US and the Bank give for cutting off funds to Nicaragua have any basis in fact? Is the Nicaraguan public sector inefficient and has the private sector been treated badly? First, it would seem that the Nicaraguan public sector is not particularly inefficient, and certainly not more so than most government bureaucracies. It may even be more efficient. Nicaragua, since 1979, has made considerable progress towards literacy, food self-sufficiency, improved living standards and increased agricultural production – all of which have been the initiatives of a public sector depleted by the loss of many of its skilled technicians and managers, never numerous, either through death during the civil war or through emigration after the war – and even the CPP admits that the Sandinistas have greatly increased the efficiency of tax collection. Second, the private sector has been treated extraordinarily well, particularly given its disruptive role. Desperate to keep the private sector producing and generating foreign exchange, the Sandinistas have given private producers credit on better terms than under Somoza, protection against drops in commodity prices and other incentives. They have banned strikes, placed ceilings on wages and forbidden land invasions. Keen not to frighten large agricultural producers, they resisted intensive pressure from the peasants to enact land reform; it was not until two years after the victory that a land reform act came into effect.

The land reform act, described as conservative by many observers, confirmed the Sandinistas' commitment to the private sector by projecting that 30 per cent of agricultural land would end up belonging to medium and large producers, 40 per cent to peasant associations and co-operatives, 25 per cent to the state and 5 per cent to small individual owners. It does not affect lands that are productive and places no ceilings on the amount of well-exploited land an individual can own. It also grants compensation for idle land that is expropriated; even those landowners who deliberately neglect their land in order to drain money out of the country receive compensation in the form of bonds at 2 per cent interest that mature after 25 years.[45] It was a land reform as much designed to keep the goodwill of the private sector as it was to satisfy the peasants' need for land. The Sandinistas made these and other concessions to the private sector often much to the frustration and anger of the urban and rural poor who did not see why they had fought a war only to have the well-off continue to be favoured by the government. The private sector, on the other hand, did not consider the special treatment they received to be adequate. It seems that they wanted political power as well as the economic power they already had in abundance. It seems too, despite the Sandinistas' repeatedly stressed goal of a mixed economy, that they were frightened by any intimations of socialism, of revolution or of power being given to the workers they had controlled for so long. Tensions between the private sector and the Sandinistas grew, the private sector encouraged by its power to withhold production and destabilise the country and by the sure knowledge that the US supported it against the Sandinistas.

By 1981 individuals in the private sector were deliberately carrying out economic sabotage or 'decapitalisation' as the Sandinistas called it. Decapitalisation in the agricultural sector included:

- Cutting back on cultivated acres.
- Laying off needed workers and technicians.
- Selling off machinery and livestock, often to buyers in Honduras and Costa Rica.
- Using government production loans fraudulently – converting part of the loan to dollars on the street market, then sending the dollars to foreign bank accounts.
- Over-invoicing for imported machinery, spare parts, fertilisers, pesticides and so on in co-operation with 'friendly corporations' in Guatemala or Florida.
- Faking or inflating fees and commissions to foreign firms or individuals, again as a way to siphon dollars out of the country.
- Paying excessive salaries, often in advance, to themselves and members of their family.
- Asking for a government loan on the grounds of 'saving jobs' once any combination of the above had caused financial losses.[46]

And de-capitalisation was even more vigorous in the industrial sector.

In Nicaragua, those sections of the Bank's staff that wanted the Bank to lend to the Sandinistas were at first able to process loans to Nicaragua because the Bank's senior management hoped to be able to influence Nicaraguan policies. But in its 1982 Country Program Paper the Bank complained of 'inconsistencies' in Nicaragua. When the revolutionary nature of the Sandinista government, its economic success and its overwhelming popular support became clearer, the Bank decided to stop lending. It thus in effect went along with the US view that the government should be overthrown, rather than conciliated. Presumably it considered that the situation was no longer 'in flux', as the Bank's CPP put it.

In Grenada the Bank was hostile to the New Jewel Movement government from the start, although, shortly before the US invasion in 1983, it appeared to have a change of heart. As usual, it used apparently technical objections as justification for its compliance with the US desire for a financial boycott of the Grenadian revolution by the West. It was, in this case, more compliant than the IMF. It based its refusal to lend to Grenada, which received no money from the Bank while the New Jewel Movement was in power, on opposition to the airport at Point Salines. The US government maintained that the airport was a staging post for Cuba. According to an IMF official, the Bank's opposition to it was 'purely political'.

In 1976, before the New Jewel Movement took power, the Bank had sent two appraisal missions to Grenada which concluded 'that the existing runway at Pearls acted . . . as a constraint on the development of air transport and tourism growth' and 'that taking into account the country's needs, constraints and development potential, the Point Salines site for a new airport would best serve Grenada's needs'; it added that further study was needed, in spite of the fact that six feasibility studies, all of them favourable to the project, had already been made, by various British and Canadian agencies.[47] The People's Revolutionary Government, before it turned to Cuba, asked the World Bank to finance the airport, but to no avail. The Bank not only refused to finance the airport itself, but, according to the Grenadian High Commission in London, attempted to obstruct Grenada's access to other sources of credit; Plessey, the British contractors, were said to be willing to finance the project and the British ECGD (Export Credit Guarantees Department) to guarantee it, but there was opposition from the Bank of England, possibly inspired, say the Grenadians, by the World Bank. At the Caribbean aid consultative group meeting, the Bank refused to back Grenada's economic programme on the grounds that the airport project was not sound.[48]

The Bank at first also refused to respond, one way or the other, to the IMF's request for an evaluation of the government's investment programme, including the airport project, though such an evaluation is now usual as a basis for IMF standby or extended facility decisions. The IMF, in this case, carried on without it, and against US (and British) opposition, recognising that there was no technical basis for objection to Grenada's economic management. The US opposition to the IMF loan, as expressed by its Executive Director was, also as usual, clothed in technical language: Grenada, he said, had no balance of payments problems, therefore it did not need money from the IMF; in addition, 'he was concerned with the IMF's involvement with development aid to Grenada without World Bank endorsement'.[49] As a result of these objections the IMF management, which had approved an Extended Fund Facility in May 1981, withdrew it two days before it was due to go to the Board. The IMF nevertheless made a standby agreement with Grenada, and, in mid-1983, its Board approved an EFF for Grenada, against the vote of the United States and three other countries, including Britain. It was apparently one of the rare occasions on which a vote has been taken in the IMF. Grenada had fought a prolonged political battle, in addition to being, as an IMF official put it, 'on top of the technical aspects' and able to negotiate 'on a par with the institution' and 'use the same terminology' in negotiating an 'internally consistent programme'.[50]

According to the *Free West Indian*, 21 September, 1983:

At the recent IMF meeting, unofficial reports indicate that the deliberations on Grenada's loan request created history in two major respects. The deliberations were the longest ever in the history of the IMF, much longer than it took the IMF to approve 5 billion (US) dollars for Mexico and 6 billion (US) for Brazil. This is itself a clear manifestation of the US attempts to block IMF assistance to Grenada.

Secondly, the deliberations on Grenada's application was the first such in the history of the IMF, on which every single member of the Executive directors spoke – an indication of the tremendous battle which took place within the IMF on little Grenada.

The absence of any balance of payments problem on Grenada's part, and the fact that we are up-to-date on the repayment of all foreign loans, meant that Grenada stood in a good position to counteract any arguments which detractors such as the US could muster.

Additionally, the IMF itself, based on their own documentation on the performance of Grenada's economy, was well aware of our sound approach to genuine economic development . . .

Big and powerful as the US may be, they cannot always have their way.

Bernard Coard, Minister of Finance, Planning and Trade, is said to have believed that he could take on the IMF and the World Bank at their own game, and win. He was assisted by an IMF official on leave of absence. In that he was possibly correct; at any rate the US was unsuccessful in economic destabilisation and resorted, tragically, to other means.

Meanwhile the World Bank had done some sort of an about-turn. In 1983 it finally produced a favourable economic report: it had 'come out to bat' for Grenada, said one of its officials, much to the disgust of the US administration.[51] The Bank said that as the airport had been nearly completed, on the basis of 'soft' finance provided by Cuba, its objections no longer applied. The Grenadians said that they had refused to accept the officials the Bank originally intended to send on its mission to Grenada, on the grounds of their blatant ideological hostility. The report was written by Pfefferman, a senior and occasionally enlightened economist in the Latin American and Caribbean region.[52]

It would in fact have been hard for the Bank to find technical grounds on which to criticise Grenada. During the years of the revolution, it was one of the very few countries in the world which had steady economic growth, with no balance of payments or debt crises. It had adopted a new investment code which was favourable to foreign private investment. As the IMF official said, its economic policies were 'most pragmatic'; the Grenadian Letter of Intent to the IMF, he said, should have been published as a means of refuting the allegation that Grenada was 'going communist'.[53] Similarly, a Bank official, asked why the Bank appeared to regard Grenada with more favour than Nicaragua or Vietnam, said: 'It's a capitalist country'.[54] Until the US invasion, the island was notably peaceful. In addition, Grenada was doing a lot of things of which the Bank, at least in theory, approves. It had reduced unemployment from 50 per cent to 15 per cent. It had practically eliminated illiteracy. It was making medical facilities available to remote villages for the first time. The fact that these services were free to their users could not really provide the Bank with grounds for objection, since there were no budgetary and financial problems.

As for the airport, the *International Herald Tribune* reported in November 1983 that Grenada's new US masters, worried about their ability to maintain the momentum of Grenadian growth, were anxious to press ahead with it. A USAID-financed study concluded that the airport was economically justified. And the *Financial Times*, on January 6 1984, failing to mention the fact that the airport was supposed to be explicable only as a Cuban base, reported without comment that:

> Baroness Young, Minister of State at the Foreign and Commonwealth Office, who arrived in St George's yesterday . . . is expected to offer British assistance for the completion of the Point Salines airport, a top economic priority for the development of the Grenada tourist industry.

In fact, USAID is to put up the $24 million needed to complete the project, and an Idaho-based firm has won the contract. The airport was due to be inaugurated by President Reagan, on the anniversary of the US invasion.

At the time of the US invasion of Grenada, the Bank was said to be discussing a loan in the agriculture sector. Whether or not the Bank would have followed up its report by making a loan to the People's Revolutionary Government (PRG) in Grenada in the face of US opposition will thus not be known. The Bank's embarrassment about its report could conceivably explain the fact that the Grenadian mission to the Organisation of American States in Washington, which had run out of copies of the Bank's report, was unable in September 1983 to obtain further copies from the Bank. The report is of course not published.

Probably the most blatant recent example of openly political US intervention in the operations of the Bank is in Vietnam. After the liberation of South Vietnam, the World Bank had been negotiating, apparently in good faith, for a continuation of its substantial lending programme. Negotiations in Hanoi, according to the World Bank officials who had been engaged in them, were proceeding well. The Bank was impressed by the 'quality of middle level officials' in Hanoi and the thoroughness with which the many projects presented to it had been prepared. However, McNamara, returning from a trip abroad, was met by Ernie Stern, Senior Vice-President of the Bank, and told that the US Executive Director had warned him that any World Bank lending to Vietnam would jeopardise the prospects for IDA replenishment. This official presented McNamara with a draft of a personal letter to Congressman Clarence Long, Chairman of the Sub-Committee on Foreign

Operations of the House Appropriations Committee, giving an undertaking that lending to Vietnam was not presently contemplated. McNamara signed it. So far no more loans have been made to Vietnam. In 1973, when the US Congress began cutting aid appropriations to the corrupt and doomed Saigon regime, the World Bank was wheeled in to take over the burden of supporting Saigon; it presided over aid co-ordinating meetings in Paris in 1973 and 1974, providing favourable economic reports as background to the meetings and arguing for more aid to Saigon. At that time the Bank was apparently warned that IDA replenishment would be jeopardised if the Bank did *not* lend to South Vietnam.

In Peru, during the period when the country had a military government which the Cubans optimistically described as revolutionary, the Bank made only one loan between 1968 and 1973. The main problem was apparently the question of compensation, mainly for the US oil company IPC, which the Velasco government had nationalised. When Peru came to terms with the US government in the Greene agreement in 1974, money from the Bank and other aid agencies poured in.[55] In Ethiopia, the Bank carried on lending to the military government which overthrew Emperor Haile Selassi for some time, apparently on the basis of promises to compensate foreign interests, but then stopped. In Egypt under Nasser, the Bank, at the behest of the United States, reversed a decision to finance the Aswan Dam, which was then financed by the Soviet Union. The Bank stopped lending to Brazil under the left-leaning government of Goulart; it resumed lending when Goulart's elected government was overthrown in the 1964 military coup, and it continued throughout the subsequent period of extreme repression and anti-working class economic policies.

So much for the Bank's political impartiality.

The World Bank and poverty

The question of the alleviation of poverty is, for the Bank, a separate one. One of the more progressive and intelligent Bank officials said, straight-faced: 'There are countries where poverty is perhaps [sic] the most important issue.'[56] But in fact, the position of this section, at the end of the chapters on the Bank, and its relative length, parallel the position the subject usually occupies in Bank documents.

Until the 1970s, the Bank went no further than the so-called 'trickle down' theory: economic growth would automatically produce benefits for the poor, which would trickle down to them from the rich. Growth is supposed to be possible once stabilisation has been achieved under IMF-type programmes, so even growth was, and still is, a secondary objective. Under McNamara there was some recognition that even when growth occurred, it did not automatically do very much for the poor and might actually result in increasing poverty and inequality, and that the problems of poverty were pressing. Even if McNamara reached that conclusion merely because he believed, as he said in 1966, that 'order' and 'stability' were not possible without 'internal development of at least a minimal degree',[57] rather than because of a more genuine concern about 'basic human necessities', in the changed rhetoric of the 1970s it is clear that this represented a relatively liberal view of how to contain unrest. Kissinger, for example, is said to have believed that starving people don't make revolutions, and the current US administration obviously considers military force a more effective method of containment than economic aid. Also it is undoubtedly true that many Bank officials, especially those recruited during McNamara's presidency, had a genuine commitment to improving the conditions of the poor.

But the counter-insurgency goals take precedence, and this can itself impose limitations on the Bank's anti-poverty programmes. The Bank, as has been said, is very clearly interested only in reforms within the system and not in any disruption of it. It backs off if the reforms it has supported show signs of implying more revolutionary changes. The case of the Philippines provides a particularly clear example of the Bank's policies and their limitations. Bank projects were deliberately undertaken in areas with high levels of rural discontent and opposition. The Bank supported the publicised intentions of the Marcos regime to carry out a land reform. When it became clear that the Marcos land reform was in words only, one Bank official proposed greater Bank involvement in 'a program of major importance to low income farmers' and another wrote: 'It is my belief that we cannot go on much longer with our agricultural program in the Philippines without contributing to the government's efforts in the field of agrarian reform.'[58] But as Bello, Kinley and Elinson comment:

the only real alternative to Marcos' brand of reform was . . . one that would drastically alter the balance of power in the countryside. Yet the Bank shrank from recommending such a move, and, as an alternative to the discontent and confusion created by Marcos' halfway measure, it eventually proposed *stepping back*: 'Some former tenants, and other potential tenants,' stated the [World Bank's confidential report on *Poverty, Basic Needs and Employment*, January 1980], 'were not really ready for a shift in tenure status; they need and prefer the protection of the landlord, who is also their creditor, particularly for insurance against bad harvests.' Indeed, it complained that agrarian reform contributed, 'in many areas [to] disruption of healthy landlord/tenant relations'.[59]

In contrast, when the Bank was pursuing an objective central to its beliefs, that of import liberalisation, it was willing to force Marcos to abandon another pillar of his support, the bourgeois nationalists who had made their fortunes from import-substitution (see above).

Bank officials are prone to defend their failure to support reformist and populist measures on the grounds that halfway measures result in economic chaos, inefficiency, and inconsistency in objectives. This type of accusation was levelled, with some justice, by the Bank at Chilean policies under Allende, Jamaican policies under Manley, Nicaragua under the Sandinistas (at least in the early years after their victory), and elsewhere. As one official in the Latin American division, who described himself as 'on the left' in the Bank, rather lucidly explained, the Jamaican government under Manley was attempting to 'put a squeeze on the private sector' at a time and under conditions in which they had no capacity in the public sector; this was 'the dilemma of all revolutionary systems'. When Castro and Mao decided to move against the private productive system, they were ready, and they knew they could not rely on the private sector; but when Manley moved 'gently' against the private sector, removing incentives, in the naive belief that they would nevertheless continue to invest, he wasn't ready with an alternative plan of what to do 'if the capitalist class refused to play'; the quite foreseeable result was economic chaos. Reminded that there had also been external pressures, the official said that they were equally foreseeable. 'That is why I'm not a revolutionary,' he concluded.[60] He should in fact have said that that was why he was not a reformist; a case against revolutions would have to be made on different grounds. The Bank's argument that 'governments cannot just hand out to everybody' is perfectly correct, and could be taken in several ways. The problem is that it is clear, when it comes to the crunch, which 'handouts' the Bank thinks ought to have priority – as the accounts, in the previous section, of the Bank's treatment of Nicaragua and Grenada should have sufficiently demonstrated.

In fact throughout the 1970s, although the Bank continued to pay lip-service to the problems of income distribution, the need for higher social expenditures, and so on, in practice the conclusion that, for the time being, the government in question was 'living beyond its means' (as the Bank's 1979 economic report on Pakistan put it)[61] and must therefore cut down on social expenditures, was probably just as widespread. Even in Haiti, where the Bank's CPP spoke of the government's 'contempt for the needs of the Haitian population', the Bank joined the IMF in demanding drastic cuts in government expenditures. Its solution to the government's resultant inability to provide counterpart funds for the Bank's own projects was to propose that the Bank should provide them itself; whether this will actually happen is another matter. The Bank's 1978 economic report on Bolivia, where the conditions in which the tin-miners live are notoriously harsh, said that the mining industry suffered from 'excessive welfare expenditures'.[62]

Bank officials say that, whereas in the 1960s the Bank criticised the Frei government in Chile for 'favoring social investment', [63] nowadays the Frei government's policies might be considered satisfactory. But there is no evidence to this effect. McNamara is said to have viewed the reformist policies of Sri Lanka with some favour. Studies had shown that Sri Lanka's 'social variables' (infant mortality, life expectancy) were much better than in other countries with similar levels of income per head, and that if Sri Lanka had gone for growth the resulting income per head levels would not have produced equivalent social achievements, on the basis of comparisons with other countries in Asia. McNamara is said to have been impressed by the evidence.[64] The World Bank nevertheless joined the IMF in pushing, eventually with success, for the re-imposition of orthodox economic policies in Sri Lanka.

Keeping down wages has always been high on the list of the Bank's priorities. In the 1970s its opposition to wage increases persisted but was couched in different language: thus 'high' wages in the formal sector were now said to be the privilege of a labour aristocracy and bad for the poor. But the effect was the same. For example, the 1981 Bank report on the manufacturing sector in Peru says that the reformist military government's 'industrial community' legislation had an 'adverse impact on industrial employment generation, productivity and income distribution', principally by giving workers in the formal sector too high wages and too much job protection. While the situation had improved, 'the labor stability law, which provides nearly full job security to formal sector workers, and the minimum wage legislation granting excessively high wages to formal sector workers, are still in operation'. This needed to be changed.

> This [proposed] move toward low real wages in formal
> sector manufacturing – and with it, the tendencies toward
> higher job creation, reduction of the formal-informal sector
> wage gap, higher labor productivity and improved export
> competitiveness – is currently thwarted by the job security
> legislation and rising real wages granted within the system
> of Government determined minimum wages.[65]

The evidence given for 'rising real wages' was that the minimum wage had been revised upward. Average wages in the unionised formal sector, according to Ministry of Labour figures, in the period from mid-1980 to mid-1981, had merely been maintained at the very low level to which they had fallen over the previous period. In the non-unionised, but still 'formal' private sector, in which the legislation was flouted, they were continuing to decline.

Under the heading 'The Informal Sector', the Peru report alleges that workers in the formal sector are opposed to any government help for the informal sector:

> Both formal sector workers and entrepreneurs resent any
> closer relationship with the informal sector. The formal
> sector workers have reached – with the support of the
> Government and their trade unions – a privileged position
> in terms of job security and wage level (although the latter
> has eroded in recent years) which could only be negatively

affected, if related to the depressed situation of informal
sector workers.[66]

The report fails to mention that wages in Peru, as in other Third
World countries, are generally widely shared among many depen-
dants. It also complains that, because high wages in the formal
sector and 'general subsidisation of the urban population' cause
people to migrate to the cities, there is 'sharp competition' in the
informal sector, which means that returns are too low, which
means that investment is inadequate, so the informal sector
'cannot be expected to absorb a large number of workers productively, improve product quality, raise labour productivity or, in
general, help to reduce the gap to the formal sector'. Thus all
would apparently be well if only the 'formal' workers would take a
bigger wage cut.

In order to show how well the Belaúnde government was doing
under the guidance of the World Bank's men (see above, p. 95),
the Peruvian Central Bank's research department, headed by
Richard Webb, formerly of the World Bank, published figures on
'improvements in the distribution of income'. The figures showed
that more was being spent on maids, dressmaking, and hairdressers,
a sign, one might have thought, that income was being redistributed
to the rich. Richard Webb, a Peruvian national, had previously
achieved newspaper headlines in Brazil as the 'young World Bank
economist' who had written a report 'proving' that income
distribution had improved under Brazil's military governments.
He claimed that he had been subjected to pressures within the
Bank to make him do so.[67]

Nowadays Bank officials say that balance of payments crises
have meant that considerations of 'efficiency' are again central.
The fact that the high priority supposedly attached to questions of
distribution and basic needs is so easily abandoned in times of
crisis tends to prove that it was never well integrated into the
Bank's general policy prescriptions. The 'poverty-orientation' was
effectively confined to projects. Thus an official close to McNamara,
asked to give examples of pressure being put on governments to
pay more attention to poverty and income distribution, cited the
case of Brazil. Pressure was indeed put on Brazil: the government
was told it had to begin negotiations on a rural development
project before the Bank would negotiate on other projects. There

was no fundamental reappraisal of development strategy and certainly no reassessment of the orthodox IMF/World Bank methods of achieving 'stabilisation'. The emphasis on overall demand limitation and market mechanisms for this purpose was undiminished, in spite of the heavy impact of these policies on the poor. As one Bank official put it, there was a 'brief flirtation with basic needs' but it was 'never well articulated intellectually' and it 'got overtaken'.[68]

In order to avoid the accusation that the Bank's poverty-orientation was merely a question of hand-outs, McNamara or his advisers hit upon the idea that the Bank's new policies involved 'increasing the productivity of the poor'. The Bank was not just going to provide one-off improvements in their situation; it was going to help them to help themselves. Thus it would not only help the poor but would comply with the Bank's duty, as expressed in its Articles of Agreement, to use its resources for 'productive purposes'. This was perhaps the central argument in the major theoretical work produced by the Bank in its basic needs period, *Redistribution with Growth*: growth would be as good with redistribution as without it, if not better.[69] This involved its own contradictions. The poor who could be helped tended to be those who had some assets on which to 'build'; hence, partly, the Bank's emphasis on small-holders, and on self-help but paid-for housing. The idea that the Bank might also assist small-scale industrialisation came to very little; the development banks supported by the Bank, for example, lend largely to large-scale foreign-owned businesses.[70] But in any case the argument related mainly to projects and to the rates of return to be achieved on them. As one Bank official put it, there was 'a lack of interface' between projects and general economic policies. In addition, there was of course a considerable lack of interface between the relatively progressive intellectuals who worked in Hollis Chenery's research department in the Bank, which has been compared to the research department of an outsize university, and the officials who actually made the decisions on the day-to-day operations of the Bank. With the arrival of Clausen in 1981 Chenery left, and the research activities of the Bank have been cut and reorganised, with the stated purpose of making them more immediately operational, as well as redirecting them to a concentration on trade liberalisation and pricing policies.

Projects financed by the Bank, as has been said, amount to less than 2 per cent of total investment in the Third World. Of these projects, only a minority have a specific poverty orientation. The majority of commitments continue to be in the Bank's traditional lending areas: development finance companies, energy, industry, telecommunications, transportation, technical assistance and 'non-project'. Between a third and a half of Bank commitments in recent years have been for projects in sectors which might be considered to be of interest to the poor. But by far the largest category is agriculture, which does not necessarily mean that income is redistributed to the poor, and may mean the opposite (see Table 10). According to the 1982 *Annual Report*,[71] the percentages of IBRD/IDA commitments to these sectors were as follows:

Table 10 Distribution of IBRD/IDA commitments by sector

	1980	1981	1982
	%	%	%
Agriculture and rural development	30.1	30.6	23.7
Education	3.8	6.0	4.0
Population, health and nutrition	1.2	0.1	0.3
Small-scale enterprises	2.3	1.9	2.2
Urbanisation (mainly housing)	3.0	4.1	2.9
Water supply and sewerage	5.5	4.3	3.4

Source: World Bank *Annual Report*, 1982, p. 125.

The question then of course arises of the extent to which these projects' benefits actually accrue to the poor. During the McNamara period the Bank's project evaluations, like its economic reports, included an assessment of the effect on income distribution. This is no longer required. In any case the figures are notoriously fudged. They may even at times amount to no more than claims that because a certain percentage of people living in the area covered by a project are poor, the same percentage of the benefits of the project accrue to them.[72] Because the Bank's method of working is to send officials for short visits, the possibilities of abuse are great. Even supposing the Bank is genuinely concerned with the effects of its projects on the poor, its ability to do anything about it is limited (see Chapter 8). Bank officials usually accept that in practice the benefits of their projects go overwhelmingly to the better-off. They do so with varying degrees of resignation, concern, cynicism or rationalisation. They rationalise by saying that the Bank has to take things as it finds them, that it is necessary for its projects to be of benefit to broad sections of society if they are not to incur the hostility of local hierarchies, and so on. But there is also much evidence that the Bank does not want too much disruption of patterns of ownership in rural areas, apart from the return to private ownership of state farms.

Even in the Bank's poverty projects, its commitment to the neo-classical theory of full-cost recovery can, yet again, intrude. This is particularly so in the 'urbanisation' or urban housing projects. The Bank is fully aware that governments' methods of eliminating slums frequently involve merely bulldozing them, and, where relocation does occur, people are moved to distant suburbs. As McNamara eloquently put it, 'there is one thing worse than living in a slum or a squatter settlement – and this is having one's slum or settlement bulldozed away by the government which has no shelter of any sort whatever to offer in its place'.[73] So, in the Philippines, the Bank set out not to destroy slums, but to upgrade them. But, because of the principle of full-cost recovery, and in theory also so that the projects would be 'replicable', it wanted the inhabitants to pay for the improvements. The end result was likely to be the same: they couldn't pay, so they had to go.[74] In general, the Bank finds it difficult to deal with the very poor, for the simple reason that they have no money, and the Bank doesn't like government subsidies.

Some people, including some people within the Bank, both on the left and on the right, were critical of the 'basic needs' strategy on the grounds that it implicitly relegated developing countries to wood-hewing and water-drawing, postponed their adoption of technology-intensive methods of production, and might also slow down growth. But that was not its biggest problem. It was a half-hearted attempt to impose some poverty-orientated projects on Third World regimes which were not interested in reforms and could not afford them; at least, not in addition to providing for their own luxuries and those of foreigners.

> Distribution and redistribution are functions of the total socio-economic system. Their pattern cannot be seriously and durably affected by selective projects, programs, policies and even institutions if these run counter to the long run, basic tendencies of the system.[75]

The 'basic needs' school of thought will probably soon be relegated to historical accounts of the Bank, as an episode which moreover had more to do with rhetoric than reality, whatever the idealism of some of those promoting it.

PART III

Conclusions and Proposals

10. Current forms of aid from the West

Purposes

Most of this book has been about the World Bank. But much of what has been said applies to government 'aid' from the West in general. The Bank is widely recognised as the most powerful of the 'aid' institutions. Bilateral donors have much less influence on the policies of governments and often deliberately mediate their demands through the Bank and the IMF. Mostly they just go along with their ideas and prescriptions. The US government has at times intervened to stop the Bank lending to certain left-wing governments, but usually this is unnecessary. Some Scandinavian governments, especially the Swedish government, have on the other hand been critical of the Bank's refusal to lend to such governments. 'The Scandinavians' thus figure in the demonology of Bank officials, and some of the following generalisations about aid from Western governments do not apply to Social-Democratic governments in Scandinavia, or to the Netherlands during the 1970s.

There is no doubt an element of humanitarianism, or guilt, in the provision of aid. The motives of many people engaged in the business of aid are mixed and the people themselves vary. For many of them, a concern about poverty in the Third World must be the main reason for their involvement and they may genuinely believe that their activities are beneficial to the poor. Others may have a different vision of the purposes of aid and be committed to different goals. Others, again, are probably just cynical, aware that they are doing nicely out of the gravy train provided by the aid business and unable to find another one with the same rewards. Even governments which include a provision for aid in their budgets may do so partly out of a sense of obligation and are not immune to high-minded pleas for international goodwill put forward at international forums.

But there is of course much more to it than that. Aid is also seen as a means of promoting political and strategic objectives. To the extent that it is an alternative to more violent methods of achieving these ends, it has aspects of humanitarianism. Thus McNamara, during his period at the World Bank, and the authors of the Brandt report, can be said to have been more progressive than Reagan or Thatcher in the simple sense that they saw economic development as a means for the containment of rebellion preferable to the use of military force. But the political and strategic goals themselves are far from progressive, even though the anti-communist crusade is carried out in the name of 'freedom and democracy'. The majority of the Third World governments supported by the West are authoritarian, often military, regimes of a brutally repressive nature. The governments that are overthrown, or subjected to 'destabilisation' through, for example, the withdrawal of aid, are usually much less repressive and they have sometimes been elected under the usual constitutional processes.

The Popular Unity government in Chile is the most famous example; military methods were used in Chile only after Popular Unity had increased its share of the vote in the mid-term municipal elections and the prospect of defeating it by democratic means had receded. Manley's government in Jamaica, Goulart in Brazil, Cheddi Jagan in Guyana were all elected. The New Jewel Movement in Grenada had won elections held under Gairy, but had been told by Gairy that his 'boys' were re-counting the votes; after they took power, one of the achievements of which they were most proud was the building of 'Participatory People's Democracy'. The US invasion, which was planned long before Maurice Bishop was murdered, has resulted in rule by the US military; elections will not be held until the US can be certain that the New Jewel Movement has been effectively destroyed (for what would be the point of invading if the NJM came back through elections?). The US helped to prevent the fulfilment of the undertaking in the 1954 Geneva Accords that elections would be held in the South of Vietnam; if elections were held, Eisenhower said on television, 'that dictator [Ho Chi Minh] would get 100 per cent of the votes'. When the Sandinistas announced that they were keeping to their plan to hold elections in 1985, and then that they were bringing them forward to 1984, the US government switched to another demand: that they should reduce the size of their military forces, which unfortunately they need in order to defend themselves against us-backed invasion.

These governments are less repressive than the governments commonly supported by the West precisely because they are seen to be acting in the interests of the majority of their own people, who usually give them their overwhelming support. The purpose of economic destabilisation is to undermine that support by making it more difficult for left-wing governments to deliver tangible benefits to their people. In Chile, military force was resorted to when destabilisation had been partially successful but not successful enough, presumably, for the ruling class to risk waiting for elections. In Grenada, economic destabilisation was notably unsuccessful. But political dissension, tragically and perhaps with the help of the CIA, provided the pretext for the invasion the us had long been planning. These governments nevertheless encounter the hostility of the West precisely because they are successful and popular and provide an alternative and more attractive model of development.

This alternative model is seen as a threat to the West partly for strategic and political reasons. Although the claim that countries as small as Nicaragua and Grenada constitute a military threat to the United States is clearly ludicrous, and the idea that they might provide bases from which the Soviet Union could attack the United States is hardly less so, the Soviet Union and Cuba can provide some form of military support for struggles elsewhere. Even very small countries, such as Grenada, which do not constitute a military threat, can nevertheless provide an example to be followed by others if they are allowed to succeed. The domino theory is far from dead. If such models of development become widespread in the Third World, they will be the opposite of a threat to freedom and democracy, in the Third World or anywhere else. But they will threaten the political system in the imperialist heartlands. And some people, even those who would not applaud the political system in Paraguay, the Philippines or Chile, nevertheless presumably feel that the relative freedoms that exist in prosperous Western parliamentary democracies can justifiably be defended by propping up right-wing dictatorships in the Third World.

But economic considerations provide an even more compelling justification for the existence of aid. As the Brandt report correctly points out, not only is the 'South' dependent on the 'North', but the North is dependent on the South.[1] Anxious though the Brandt report was to change the geographical terminology, this is primarily a dependence of the major Western powers on their former colonies and semi-colonies in the Third World. Having built up a system under which the Third World provides it with cheap and abundant raw materials and primary commodities, markets for its manufactured goods and super-profits for some of its major firms and banks, the West would find it difficult to adjust to the loss of these advantages. Some raw materials crucial to Western industries are to be found only or mainly in the Third World. A large part of the proven reserves of oil are in the Third World. The Brandt report is concerned that multilateral mining companies, whose super-profits are threatened by Third World nationalism, may become reluctant to invest in new capacity. Western consumers would suffer from any diminution in the willingness of Third World countries to turn over their land to export crops in their desperate attempts to satisfy the requirements of their urban elites for Western manufactured goods. If more land was devoted to food crops for local consumption, there could be shortages of tea, coffee, bananas and other tropical crops and their prices could go up, feeding inflation; the Thatcher government's 'success' in bringing down inflation was said by the Bank of England to be mainly a consequence of the decline in the prices of commodities supplied by Third World countries.[2]

Between a quarter and a third of the exports of developed countries and nearly 40 per cent of US exports go to the Third World. The big redundancies at British Leyland Trucks in 1984 (which were followed by its threatened total closure) and the failure of Vauxhall to reduce its losses in spite of its success on the British market were ascribed to their over-dependence on Third World markets and the contraction in these markets caused by the debt crisis.[3] Economic policies in the Third World directed primarily at meeting the needs of the poor might reduce the need for imports and would certainly mean that different types of manufactured goods were imported; more medical equipment and fewer cars, for example. Western industry might have difficulty in adjusting to the new demands. Socialist countries in the Third World would nationalise the subsidiaries of multinational companies, probably without compensation. The profits made by multinational companies are higher in the Third World than they are at home and in other developed countries, mainly because wages are much lower; some of the major multinational companies make most of their profits and in some cases most of their sales in the Third World. Left-wing governments might be more interested in a debtors' cartel, which would threaten major banks.

Methods

Aid is one means of safeguarding these interests. It does so in a number of direct and indirect ways. The most obvious is that aid is allocated between countries so as to reward friends and penalise enemies and, in some cases in which aid is provided to left-wing governments, to keep open or enlarge the possibility that they will adopt policies favourable to Western interests. At times the threat of cutting aid is used as a means of preventing governments from adopting specific policies of which Western donors disapprove; for example, trading with Cuba or nationalising some foreign asset. Aid is known to be unavailable to governments which fail to reach agreement with foreign investors and creditors. The offer of aid is used, perhaps consciously, to ensure that governments become dependent on its continuation. Once a country is 'hooked' on aid and loans from abroad, its economy becomes orientated towards foreign trade and it needs new loans to service old ones. The threat of non-renewal of aid is harder to deal with than its absence from the outset.

Aid is used to open up markets. Once a country has imported a steel mill or railway equipment partly financed on 'soft' terms or with grants, it is almost bound to have a continuing need for imports from the same source. Abandoned equipment in many parts of the Third World testifies to the fact that this need is often not met. But it increases the willingness of many governments to do what is necessary to obtain the favours of the West. If the aid had not been available in the first place, the materials and skills might, in many cases, have been provided from local sources. A foreign firm's bid may be supported by offers of aid. Thus the *Financial Times* reported that Bharat Heavy Electrical (BHEL), India's state-owned power station contractor, 'was overtaken by GEC . . . backed by the UK Government. The fact that a substantial proportion of the cost of imported equipment will be covered by grants reduced the power of BHEL's arguments.'[4] The drastic cuts in imports being imposed by the IMF and the banks on the debtor countries are, paradoxically, causing some of them to find ways of reducing their dependence on imports: thus Mexico is using glass bottles rather than imported tin cans, and wood rather than imported plastic in the manufacture of furniture and other household goods.

Aid also finances projects in the economic infrastructure, such as harbours and telecommunications, which are essential for the profitable operation of foreign investors but which the private sector itself will not invest in, because they are not profitable enough. This is also a means of ensuring that governments' revenues are used for these purposes, since aid seldom finances the total cost of a project or its recurring costs, and the loans must be repaid. Projects in social sectors such as education and health are sometimes justified in publications about aid as a means of ensuring that the private sector is supplied with a sufficiently healthy and competent workforce. It can also be justified as a contribution to quietening unrest, and is in that sense equivalent to reforms within industrialised countries, though on a far smaller and more haphazard scale. Projects in agriculture are in line with the interests of the increasingly powerful and expanding agribusiness firms which supply the inputs of fertiliser and improved seeds used in Green Revolution projects. They are also of course a means of helping to secure continued supplies of agricultural commodities for consumption in the West.

Aid is in a sense a transfer from taxpayers to private firms and banks, enabling them to get rid of otherwise uncompetitive products or to get their money back. For this reason it has its right-wing critics, who do not deny that aid is useful to parts of the private sector but who are opposed to public subsidies as such. This type of criticism partly accounts for the failure of the Reagan and Thatcher governments to support aid, and is related to their general hostility to all public spending, except spending on the military and the police. They are clearly also unconvinced of the general political usefulness of aid, preferring to rely on military methods. The Thatcher government has abandoned much of the sentimental rhetoric surrounding aid and directed that it should be more closely related to British commercial interests. These governments' hostility to aid extends even to the World Bank, though they are forced to concede that the IMF is indispensable to the recovery of debt and must have its funds replenished to some extent.

Less doctrinaire right-wing governments, including previous US governments, and also the US Treasury Department (see p. 197) have nevertheless perceived the usefulness of the multilateral organisations in the more indirect function of aid: that of securing the adoption of general economic policies compatible with Western interests. These institutions are recognised to be better instruments for achieving policies favourable to the West than bilateral aid institutions because of their veneer of political neutrality. Thus their promotion of import liberalisation, integration into the world market and increased borrowing from Western financial institutions, together with reliance on market forces, and their opposition to the establishment of industries which would compete with those of the major Western powers, are justified on supposedly technical, value-free grounds; they are not promoting capitalism, or the interests of the West, they say, just 'efficiency'. The multilateral 'aid' institutions specialise in active intervention in the economic policy-making of Third World governments, and their aim is to buttress their efforts through the support of bilateral donors, other lenders, including the banks, and private investors. They are the self-appointed guardians of the profits and assets of the banks and the private sector in general.

The World Bank and the IMF are sometimes described as the police of the international financial (capitalist) order. In their efforts to ensure its survival, they devise programmes of 'adjustment' to the shocks which it administers to the economies of Third World countries. These adjustment programmes are supposed to enable countries to avoid financial and economic chaos and are presented as being in the interest of the developing as well as the developed countries. But because of the inherent difficulty of providing for the needs of the poor as well as for those of local elites and foreigners, they end up as austerity programmes whose major emphasis is, as always, on squeezing the poor: through cuts in public expenditure, increases in the prices of basic goods, and wage cuts. The prospect that they will lead to a resumption of growth in the Third World and the ability to service and repay existing debts, let alone reduce the incidence of poverty, is minimal.

Effectiveness

It is of course hard to tell whether these efforts to change the policies of governments have any effect. Recipient governments invariably claim that their policies are unaffected by aid. They would have done it anyway, they say. Government officials and politicians say, as for example Algerian officials did, that they know their own minds and cannot be pushed around. Indian officials say, implicitly, that they are cleverer than Fund, Bank and other aid officials and can out-manoeuvre them. There is much truth in these claims. Government officials elsewhere make similar claims; although not all of them are as tough or as intellectually powerful as Algerian or Indian officials, their knowledge of local conditions is necessarily greater than that of the aid agencies, and they are often more competent as well. Some of them are, in any case, former officials of the Bank or the IMF, or former employees of Wall Street banks. Governments may say they will do one thing and in fact do something else. And aid agency officials do not usually claim to be able to bring about radical shifts in policies, but merely to be attempting to move them some way in the desired direction. Thus neither in Hungary nor in Algeria would they dare to propose the wholesale privatisation of state enterprises; and the degree of import liberalisation pressed upon India, or the opening up to the world market urged on China, is nothing compared to the wholesale dismantling of import restrictions embarked upon in some Latin American countries. Clausen is reported in the Indian newspaper *Business Standard* as saying: 'We would never hold a gun to anyone's head' to make them accept conditions; 'I know that the political ice in some of these countries can be too thin for the right economic policies to be put into gear'.[5] Excessive pressures may even be counterproductive from the point of view of the donors, pushing governments into open displays of defiance; governments do not wish to be seen to be bowing to the pressure of foreigners. Thus an Indian government employee, on leave of absence from the World Bank, claimed that the IMF's support for import liberalisation, far from being useful, was 'an albatross around our necks'.[6] The whole exercise, one is frequently told, is a 'sensitive' one; hence the desire for secrecy.

But it is obvious that, however limited the power of the aid agencies, they do have some effect on the balance of power within countries. For example, identical 'rural development' projects appear in Colombia, Nigeria and the Philippines. The aid agencies' success depends on identifying and supporting local allies who favour the policies of the West. Such people are to be found in every country. Their position within governments can be reinforced by the support of the aid agencies. They can argue that the money will not be forthcoming unless certain policies are adopted. Allies can be created by more or less obviously corrupt methods, ranging from the prospect of jobs in the World Bank to outright pay-offs. The financial wellbeing of local elites may be closely related to aid. The burgeoning urban elite of Bangladesh owes its position almost entirely to aid; the creation of luxurious residential and shopping areas in Dhaka is the one tangible effect of all the aid money that has been poured into Bangladesh since its independence from Pakistan.

In the current world crisis and with acute balance of payments problems in most Third World countries, the position of many governments is abject. The aid agencies congratulate themselves on the current 'greater receptivity' to foreign advice among Third World governments, much as employers in the industrialised countries are able to assert their 'right to manage' because workers fear redundancy. Governments which wish to reach agreement with their bank creditors now have to go to the IMF. Having been forced to take this step, they may be more open to pressures from other quarters and the proffering of 'solutions' to their crisis in the form of import liberalisation, 'reform' of their public sector, and so on.

Moreover, while the policies promoted through aid hurt many sectors of the population, especially the poor, the money is likely to benefit more crucial sources of support to the government and thus enable it to survive. Aid can bolster reactionary regimes. But the threat of its withdrawal is taken seriously by most governments. It can be especially effective as a deterrent to governments whose commitment to a radical redistribution of income in favour of the poor is not whole-hearted, such as the Manley government in Jamaica. But even governments with a clearer commitment to left-wing policies or a more radical tradition are wary of becoming embroiled with the major aid agencies. The fact that the government of Zimbabwe successfully pursued a policy of getting money from the World Bank no doubt played a part in its shift to the right. The

Sandinistas in Nicaragua were determined to have nothing to do with the IMF and divided on their attitude towards the World Bank. A Filipino revolutionary, asked whether, supposing the left won power in the Philippines, they should try to get money out of the World Bank, thought it over and eventually said he would prefer 'not to ride the tiger'.

11. Alternatives

Reforms

Third World governments and their supporters have put forward proposals for reform. These consist mainly of proposals for larger quantities of aid, with different conditionality or no conditionality, and increased control by Third World governments of the World Bank/IMF. There are those who argue that the World Bank/IMF should support a different though still capitalist model of development: more expansionist policies, less hostility to import controls, more support for attempts to build an integrated industrial structure even when the resulting manufacturing capacity would compete with the established industries of the West, a less doctrinaire attitude towards the public sector, and more attention to the needs of the poor, including support for income redistribution and land reform. Others expect the World Bank and the IMF to support socialism. They argue that the representatives of Third World governments should have more control over decisions in the Bank and the IMF. The Grenadian government under Maurice Bishop proposed that there should be an Advisory Commission set up in the Bank to mediate between the Bank's staff and governments, and these proposals were taken up by the Group of 77, as the representatives of Third World governments are called.

The Brandt report proposals are the product of an alliance between members of the ruling elite in Third World capitalist countries and enlightened members of the ruling class in the North. They are progressive mainly in the sense that they favour non-military solutions to the problem of containing rebellion. The two Brandt reports do contain some muted criticisms of the IMF and the World Bank, particularly of their insistence on import liberalisation in Third World countries, which, they say, is a little excessive at the present time, notwithstanding their general belief in the value of free trade. But the main way in which they differ from the ideological positions currently dominant among the major powers is that they favour more expansionist policies: they are international Keynesians. They argue that the crisis in the world economy will not be resolved by competitive deflation. They might extend the argument to say that it will not be resolved by competitive wage cuts either, but that would be expecting too much of a body of people who do not stray very far from the paths of orthodoxy, and whose proposals are basically aimed at the survival and expansion of capitalism on a world scale.

Both sets of proposals are unrealistic. There is no possibility that the World Bank and the IMF will support policies that are not at least compatible with the perceived interests of the ruling class in the major capitalist powers which finance them. Unless the governments in these countries, including the United States, change, the Bank and the IMF cannot change to any significant extent. It is true that the economic and therefore political weight of some Third World countries is greater than it was at the time of Bretton Woods. But even as things are, multilateral agencies are having difficulty in getting money out of the United States and other right-wing governments; the IDA is having its funding cut. But the IDA itself was set up because the United States would not support an organisation controlled by the United Nations; the rich governments would be even less willing to fund institutions whose policies they do not control. If the IMF was not seen to be acting in the interest of the banks and other creditors, its 'seal of approval' would be useless.

It is perhaps conceivable that these institutions could take a more long-term view of the interests of capitalism. They could argue that the cuts currently being demanded in imports and investment in Third World countries may be in the short-term interests of the banks but are not in the long-term interests of capitalism, of exporters to the Third World or even of the banks themselves. They could take up and promote some of the proposals in the Brandt report, which have so far received rather a frosty reception, even from McNamara who commissioned the report. But expansion on an international scale is clearly not considered a feasible option by the authorities in the industrialised powers, any more than Keynesian ideas have provided the solution to the problems of capitalism within these countries. Inflation continues to be the great fear. No solution has been found to the problem of how to grow under capitalism without fuelling inflation, and how to keep profits up in the face of the aspirations of the working class without mass unemployment. The most likely prospect for the developed countries over the next period is semi-stagnation. In that situation any enlightened view of the long-term interests of capitalism is likely to go by the board. For the Third World, the prospect is that the developed countries will do what they can to protect their own industries and shift the burden of the crisis from themselves to the Third World, especially the poor. Whatever spurious rationalisations are used, the World Bank and the IMF will assist them in that task, principally by attempting to impose a combination of austerity and import liberalisation on the governments of the Third World.

Even supposing growth does resume in the developed countries, it would not automatically resolve the problems of the Third World, though it would alleviate them. The boom period of the 1950s and 1960s, in retrospect, seems like halcyon days. Some capitalist Third World countries had impressive rates of economic growth and the manufactured exports of a few of them grew at over 10 per cent a year over a number of years. The industrialisation that took place in some countries confounded some of the predictions of dependency theorists, who had argued that industrialisation in the Third World would not be possible under capitalism. Significant progress in industrialisation was confined to a few countries; it is hard to imagine that the markets of the industrialised countries could absorb the production of a South Korea multiplied worldwide, and moreover in most of the new exporters the export-orientated industrialisation that took place was confined to light manufactured products and was far from independent. It was nevertheless clear that industrial progress of a sort was possible under capitalism. But it did almost nothing for the poor. The advance was heavily dependent on the existence of cheap and extremely repressed labour. In Brazil, although industrialisation was extensive, the distribution of income almost certainly became worse and poverty in the slums of Sao Paolo and in the North–East increased; the Brandt report itself points out that infant mortality rates in Sao Paolo went up during the boom years. In South Korea, the most notably successful of the East Asian 'success stories', social services remain minimal, the industrial accident rate is the highest in the world, and repression is harsh. If this was the case during the boom years, the prospects for capitalist development in the Third World are even worse under the restrictive conditions of the recession, as export markets shrink and the banks cease to lend.

Some people argue, from within a Marxist tradition, that not only does the industrialisation that has occurred in the so-called NICS (Newly Industrialising Countries) contradict the theories of dependency, but that any attempts to build socialism in the Third World without first developing the forces of production under capitalism are futile. This 'stagist' view is held by some Communist parties and is put forward, for example, in Bill Warren's book, *Imperialism: Pioneer of Capitalism*.[1] Those who espouse it ought perhaps logically to welcome the activities of the World Bank and other Western aid agencies, although they may be critical of their bias in favour of the capitalists and multinational companies of the already developed countries. In a recent book Arghiri Emmanuel has pursued rather similar ideas to their logical conclusion. He now applauds the activities of multinational companies on the grounds that they represent the highest and most efficient form of capitalist production.[2] Such views accept implicitly that the extreme hardship associated with capitalism in the Third World, as in nineteenth-century Britain, is unavoidable in the early stages of industrial accumulation.

This perspective is rejected by those who believe that immediate attempts to build socialism in the Third World provide an alternative that is potentially superior both socially and economically to the hardship, inequality and repression that exist in capitalist developing countries, including the most 'successful'. Countries such as Cuba, Nicaragua and Grenada, before it was invaded, provide evidence that this alternative has great potential. Their biggest problem is the threat and the reality of external intervention. The major capitalist powers respond to industrial competition from capitalist Third World countries by protectionist policies and harsh World Bank/IMF conditionalities. They respond to withdrawal from the capitalist world market by still fouler means. Socialism in the Third World apparently cannot be accommodated by governments which effectively rely on the continued exploitation of the Third World. It is ludicrous to suppose that the institutions such governments finance can be expected to promote socialism, or to do anything other than attempt to undermine it. It would require, in any case, a comprehensive replacement of their existing staff.

The 1974–9 Labour government in Britain had a policy of 'aid to the poorest people in the poorest countries'. This did not mean that, like the Swedish and Dutch governments, for example, they provided significant sums of money to poor countries which had left-wing governments, such as Mozambique, Angola or Vietnam. It meant, in theory, that they tried to ensure that the aid which went, as before, to poor countries with right-wing governments actually benefited the poor within those countries. The theory was therefore not much different from that espoused by McNamara when he was President of the World Bank. There is little evidence that the practice was different either. Even supposing there is a genuine commitment on the part of those administering aid to try to ensure that the money reaches the poor, in practice it nearly always ends up in the pockets of the elites or at least of the relatively well-off, when they control the state. Official aid, whether it is from bilateral or multilateral organisations, goes through governments. Governments have many ways of frustrating the supposed purposes of such aid, either deliberately or merely from lack of concern to ensure that it reaches its 'target' and is not lost in corruption, etc., along the way. Such governments derive their power from the support of rural land-owning classes and urban elites; they have no interest in disrupting rural systems of power and patronage or in any diminution of the exploitation of the rural and urban poor. Most aid officials will testify to such difficulties. They know that their task would be easier in a country with a left-wing government with different bases of support and a commitment to redistribute income to the poor; supposing that the officials themselves have such a commitment, which of course many of them do not. The policy is unworkable.

Some people pin their hopes for reform on the so-called 'voluntary agencies', organisations such as Oxfam, War on Want and Christian Aid, which raise money from charitable donations and make grants for projects in Third World countries. These agencies do not usually channel their money through governments; in many countries with repressive right-wing governments they operate in ways which displease these governments. There continue to be problems in finding genuinely useful projects and in ensuring that a project that starts out with local grass-roots support does not become corrupted by its association with the aid-giving process. On occasion the recipients of the money themselves decide to do without it because they do not want to cut themselves off from their base of support. The voluntary agencies certainly do some useful things. But their funds are small compared with government aid. The total amount provided by all such organisations, including North American and other European voluntary agencies, is about the same as British government aid. The money provided by Oxfam, the largest of the British agencies, is not much more than one per cent of British government aid. In any case it is doubtful whether the type of projects undertaken by the voluntary agencies could be replicated on a large scale. They are admired partly because they are small. If very large sums of money were available, the projects they finance would probably depart from the principles which gave them their particular value in the first place. The voluntary organisations are no substitute for government aid.

Doing without aid

The realistic prospect for Third World countries with left-wing governments is that they will get aid only from the Soviet Union, Cuba, East European countries, perhaps one or two relatively progressive West European governments, and some of the voluntary agencies. The amounts are small compared to what right-wing governments get. This is of course a relatively unimportant problem compared to the other external problems they face. Aid is a minor weapon in the destabilisation arsenal, which ranges from credit and trade boycotts, through CIA attempts to administer drugs to Fidel Castro to make his beard fall out, the organisation of the lorry-owners' strike in Chile in 1973, and innumerable assassination attempts, some of them successful, to CIA-backed military coups and outright military intervention by the USA, Britain, France, South Africa, Israel, or the mercenaries of these powers.

To the extent that aid went to the rich, who would anyway be opposed to a left-wing government or go into exile, its loss may moreover not be much felt by the government's supporters, the poor majority. When income is radically redistributed, patterns of consumption of course change and can perhaps be more easily met from local sources. There is much to be gained in any case from a policy of greater self-reliance, a policy of using the resources of the country, especially its land, primarily to meet the basic needs of its people, and of reducing reliance on international trade and dependence on foreign products and skills. The concluding chapter to Rehman Sobhan's book on Bangladesh, *The Crisis of External Dependence*, is entitled 'Self-reliance for Bangladesh'.[3] It puts forward an economic programme for Bangladesh designed to satisfy the needs of the rural poor and to do so in the absence of aid from the West, which Sobhan considers to be an obstacle rather than a contribution to resolving the problems of the Bangladeshi poor.

There is always a tendency, bred of centuries of colonial rule and racial stereotypes, to underestimate the capacity of ordinary people to do what is needed. The prejudices extend to the highly skilled and educated. Moreover, the reasons for making use of offers of aid are frequently dubious. Thus an Algerian architect, with seven years training in France, spent much of her time in the agricultural construction institute where she worked fighting against her director's desire to accept offers of 'technical assistance', from Bulgaria or elsewhere; she said that she and her colleagues were competent to do the work; asked why her director wanted foreign assistance, she said it provided him with the opportunity to travel.[4] A considerable component of World Bank loans is for large fees to foreign consultants; their usefulness is often unclear. A US Embassy official in Brazil, asked in 1967 whether he felt quite certain that he knew what the solution to Brazil's problems were, since after all Brazil was a big country with complex problems, said: 'We have a large staff of experts here and in the AID (US Agency for International Development)'; asked whether this did not assume that there were more skilled people in the US Embassy and the AID than there were in Brazil, he said: 'Not greater in number, but in competences, yes'[5]. Such unwarranted assumptions are peculiarly widespread.

A further potential advantage of the absence of aid and other financial links with the major Western powers is the prospect of greater collective self-reliance among the countries of the Third World. The debt crisis is causing moves in this direction which will be reinforced if the debtors are pushed into using their 'debtors' power' and forming a cartel. Brazil and Mexico have started to arrange barter trade between themselves, which by-passes the

Wall Street banks. Alternative multilateral arrangements for financing trade could be made. Nicaragua's ability to withstand a trade blockade is said to be greater than Cuba's was even 20 years ago because of the ability of Brazil and Mexico to supply many of its needs, including manufactured goods and parts more compatible with its existing equipment than what might be available from the Soviet Union and Eastern Europe; the Cubans had to perform miracles of adaptation to make their US machinery function with Russian spare parts.

Historically the industrialisation of Latin American countries proceeded most rapidly when imports were unavailable from the North, because of wars and depression. Even though the current Chinese leadership has decided that they must import more modern technology from abroad, China has had no aid since it broke off relations with the Soviet Union. It has gone much further than more 'outward-orientated' Third World economies dependent on foreign aid in building up an industrial structure and the capacity to produce, for example, an enormous variety of machine tools whose quality is considered comparable to more expensive European and Soviet models.

India, though it is sometimes thought of as the classic aid-dependent economy, in fact receives relatively little aid in relation to its size, has a low dependence on foreign trade, and has a restrictive attitude towards foreign private investment. Because of its policy of systematically promoting industry, including heavy industry, through government planning and comprehensive import controls, it is currently able to produce virtually the whole range of manufactured goods itself and its basic technological capacity is more highly developed than that of many richer countries, including the Latin American countries, the East Asian export-orientated 'success stories' and some European countries. As one of the senior Indian officials involved in negotiations with the international agencies put it: 'I would welcome a renewed emphasis on self-reliance. Technology choices do get affected by financial offers, which reduce the incentive for the indigenous development of technology'. Another Indian official explained:

> In fertilisers, for example, we have the capacity to
> manufacture them ourselves, but this is stultified by several
> people who were bought up by the World Bank; if they are

> getting continuous assignments from the World Bank, it is too tempting for them . . . when the World Bank goes for international tender, they go for the best technology in the world, which necessarily means imports; we lose the will, energy and desire to produce our own . . . our failure to raise resources internally, which is a political failure, implies that we go to the World Bank; in the process we receive imports which are tied to specific technologies. These are developed in different conditions and are not necessarily adapted to the use of Indian raw materials . . . we lose the will to develop on our own, even though we have the technicians and the machines.[6]

However, in many countries, especially smaller countries, there are definite limits to the improvements in living standards to be derived from a policy of greater self-reliance. There are some products, notably oil, which it is hard for any country attempting to industrialise to do without. It takes time to build up industrial capacity. Imports of raw materials and spare parts are necessary to keep existing industries and infrastructure functioning. Many countries are, under existing policies, increasingly dependent on importing food. It takes time to reverse this process and some countries may never be self-sufficient in food because of a shortage of cultivable land.

More immediately, some left-wing governments are the product not of peaceful electoral transition, but of protracted armed struggles against brutal dictatorships and/or foreign powers. Vietnam, the former Portuguese colonies in Africa, Nicaragua, Algeria, were physically devastated. Most of these countries continue to be the victims of military aggression. This obviously makes it more difficult for them to provide tangible economic benefits to their people. The success of destabilisation relies on the fact that reaction feeds on shortages. In such circumstances, aid from friendly governments can be useful. Soviet aid to Cuba probably ensured that Cuba was not invaded by the USA. The Cubans have enormously helped Angola, Mozambique, Nicaragua and, until the US invasion, Grenada. Excessive reliance on aid from the Soviet Union and Eastern Europe has, however, disadvantages of its own, and the pressures exerted by the USSR are often far from progressive.[7] If these governments had more support from a number of different sources, they would be freer to determine their own policies, and they could move ahead more rapidly.

Socialist solidarity

It is tempting, considering the nature of existing forms of aid from the West, the fact that reforms are unworkable, and the possible advantages of doing without aid, to take an attitude of total rejection of aid. Moreover, the very existence of aid implies the existence of inequality. Under socialism, there can be no question of the rich giving away part of their unfair gains to the poor.

But meanwhile inequality exists, in a particularly acute form on an international level, and will no doubt persist for many years. During this long transitional period, socialists must argue for solidarity with the poor in the Third World in order to mitigate the effects of injustice and exploitation. Direct transfers of financial resources in the form of 'aid' are one way of expressing solidarity. Given that in industrialised countries part of the government's budget is normally allocated to what is called 'aid', there is some point in putting forward proposals for using this money better, especially if, as is the stated intention of most political parties, the volume of aid is increased. In Britain this can take the relatively concrete form of proposals about what might be included in the manifesto of a future Labour government, with some expectation that such a government might be elected on a left-wing platform. But much of what follows would apply to any left-wing government anywhere so long as international inequality persists.

Up to now the record of the British Labour Party on internationalism has been unimpressive. Labour governments have deviated little from preceding Tory governments on colonial questions, on Ireland, or on any other international issue. The attention devoted to international questions including aid at annual party conferences has been minimal. On aid, the party has tended to adopt an uncritical attitude towards the Brandt report and a peculiarly myopic and naive attitude on, for example, the World Bank (see p. 110). A fringe group of the Labour Party, the Labour Aid and Development Committee, has taken similarly ill-informed positions, proposing, for example, that aid channelled through the European Development Fund should be diverted to more 'efficient' institutions such as the IDA. The slogan 'aid to the poorest people in the poorest countries' is still party policy, insofar as the Labour Party has a policy on aid.

However, *Labour's Programme 1982*, the document on which the Labour Party's manifesto for the 1983 elections was based, contains some more encouraging statements. For example, it proposes that there should be 'a generous aid programme to progressive governments in Nicaragua and Grenada', economic aid for Vietnam and support for Tanzania, Zimbabwe, Mozambique and Angola. It says that: 'Labour favours a consistent and far-reaching socialist policy towards Latin America which will put pressure on dictatorial regimes, actively support progressive governments, and will give help and comfort to opposition democratic and socialist movements fighting for liberty and self-determination.' And: 'Central America and the Caribbean . . . has become a key area for social change, where bold and radical socialist experiments are being attempted and where long-standing regimes of exploitation and brutality are being challenged by newly emerging popular movements'.[8]

Although the Labour Party document reasserts 'the principle that aid . . . should go first and foremost to the *poorest people in the poorest countries*' (original emphasis), it adds that: 'Preference will be given to governments which are carrying out policies which benefit the poorest (such as land reform), have a good human rights record and respect trade union rights'. Unfortunately, and still somewhat unrealistically, it continues: 'In the case of countries which do not meet these criteria, Labour will attempt to help the poor by financing particular projects of interest to poor people or', says the document, in cautious and ambivalent language, 'by supporting independent organisations engaged in lifting the burden of poverty and oppression'.[9] In the section on Latin America and the Caribbean, it provides a more promising interpretation of the Labour Party's commitment to 'aid to the poorest people' by proposing that:

> Labour will where necessary rechannel our development assistance, following on from our work in Chile . . . to relief work within countries with repressive regimes. We would provide financial support for community projects, helping to provide employment for poor people. Such projects while coming clearly within our policy of 'aid to the poorest'

> would also, by helping the victims of repression,
> demonstrate clearly where our sympathies lie . . . our
> emphasis on rural development cannot be used to enable big
> landowners to benefit from British aid.[10]

The Labour Party ought to abandon altogether the slogan 'aid to the poorest people in the poorest countries' and replace it with a much clearer commitment to solidarity with socialist movements and governments in the Third World. If the Labour Party is committed to the construction of socialism in Britain, it should support attempts to build it elsewhere. Unless it believes that there is no alternative to going through the harsh process of the early stages of capitalist accumulation in the countries of the Third World, there is no good reason for it to support that process. Hard though it may be to establish a precise balance of the advantages and disadvantages of aid to right-wing governments from the point of view of the poor, there is no doubt that such advantages as may 'trickle down' to the poor in those countries are very slight, if any, and that they may well be outweighed by the disadvantages of bolstering oppressive governments and the luxury consumption of elites. Since the amounts that are likely to be spent on aid are limited, they might as well be concentrated in countries where aid is more likely to be used for the benefit of the underprivileged. Such a concentration, in any case, would do something to counteract the prevailing bias in the aid programmes of Western governments.

The accusation is sometimes rather strangely made that this would be another form of 'neo-colonialism'. The alternative would presumably be to allocate the money according to some automatic formula based on population and perhaps per capita income. But since there is no chance that all governments, intent on using aid to support their interests in the Third World, would agree to do the same, the gesture would be futile. The British aid programme, currently some $1.75 billion, is not particularly large. Spread among more than 100 countries its effect would be small. It certainly would do little to reduce the external pressures on left-wing governments in the Third World, or to counteract the inducement to governments to adopt right-wing policies so as to escape from the pressures of destabilisation and gain access to Western aid. But $1.75 billion, or the bulk of it, concentrated in a dozen or so countries, could make a substantial difference to their situation.

It would clearly be difficult, and undesirable, for a Labour government to cut aid immediately to all of the rest of the Third World. But there are governments, such as the Pinochet government in Chile and many others, to which aid could and should be stopped immediately. In such cases it would be possible to make contact with opposition groups and to find out their view on the desirability of continuing aid. They are likely to be in favour of cutting it. An interesting case was the visit by a British miners' delegation to their union counterparts in Bolivia. The miners wanted the British government to cancel a planned aid project in the Bolivian mines, on the grounds that it would merely strengthen the Bolivian military dictatorship. The NUM delegation went back and persuaded Judith Hart, then Minister for Overseas Development in the Labour government, to drop the project. The Sandinistas in Nicaragua were of course bitterly opposed to the IMF's decision to make a loan to the Somoza dictatorship, in a situation in which the normal conditionality could not operate, shortly before Somoza was overthrown; as they correctly foresaw, the money went straight into a Swiss bank account, from which it could not be retrieved when the Sandinistas took power; it was partly because of this that the Sandinistas refused to enter into negotiations with the IMF. There are many other governments, especially those in which the opposition is strong and well organised, which should receive no money from a Labour government; the Labour Party's 1982 document said that it would review the previous Labour government's decisions to lend money to Paraguay and Brazil.[11]

There are other countries where decisions about aid are more difficult. Their governments may not be outstandingly repressive; the opposition may be weak and divided; they may be heavily dependent on aid, for example for importing food. The sudden withdrawal of aid is unlikely to strengthen popular opposition and may merely mean that the rich appropriate an even larger share of what is available and the poor therefore suffer even greater hardship. There is certainly an argument for not cutting aid that is already committed to such governments, particularly commodity aid. But the argument can be taken too far. There are very few governments sufficiently dependent on British aid for a unilateral withdrawal to make much difference. In Bangladesh, for example, the influence of the British is insignificant compared to that of the World Bank and the United States. A mass withdrawal of Western aid from Bangladesh, on the grounds of human rights violations for example, is extremely unlikely. But even a total cut would not necessarily hurt the poorest people, even in the short term. As Rehman Sobhan and others have made clear, there were many in the post-liberation government of Bangladesh who argued against falling into the trap of dependence on Western aid. They believe that the rural people of Bangladesh would have been better off, and still could be better off, if Bangladesh had held out against the inducements offered by aid from the World Bank and the major Western powers.

In addition to supporting left-wing governments, a Labour government could also use aid to support opposition to right-wing governments. The amounts of money involved are likely to be less. But the British Labour Party already has contacts with or supports a number of opposition parties, liberation movements, and trade unions in the Third World. At least 17 such organisations are referred to in *Labour's Programme 1982*, and support is promised. They include, for example, liberation movements in Southern Africa and Central America, the Sandinistas, the New Jewel Movement, the Eritrean People's Liberation Front, and the labour movement in Chile. Thus the basis exists in Labour's published policy for supporting, financially where this is possible, such movements and organisations in the Third World. The document also proposes that aid could be *'rechannelled'* (emphasis in original) rather than simply cut off from 'regimes with un-acceptable human rights records' and that one use for it would be study grants for refugees and funding the refugee programme in general.[12]

The means of supporting opposition groups within countries with right-wing governments is not always clear. At times the distinction between supporting 'the poorest people' in such countries and supporting the opposition seems blurred. Supporting 'the poorest people' in repressive societies can be a subversive activity in itself, which is one reason why it usually fails in its ostensible purposes. Supporting 'community projects, helping to provide employment for poor people', as the Labour document proposes, may be no more realistic as a policy. It ought therefore to be made clear that it means channelling money directly to organisations which are clearly and completely independent of governments, such as left-wing political parties, liberation movements, and independent trade unions. The Labour Party could follow the example of, or support, the London-based El Salvador Solidarity Committee and finance or help to finance projects in the liberated zones in El Salvador. And it could give much more financial support to labour movement delegations to observe conditions under right-wing regimes, to help the victims of repression, and to provide solidarity with repressed trade unions and other resistance movements. Such delegations can sometimes deter governments from some of the more vicious forms of repression and denial of human rights, and they can also help to build support within Britain for the struggles of people elsewhere. British trade unionists are becoming increasingly aware that their interests are linked with those of their fellow-workers in the Third World. They often face the same multinational employers, and have an immediate interest in preventing the multinationals from playing them off against each other, in addition to the more general concerns of international working-class solidarity.

But the biggest call on British aid funds should be independent left-wing governments. It is often said that it would be difficult to decide which governments should be supported. But clearly, in the absence of some automatic formula, the allocation of aid involves political choices. Such choices are currently made by all the governments which provide aid, including the Soviet Union, Cuba, the United States, the EEC and Britain. A Labour government cannot eschew political choices. It should merely make different ones. Difficult though it may be to decide whether Tanzania should get more than Zimbabwe or as much as Vietnam, the choice is no more difficult than current choices, except in the sense that it is less determined by routine and colonial tradition. Whatever criticisms may be made of governments in the Third World that profess adherence to socialist ideas, there is little doubt that most of them are attempting to provide benefits primarily to the people who suffered most under previous right-wing regimes. Their chances of success will be greater, and the scope for criticism less, if they have the support of a larger number of friendly governments, such as European governments, who can supply them with most of the things which they find it essential to import, and support them politically. They in turn can provide an example to the rest of the world and demonstrate that, freed from some of the weight of external hostility, socialism can flourish and give hope in a frightening world.

It is sometimes said that there are not enough governments worthy of support to absorb all the available British aid. But the number is likely to increase. In addition, part of the problem of 'absorption' is caused by the form that aid has traditionally taken. The identification of suitable projects takes time and their direct requirement for imports may not be great. On the other hand, as is frequently pointed out even by orthodox critics of current aid practice, the needs for current imports, including spare parts for aid-financed equipment, are often unmet. Aid should be provided in the form of foreign exchange, untied to procurement from any particular source, and unencumbered with conditions. Such aid can be immediately disbursed. It can then be used as the recipient government thinks best. The government may make mistakes. But the history of aid and of so-called 'experts', however well-meaning and even socialist they may be, is littered with costly mistakes. These mistakes often spring from an ignorance of elementary aspects of local reality. The capacity of ordinary people to make their own decisions, on the other hand, is continually underestimated. If there is really a need for particular foreign skills, the money provided under aid can be used to hire them. Similarly the choice of technology should not be determined by the source of the funds. One of the ultimate goals of socialism is, after all, to enable people to control their own lives.

It is sometimes said, conversely, that British aid is too small to make much difference. That is partly true. There is scope for increasing the effect of changed policies by urging changes on other European governments. This would also make it harder for the us government to retaliate; for example, when the Mitterrand government in its early days issued a joint declaration with Mexico in support of the opposition forces in El Salvador, the us government threatened to destabilise the French dependencies of Guadeloupe and Martinique. There is another way of increasing the potential size of financial support for left-wing governments in the Third World: by British withdrawal from the World Bank. British opposition to World Bank policies and pressure for changes from within could possibly have some effect on the policies of the Bank, but not much. A British Labour government might wish to use the threat of withdrawal from the Bank, perhaps in conjunction with other governments, as a means of increasing pressure on the Bank to reform itself. It could support the Grenadian initiative to create an Advisory Council to provide an element of outside control, as was originally proposed in Article V, Section 6 of the World Bank Articles of Agreement. It could support the Nicaraguan contention that it is unlawful for the Bank to discriminate against governments on political grounds. It could press for changes in membership and voting power. It could argue for decentralisation of the Bank's operations outside Washington, in the hope that this would loosen the grip of reactionary staff members based in Washington. It could argue that the way leverage is used should be a matter of explicit policy formulation by executive bodies rather than being left to the ingrained prejudices of the Bank's senior management, and that the Bank's policies and documents should be made public. It could oppose loans to oppressive regimes on human rights grounds, as the Carter administration in fact did. It could also argue for lending to left-wing governments, although this would have its dangers unless the nature of the Bank's attempted interventions in the balance of power were changed as well.

But unless there are major changes in the United States itself, and probably also in the nature of ownership and control of the major Wall Street and other private institutions through which the Bank raises the bulk of its capital, the effect of any British votes and pressures, even if they were combined with those of other European governments, would be slight. The advantages to be derived from withdrawal are undoubtedly greater than the advantages to be derived from threatening to withdraw. Withdrawal would make a small dent in the post-war hegemony of the World Bank in Western aid policies. It would somewhat weaken the Bank, both by depriving it of finance and by depriving it of some of the political legitimacy which enables it to maintain the pretence of impartiality. And a similar policy could be adopted towards the IMF.

When the Labour Party takes office, however radical the programme on which it has been elected, it invariably makes concessions and compromises in carrying it out, or failing to carry it out. That was of course the experience of the Mitterrand government in France which not only back-tracked in its support for opposition forces in Central America, but also rapidly resumed its cosy relationship with the governments of former French colonies in Africa when the latter threatened to 'go to the United States' if they had any difficulty in getting aid from the French. A future Labour government would be subjected to similar pressures and there is no evidence that it would be more effective in resisting them. Apart from the apparent political difficulties of a clear commitment to support socialism in the Third World, which are evident even during periods of opposition, there would be many economic pressures. Aid, as has been said, is used above all to subsidise exports and, in addition, to secure supplies of raw materials and primary commodities. No doubt a Labour government would find it difficult to sacrifice the economic advantages to be derived from aid as well as from the exploitative relationships with the Third World which aid is used to support. Some metropolitan-based companies are heavily dependent on Third World markets, and some secure their supplies from countries whose governments would be opposed to a socialist aid policy. Some adjustments might not be too difficult to make; some industries could switch to different markets and sources of supply and new markets could be developed in socialist countries, possibly for different products. But there would be great pressure to maintain established economic relationships. This means that a change in aid policies can clearly not be seen in isolation from other aspects of a socialist programme for Britain, such as the social ownership of the means of production, and its reorganisation in the interest of the genuine needs of ordinary people, rather than of profits for capitalists.

The supporters of Western aid are right about one thing: the interests of those who provide it and those who receive it are closely linked. The problem is that they are talking about the ruling class. It is equally true to say that the interests of the underprivileged majority throughout the world are closely linked. One of the great contributions made by the peoples of the Third World is that they have made revolutions. They have not yet, it is true, created perfect and complete models of socialism. Armchair critics, including many who call themselves Marxists, affected no doubt by the sour cynicism of late capitalism, love to run them down. They issue blue-prints of what revolutionaries elsewhere ought to do. They write books describing the failings of the Cuban revolution. They tell the Sandinistas that the wage demands of the working class must be met under all circumstances. They expect the instant achievement of revolutionary socialist democracy. Many of their criticisms are valid. But reality is hard; socialism cannot be instantly achieved, worldwide. Great progress *has* been made in some countries of the Third World. Education and health services have been made widely available, illiteracy has been virtually conquered, unemployment has been greatly reduced, popular democratic institutions have begun to be built, and the enthusiastic support of the people has been won and retained. We should greet this progress with enthusiasm, learn from it, and support it.

Appendix

Working at the World Bank
Catharine Watson

I started work at the World Bank the day after I turned 23. I mention that because as a young woman I had a particular experience at the Bank: I was able to be critical, nosey and outspoken precisely because I wasn't taken completely seriously, or seen as a real threat.

I went to work at the Bank because I was concerned about the impact of development on the environment and wanted to work with the ecologist, Dr Robert Goodland. Goodland, one of three environmentalists employed by the Bank's Office of Environmental Affairs, was the author of *From Green Hell to Red Desert*, a study of the damage done to the Brazilian Amazon and its inhabitants by the building of the Transamazon Highway. The study had said the Transamazon would be an economic disaster – and the study was right. No ecologist had dared challenge economics and geo-politics like that before.

I was hired to write environmental guidelines for agricultural projects. This was Goodland's idea. They were to be recommendations on how to prevent the consequences of conventional agricultural projects – loss of top soil, the destruction of forests, the rise in pesticide-resistant insects and others. We hoped that these guidelines would eventually become official Bank policy and that the Bank agriculturalists would accept them. But in the end, they became neither official nor accepted, although they did set off a modest amount of introspection among the agriculturalists and the Bank did give us permission to publish them outside the Bank with a commercial publisher.[1]

I also helped Goodland to scan agricultural projects for environmental problems and to prepare and present our case if we found problems. This sounds more systematic than it was. We had to look at projects in all parts of the Third World, and there were far too many projects to review them in any depth – about 100 agricultural projects a year were prepared in the early 1980s – and Goodland had to review hydroelectric projects for environmental impact as well. Furthermore, the documents often gave no hint of potential problems so that unless we knew the area personally (and knew, for example, that there was a threatened watershed), we had to give the project the go-ahead. If we took the time to research one project, a dozen would slip by.

Sometimes environmental problems would surface late in the project when the documents became more informative, as in the El Retorno case (see p.191). But by then we were not meant to suggest major changes as the Bank would already have invested hundreds of thousands of dollars and many staff hours in preparing the project.

Project staff treated us like scourges. As far as they were concerned, we were trouble. We could hold up projects and we could impose new costs on projects, insisting, for example, on reforestation – although we did both extremely rarely. Often they successfully blinded us with detail. They knew that they knew the project area and that usually we did not. For example, if we queried the wisdom of clearing steep slopes for cultivation and leaving erosion control up to a powerless and under-funded agricultural agency, the project staff would look pained and say, 'That's only in the south-west corner of the Rio Negros district and we were particularly impressed by the commitment of the agricultural extension workers there . . .' After a point we could argue no further.

Project staff would also tell us, sometimes patiently, sometimes impatiently, that worrying about the environment was a luxury the Third World could not afford. Then we would have to explain to them that we were talking about rivers flooding, about firewood running out, and about soil being depleted – factors that would determine the peoples' survival *and* the viability of projects – and not about preserving rare toads and snakes (although of course we were also concerned about the preservation of habitats and species).

Some members of Bank staff were sympathetic to our work and some did approach us with environmental problems they had come across in their projects. But by and large, we were viewed by project and technical staff as an unessential office which at best put useless icing on the cake and at worst could slow or halt projects. In response to this attitude and to the unrealistic work load, we developed a strategy: we took on only cases which we knew we could win, or at least make some impression on, and these tended to be projects in Latin America's tropical forests.

Several months after I started work at the Bank, we began to look at the impact of Bank projects on tribal peoples. The trigger for this new direction was a massive development scheme in the north-west of Brazil, in the states of Mato Grosso and Rondonia, which the Bank was to fund in part and which was to affect several Indian groups. We started watching projects with the aim of preventing them from impingeing on the land and resources of tribal groups and began putting together guidelines for projects to follow if tribal people were involved. These guidelines had more success than our agricultural ones, partly because there were no experts in the Bank on tribal peoples (the agriculturalists who resisted our guidelines on agriculture felt that we were usurping their role) and because the Bank was vulnerable to arguments that it was violating the human rights of tribal peoples. In 1981 the tribal peoples guidelines became part of official Bank protocol, with arguable effectiveness.

As a workplace, the Bank was like any large company in that it was run by white middle-aged men with few women or people from the Third World in senior positions. Some people were good at their jobs, others did little and still others were not coping well due to difficulties like drink. Rumour had it that the Bank never fired its staff; instead it sent them to work in the Personnel Department or to an overseas posting. Most Bank staff are in Washington and no one, apparently, wanted to be posted overseas. It was spoken of as a term of exile in an uncomfortable place. The Bank's East Africa office in Nairobi was said to be the worst place to be sent. The crime rate was terrible and you had to live in a compound wired up with burglar alarms to your neighbours.

Going on missions to prepare and supervise projects was also looked upon by most as a trial. After a certain number of nights of deprivation away from their wives in Washington, male Bank staff members were entitled to take their wives with them on a mission. (I don't know if this applied to female Bank staff as well.) I found this general attitude to going overseas odd as I was constantly *trying* to get there.

The Bank was obviously different from most companies in that the staff came from over 100 countries. In practice, however, it did not feel particularly international, as the majority of staff are British and American. It was possible to go to many meetings without sitting at the same table as someone from the Third World. What Third World staff members there were tended to come from the affluent class of their countries and to have Masters degrees or PhDs from the top North American or European universities. They tended to be as sophisticated as their Northern counterparts, if not more so, and arguably were as removed as the Northerners from the population at whom the Bank's projects are aimed. Certainly they did not make the First World staff more delicate in the way in which they spoke about the Third World.

It is not too strong to say that I loved working at the World Bank. First, there was the physical comfort of it all. There was sheer pleasure in north-west Washington – the cafes, the shops, the wide streets and the bookstores. The Bank offered gleaming attractions too – delicious and heavily subsidised food in the canteens and restaurants, the white stone courtyard where we sat in the spring and summer, the cosmopolitan bookstore in the main foyer, the air conditioning and the tax-free international civil servants' salary which enabled me to buy silk shirts and linen skirts.

Second, the work was gripping. I learnt about tropical agriculture and the procedures of aid. At that time information moved quite freely around the Bank. There was an atmosphere of confidence, privilege and inviolability, and it was possible to dig through files on old projects and to obtain project evaluations and rarely did anyone ask to see an identity card though security on information has become much tighter since.

Work was also exciting because of the difficulties we faced in getting our ideas accepted and because, I felt, of the absolute correctness of what we were saying. There was almost daily drama – the Brazil project was going through, the Ecuador project was coming up and I'd tear off to the Library of Congress to find out which Indians lived in the west of Ecuador and what the soils were like.

The third fascination of the Bank for me was the people who worked there. Roughly speaking, there were four sorts of Bank types, excluding the secretaries who were mostly beautiful young Latin American or Philippine women who wore expensive clothes, or redoubtable British women who had been with the Bank for years, who treated their bosses as though they were ever so slightly daft, and who no doubt would have had a shot at being bosses themselves had they been born 20 years later.

The four categories were: the ex-colonials; the First and Third Worlders in their early thirties with post graduate degrees in economics or international relations; the career men who had entered the Bank in their youth, much as other men of their generation went into the US State Department or the British civil service; and the most rarefied group, the men who had become interested in development in the 1950s and 1960s, long before it was fashionable, and had spent their lives rotating through influential jobs in universities, development agencies and think tanks. I didn't have much contact with this group. They were the strategists and the high-flyers of whom Montague Yudelman, Director of Agriculture and Rural Development from 1973 to 1984, is a good example.

The career men at the Bank were the ones who impressed me the least. They usually had little academic knowledge of development, having entered the Bank before development became a competitive field. They tended to base their work on personalities – in the Bank and in their Third World 'patch'. They'd been around for so long that they were expert at using the Bank's rules of the game, knew all the higher-ups' weaknesses and foibles and, with respect to their Third World responsibilities, could remember the Minister of Transport when he was a junior civil servant in the Ministry of Health. They could dazzle you and themselves with the minutiae and yet have no overview, and they often resisted innovations and new directives on Bank strategy. I'm thinking of one person in particular, but there were many like him.

The young Bank staff members recently out of graduate school were good on theory; but only conservative theory. They had usually swallowed whole what they had been taught, which tended to be orthodox economics. Some had had a spell with the Peace Corps, but most had no experience of the Third World. Nowadays it is extremely difficult to get a job with the World Bank – there were 5,000 applicants for the 25 spaces in the 'Young Professionals' programme this year – so most of these types were enjoying their position and cosseting their careers. They were supremely irritating. They weren't, or so it seemed to me, particularly curious about the Bank or their work. For example, it always seemed odd to me that more people at the Bank, but especially among this group of staff, hadn't read Teresa Hayter's first book on the Bank, *Aid as Imperialism*, particularly as only half a dozen books have been written about the Bank. I remember one argument I had with a prime example of this type of Bank employee about the project his office was preparing. I said that if I were them, I would bend over backwards to make sure that the new projects addressed the problems of land tenure, given the mess the earlier projects had made of it. As it turned out, he apparently had no idea of what projects his office had funded in the 1970s and 1960s and hadn't even glanced at the project evaluations of those projects. How could he be so sure of the soundness of the projects he was preparing now?

I had another argument with another young professional about the first Caqueta project in Colombia (see page 185). He insisted that the project had been a success since the rate of return had been calculated at 13 per cent. I insisted that it hadn't because the roads had washed out, the rivers were no longer navigable, and only the rich farmers had benefited. We reached an impasse; and later when we met at meetings, we pretended that we didn't know each other. If it was hard to respect this breed of young professionals, it was much easier to respect the ex-colonials. Undoubtedly they were the best of the lot. They were usually British or Australian and they were concentrated in technical posts – as agricultural advisers, engineers, water experts and so on. I knew the agriculturalists best. Most had worked in the Third World in the 1950s and 1960s for colonial governments, often being in charge of the agricultural production or forest resources of vast areas. Many had gone on to work for national governments after independence and others had worked for big companies like Tate & Lyle. They all knew at least one Third World country in great depth, had usually learnt the local language and quite a number of them had married local women. Most of the agriculturalists had, it seemed to me, brilliant knowledge of tropical agriculture, although not usually of peasant agriculture. A lot of them felt that the quality of the Bank agricultural projects was much poorer than the work they themselves had done in the 1950s and 1960s with governments.

On the negative side, these agriculturalists were largely unquestioning when it came to the Bank's agricultural strategy. They seemed completely unaware, and this always amazed me, that there was an entire body of theory, research and practice showing that Third World countries need to, and can, regain their self-sufficiency in food production. I doubt that more than a handful of the agriculturalists had read *Food First* or even knew of its existence. With respect to new ideas about the Third World and development, they were out of touch. One of the reasons for this, besides plain human laziness and inertia, was that the ex-colonials felt that theirs had been the authentic experience in the Third World, and, in comparison with most Bank staff, they *had* had a relatively reciprocal and honest experience in the Third World. However, this attitude bred smugness and limited their curiosity about what had happened to the Third World since they had left.

I do not mean these descriptions to dismiss out of hand the staff of the Bank – there were decent and thoughtful people there – nor do I want to reduce the errors of the Bank to the level of individuals. It is difficult to know who would be knowledgeable and wise enough to do a good job of administering billions of dollars of aid to the Third World each year. Nevertheless, it is alarming the extent to which the current debate on aid and development passes by the majority of Bank staff members and the isolation and ignorance in which most Bank employees carry out their jobs.

I am beginning to forget why I left the Bank, particularly because I liked the work so much, but there was something I wanted to do in England. I was also beginning to be weighed down by the feeling that Goodland and I and the other environmentalists constituted a token office within the Bank. When our proposals were accepted it was because they enhanced the progressive image of the Bank and cost the Bank little. When our proposals threatened the future of a project, or had major implications for Bank practice, they and we were dismissed as unrealistic and impractical. Reform was possible, but only insofar as it left the Bank's basis unchanged.

This was why our environmental guidelines for agriculture never won support. In them, for example, we maintained that using the best land for export crops had environmental implications. The population is forced to open up marginal areas in order to produce food for itself: forests are destroyed, the top soil is lost, rivers flood and then run dry, and eventually the agricultural potential of the country decreases. We recommended that more emphasis be put on domestic food production, including the use of some of the prime land for food production. This was far too fundamental. The Bank could not approve this guideline, no matter how environmentally sound and reasoned it was, as the Bank firmly maintains that growth must be export-led and that it is money earned from exports and not local food production that makes food available.

Our tribal peoples guidelines, on the other hand, found approval precisely because they challenged no basic Bank tenet and the Bank knew that it was an exercise in humanity it could afford: there are not many tribal peoples left in the world. Had we put forth a guideline confirming the rights of peasants to their land, the Bank would have reacted differently. The Bank reasons rightly that in a project worth several hundred million dollars, an allocation of one million dollars for the needs of tribal people is a pittance, particularly if the Bank gains favourable publicity by it. Furthermore, it has yet to be seen whether a project would be halted because of the presence of tribal people.

A big powerful organisation can afford to have, indeed benefits from having, critics on its payroll. Our office was like the Bank's office on women and the office which promoted appropriate technology – good for the image but mouse-sized in impact. Because of the work of our office, the Bank won a prize for its contribution to the environment; it can advise other development banks on their environmental policies; and it can, and does, make the claim that all Bank projects are carefully reviewed for environmental problems and that steps are taken to correct any that are found – a claim that simply is not true.

I left the Bank in 1980 with two main stories to tell – the account of how Bank projects in Latin America held back land reform and land distribution, and the story of the environmental devastation wrought by the Bank's funding of settlement projects in the tropical forests. Then, two years after I left the Bank, I was given the documents on Nicaragua. All this was too important to leave unwritten. My main hope is that these chapters generate more criticism of the Bank and damage its credibility.

Notes and References

Preface

1. Edward S. Mason and Robert E. Asher, *The World Bank since Bretton Woods*, The Brookings Institution, Washington DC, 1973 (which is the semi-official history of the Bank), and Robert Ayres, *Banking on the Poor: the World Bank and World Poverty*, Cambridge Mass.: MIT Press 1983 (a favourable account of the Bank from a liberal point of view).

Introduction

1. *Financial Times*, 'The international debt crisis: the pressure mounts for a new initiative', 10 May 1984.
2. *North-South: A Programme for Survival, The Report of the Independent Commission on International Development Issues under the Chairmanship of Willy Brandt*, Pan Books, 1980.

PART I – Capital flows to the Third World

1. Definitions

1. *Financial Times*, 'Indonesian cuts may hit British contractors', 13 May 1983.
2. *Financial Times*, 'UK faces challenge over Kenyan projects', 24 March 1982.
3. *Financial Times* leader, 'The value of British aid', 21 September 1982. See also *Real Aid: A Strategy for Britain*, distributed by the Overseas Development Institute, Oxfam, Christian Aid and the World Development Movement, London 1982.
4. OECD, *Development Co-operation, Efforts and Policies of the Members of the Development Assistance Committee, 1982 Review*, November 1982, p. 57.
5. See T. Hayter, *The Creation of World Poverty*, London: Pluto Press 1981, pp. 77–79, and Richard J. Barnet and Ronald E. Muller,

Global Reach: the Power of the Multinational Corporation, New York: Simon and Schuster, 1974.
6. OECD, *op. cit.,* p. 56.
7. Deepak Lal, 'Time to put the Third World debt threat into perspective', *The Times*, 6 May 1983.
8. OECD, *op. cit.,* pp. 87–88.
9. OECD, *op. cit.*, Table 1.15, p. 192.
10. OECD, *op. cit.,* Table II.B.1, p. 222.
11. Rehman Sobhan, *The Crisis of External Dependence: The Political Economy of Foreign Aid to Bangladesh*, The University Press Ltd, Dakha, 1982.
12. OECD, *op. cit.*, Table VII-3, p. 69.
13. Calculated from OECD *Geographical Distribution of Financial Flows to Developing Countries,* OECD 1981.
14. *Statistical Yearbook 1979/80*, United Nations, pp. 401–3.
15. OECD *Geographical Distribution op. cit.*

2. Private banks

1. OECD, *Development Co-operation, Efforts and Policies of the Members of the Development Assistance Committee, 1982 Review,* Table V-5, p. 55.
2. *Wall Street Journal*, 2 March 1981.
3. OECD, *ibid.* Table II. D.8, p. 239.
4. *World Bank Annual Reports 1982 & 1983*, Statistical Annex Tables 4, and *Financial Times*, 'Zambia and IMF agree standby credit', 9 March 1983.
5. *World Bank Reports, op. cit.*
6. *Financial Times*, 27 April 1982.
7. Interview with IMF official by Teresa Hayter, September 1983.
8. The Brandt Commission, *North-South: A Programme for Survival,* Pan Books, 1980 and *Common Crisis*, Pan Books, 1983.
9. International Bank Credit Analysis Report, quoted in *Financial Times*, 31 May 1983.
10. For a convincing fictional account of a banking crash, written in gaol by a former banker, ending with the hero living off the land in California deprived of his Martinis, see Paul E. Erdman, *The Crash of 79*, Sphere Books, 1977.
11. *Financial Times*, 29 May 1984.
12. *Ibid.*
13. 'The Micawber approach to debt', *Financial Times*, 10 February 1983.
14. The Brandt Commission, *Common Crisis*, Pan Books 1983, p. 47.
15. Jonathan Agnew, Managing Director of Morgan Stanley, reviewing

Anthony Sampson, *The Money Lenders – Bankers in a Dangerous World*, in the *Observer*, September 1981.

16. Carlos Langoni, 'The way out of the country debt crisis', *Euromoney*, Fall 1983. See also, on Brazil, Celso Furtado, *No to Recession and Unemployment*, Third World Foundation 1983, with an introduction by Teresa Hayter.

17. For example, rather obliquely, in Deepak Lal, 'Time to put the Third World debt threat into perspective', *The Times*, 6 May 1983.

18. 'Poor get poorer in Brazil as IMF discusses terms', *Financial Times*, 15 November 1983.

19. 'The IMF toughens its brief', *Financial Times*, 11 June 1982.

20. *Financial Times*, 9 March 1983.

21. 'The Micawber approach to debt', *op. cit.*

22. 'Why the bankers put the boot into Brazil', the *Guardian*, 15 July 1983.

23. *Financial Times*, 11 August 1983.

24. *Financial Times*, 15 August 1983 and 16 December 1983.

25. World Bank estimate, quoted in the *Financial Times*, 27 January 1984.

26. *Panorama*, 20 June 1983. See also report in the *Guardian*, 21 June 1983.

27. *Financial Times*, 10 August 1983.

3. The International Monetary Fund

1. *IMF Annual Report 1981*, Washington DC.

2. But see *The Poverty Brokers: the IMF and Latin America*, London: Latin America Bureau 1983, for a clear brief description.

3. *IMF Annual Report 1981*.

4. The Brandt Commission, *Common Crisis*, Pan Books 1983, p. 60.

5. See Teresa Hayter, *Aid as Imperialism*, Penguin 1971, p. 38 and footnote, for sources.

6. T.M. Reichmann and R. Stillson, 'Experience with programs of balance of payments adjustment: stand-by arrangements in the higher credit tranches', *IMF Staff Papers*, 25(2), June 1978; and T.M. Reichmann, 'The Fund's conditional assistance and the problems of adjustment', *Finance and Development*, 15(4), December 1978, quoted in Tony Killick, 'IMF Stabilisation Programmes', London: Overseas Development Institute Working Paper No. 6 1981. See also Tony Killick, Ed., *The Quest for Economic Stabilisation – The IMF and the Third World*, Heinemann 1984, pp. 229 ff.

7. For example in a document commenting on the Brandt report, referred to in Killick, 1984, *op. cit.*, p. 185.

8. Killick, 1984, *op. cit.*, p. 217.

9. Margaret de Vries, *The International Monetary Fund, 1966–1971*, Washington: IMF 1976, p. 363, quoted in Killick, *op. cit.*, p. 217.

10. Killick, 1984, *op. cit.*, pp. 193–6.

11. Table 6.1, p. 188.

12. *Financial Times*, 'Man in the News: Brazil's inflation expert', 21 May 1983.

13. See also *The Poverty Brokers, op. cit.*, pp. 9–10.

14. See Teresa Hayter, *Aid as Imperialism, op. cit.*, especially for references to some of the massive Latin American literature on the subject.

15. David Tonge, 'An IMF success story – but the strains show', *Financial Times*, 11 August 1983.

16. *Ibid.*

17. Mohsin S. Khan and Malcolm D. Knight, 'Stabilisation in developing countries: a formal framework', *IMF Staff Papers*, Vol. 28(1), March 1981, quoted in Killick, 1984, *op. cit.*, p. 218.

18. Killick, 1984, *op. cit.*, pp. 46–7.

19. Carlos Langoni, 'The way out of the country debt crisis', *Euromoney*, Fall 1983, p. 24.

20. Killick, 1984, *op. cit.*, p. 219.

21. See Jim Morrell, 'A billion dollars for South Africa', *International Policy Report*, Center for International Policy, Washington CDC, April 1983.

22. *The Poverty Brokers, op. cit.*, pp. 44–47.

23. Norman Girvan, Richard Bernal and Wesley Hughes, 'The IMF and the Third World: The Case of Jamaica, 1974–80', in *Development Dialogue*, 1980: 2, Dag Hammarskjold Foundation, Uppsala, Sweden, pp. 113–15.

24. Quoted in *ibid.*, p. 126.

25. *Ibid.*, p. 127.

26. *Financial Times*, 'Jamaican cloud's silver lining eludes businessmen', August 9 1982. See also *The Poverty Brokers, op. cit.*, pp. 85–108.

27. Published in *Development Dialogue, op. cit.*, pp. 7–8 and see also Chapter 9.

28. *Business Standard*, 20 August 1982.

29. *The IMF loan: Facts and Issues*, Government of West Bengal, November 1981.

30. Stephany Griffiths-Jones, 'The evolution of external finance, economic policy and development in Chile, 1973–78', Institute of Development Studies Discussion Paper, University of Sussex, 1981. See also Stephany Griffiths-Jones, *International Finance and Latin America*, Croom Helm, 1984.

31. *Ibid.*

32. *Ibid.*, p. 18.
33. Interview in *Chile America*, 1975, quoted in Griffiths-Jones, 1981, *op. cit.*, p. 31.
34. See Andre Gunder Frank, *Economic Genocide in Chile: Monetarist Theory versus Humanity*, Spokesman Books 1976.
35. Griffiths-Jones, 1981, *op. cit.*, p. 34.
36. Quoted in Griffiths-Jones, 1981, *op. cit.*, pp. 37–8. See also I. Letelier and M. Moffitt, *Human Rights: Economic Aid and Private Banks*, Transnational Institute, Washington DC, 1978.
37. *Financial Times*, 25 November 1983.
38. 'Chile's reserves outflow could imperil its solvency', *Financial Times*, 4 March 1983.
39. See case study on Yugoslavia in Cheryl Payer, *The Debt Trap, the IMF and the Third World*, Penguin 1974.
40. Michael J. Harrington, 'The IMF: an International Methodone Fund?' speech to the House of Representatives, quoted in Howard M. Wachtel, *A Decade of International Debt*, Department of Economics, American University, Washington DC, 1980.
41. Anthony Harris, 'The end of the world – perhaps', *Financial Times*, 2 September 1982.
42. *Financial Times* leader, 24 August 1982.
43. *Common Crisis, op. cit.*, p. 62.
44. Killick, 1984, *op. cit.*, p. 39.
45. *Common Crisis, op. cit.*, p. 62.
46. Stephany Griffiths-Jones, 'International Monetary and Financial Issues for Developing Countries after UNCTAD V', *Bulletin*, 1980, Vol. II, No.1, Institute of Development Studies, Sussex, p. 12.
47. Quoted in Killick, 1984, *op. cit.*, p. 208.
48. *IMF Survey*, 19 March 1979.
49. Killick, 1984, *op. cit.*, p. 82.
50. *Ibid.*, p. 210.
51. *Ibid.*, p. 211.
52. 'The role of the Fund in recycling', reproduced in *Finance and Development*, March 1981, p. 12.
53. *Financial Times*, 'Why $65 billion looks a small sum', 4 October 1982.
54. See for example, Barbara Stallings, *Peru and the US banks: privatisation of financial relations*, Wilson Center Working Paper no. 16, Washington DC, n.d.
56. *Financial Times*, 10 August 1983.

55. *Financial Times*, 10 August 1983.
56. *Financial Times*, 31 October 1983.
57. De Larosière, press conference, Washington Sheraton Hotel, September 1983.
58. Anatole Kaletsky, 'Brazil and the IMF: a battle of wills and wits', *Financial Times*, 26 October 1983.
59. *Financial Times, ibid.*
60. *Financial Times*, 10 May 1984.
61. *Ibid.*
62. *Ibid.*
63. *Financial Times*, May 22 1984.

PART II – The World Bank

4. The nature of the beast

1. *World Bank Annual Report 1982,* Washington DC, IBRD Appendix A, p. 147.
2. *Ibid.,* IBRD/IDA Appendix 2, p. 186.
3. *Ibid.*, p. 10.
4. A.W. Clausen, Address to the Board of Governors of the World Bank and the International Finance Corporation, Washington DC, 27 September 1983.
5. *World Bank Annual Report 1983*, p. 12.
6. *World Bank Annual Report 1982*, p. 12.
7. Quoted in Edward S. Mason and Robert E. Asher, *The World Bank since Bretton Woods*, Washington DC: The Brookings Institution, 1973, p. 386. This massive book is a semi-official history of the Bank; it is nevertheless informative and at times quite critical.
8. *World Bank Annual Report 1982*, IDA Appendix E, pp. 172–4.
9. *Ibid.*, IBRD/IDA Appendix 2, p. 186.
10. *Ibid.*, p. 16.
11. *Ibid.*, p. 10 and *World Bank Annual Report 1983*, p. 12.
12. For a much more detailed description and analysis of the financial aspects of the World Bank, see Cheryl Payer, *The World Bank*, Monthly Review Press 1982.
13. *Financial Times*, 18 January 1984.
14. *World Bank Annual Report 1983*, p. 125.
15. *World Bank Annual Report 1982* and Clausen press conferences at the annual meetings.
16. *Ibid.*, p. 40.
17. *World Bank Annual Report 1983*, p. 13, and *The International Finance Corporation: in Brief.* The IFC publishes its annual report separately.

18. Mason and Asher, *op. cit.*, p. 236.
19. *Ibid.*, pp. 739–741.
20. Written comment to Teresa Hayter, August 1984.
21. See 'Politicisation of Member country activities relating to international financial institutions', Memorandum from Stanley J. Heginbotham to Howard Wolpe, Chairman, Subcommittee on Africa, Committee on Foreign Affairs, House of Representatives, 26 April 1983.
22. Mason and Asher, *op. cit.*, p. 50.
23. *Ibid.*, p. 43; see also Table 4–3, p. 68.
24. *North-South: A Programme for Survival*, London: Pan Books 1980, p. 248.
25. Interview with Teresa Hayter, April 1981.
26. *Ibid.*
27. Fawzy Mansour, *The World Bank: Present Role and Prospects, an Outsider's View* (A draft), United Nations African Institute for Economic Development and Planning, Dhakar, p. 181.
28. See Walden Bello, David Kinley and Elaine Elinson, *The Development Debacle: The World Bank in the Philippines*, Institute for Food and Development Policy, San Francisco, 1982, pp. 10–12.
29. Mason and Asher, *op. cit.*, p. 73.

5. The lender's cartel

1. Eugene H. Rotberg, *The World Bank: A Financial Appraisal*, World Bank, January 1981, p. 12.
2. *Ibid.*, p. 17.
3. *Ibid.*, pp. 33–34.
4. Quoted in Mason and Asher, *The World Bank since Bretton Woods*, The Brookings Institution, Washington 1973, pp. 156–157.
5. See Hayter, *Aid as Imperialism, op. cit.*, p. 31, footnote 7, and Mason and Asher, *op. cit.*, p. 746.
6. 'The World Bank and International Commercial Banks: Partners for Development', Remarks to the International Monetary Conference, Vancouver, 25 May 1982.
7. 'Third World Debt and Global Recovery', the 1983 Jodidi Lecture at the Center for International Affairs, Harvard University, by A.W. Clausen, World Bank, 24 February 1983, p. 20.
8. *Financial Times*, 27 January 1984.
9. 'World Bank warning on debt repayments', *Financial Times*, 19 August 1983.
10. Anne Krueger, Press Conference, 1983 IMF/World Bank meetings.

11. Barend A. de Vries, 'International ramifications of the external debt situation', September 1983, mimeo, pp. 4–5.
12. Press Conference at the 1983 World Bank/IMF annual meetings.
13. *Co-financing,* World Bank, 1983 p. 1.
14. *Co-financing*, World Bank staff report to the Development Committee, 28 March 1980, mimeo.
15. *Co-financing*, World Bank, 1983, Annex 2, Table 2, pp. 20–21.
16. Anatole Kaletsky, 'Clausenomics: how the World Bank is changing', *Financial Times*, 30 March 1982.
17. *Ibid*.
18. *Co-financing*, World Bank staff report 1980, *op. cit*.
19. *Ibid*., p. 8.
20. *Ibid*., p. 11.
21. *Co-financing*, World Bank 1983, *op. cit*., Annex 2, Table 2, p. 20.
22. *Co-financing*, World Bank staff report 1980, *op. cit*., p. 7.
23. Rotberg, *op. cit*., pp. 10–11.
24. *Co-financing*, World Bank staff report, 1980, *op. cit.*, p. 2.
25. *Business Standard*, 15 September, 1981.
26. *Financial Times*, 11 November, 1983.
27. This might almost be achieved from a single source: see Mason and Asher, *op. cit*., pp. 335ff., 366, 378, 383, 458–459, 465, 703ff., etc.
28. Mansour, *op. cit*., pp. 57–58.
29. Interview with Teresa Hayter, January 1983.
30. *United States Participation in the Multilateral Development Banks in the 1980s*, Department of the Treasury, Washington DC, 1980, pp. 160ff.
31. Interview with Teresa Hayter, January 1983.
32. *Ibid*.
33. See Payer, *The World Bank, op. cit.*, pp. 119ff., and Mason and Asher, *op. cit.*
34. *Peru: Major Developments Policy Issues and Recommendations, a World Bank Country Study*, World Bank, June 1981, p. 20.
35. *Ibid*., p. 47.
36. For a full and interesting account of the Bank's energy lending and its relations with the oil companies, see Payer, *The World Bank, op. cit.*, pp. 185–206.
37. Quoted in *ibid*., p. 202.
38. Interview with Teresa Hayter, January 1983.
39. *Ibid*.

6. The bank and leverage

1. *Some Aspects of the Economic Philosophy of the World Bank*, World Bank, September 1968, p. 7, quoted in Hayter, *op. cit.*, p. 58.

2. See *Effective Aid*, account of conference proceedings, Overseas Development Institute 1966, p. 34, quoted in Hayter, *Aid as Imperialism*, p. 57.
3. Quoted in Hayter, *ibid.*, p. 62. For an account of the evolution of the Bank's activities in this field up to 1967, see *ibid.*, pp. 51–87.
4. Interview with Teresa Hayter, February 1982.
5. Teodoro Valencia, 'World Bank-IMF formula could sink RP economy', *Philippine Daily Express*, March 2 1981, quoted in Bello et al., *op. cit.,* p. 65.
6. Mason and Asher, *op. cit.*, p. 329.
7. Anatole Kaletsky, 'Clausenomics: how the World Bank is changing', *Financial Times*, 30 March 1982.
8. *World Bank 1983 Annual Report*, p. 10.
9. Hayter, *Aid as Imperialism, op. cit.*, Appendix, pp. 193–194.
10. Interview with Teresa Hayter, Islamabad, April 1980.
11. Michael Lipton and Alexander Shakow, 'The World Bank and poverty', *Finance and Development*, June 1982, p. 16.
12. See Hayter, *Aid as Imperialism, op. cit.*, p. 197, footnote 2.
13. See Mason and Asher, *op. cit.*, pp. 280ff.
14. 'The Bank's recent experience with program lending', a Staff Study, Annex C of *Program Lending for Structural Adjustment*, Joint Managerial Committee of the Board of Governors of the Bank and the Fund, April 2 1980, mimeo, p. 3.
15. *Ibid.*, p. 5.
16. 'Structural Adjustment Lending', Memorandum to the Executive Directors, World Bank, 9 May 1980, pp. 4–5.
17. *Ibid.*, Annex A, p. 1.
18. *World Bank Annual Report 1982*, p. 41.
19. Interview with Teresa Hayter, February 1982.
20. United States Participation in the Multilateral Development Banks, *op. cit.*, p. 32.
21. Rehman Sobhan, *The Crisis of External Dependence – the Political Economy of Foreign Aid to Bangladesh*, University Press Limited, Dhaka, 1982, p. 178, and Zed Press, forthcoming.
22. *Peru: Public Investment Program 1981–85, Consultative Group Presentation*, 27 April 1981, World Bank.
23. See also Just Faaland, *Aid and Influence: the Case of Bangladesh*, Macmillan, 1981.
24. *Development in a Rural Economy* (Green cover), World Bank, 1974.
25. Walden Bello et al., *op. cit.*, p. 14–15.
26. Quoted in Bello et al., *op. cit.*, p. 24.
27. For other specific examples of the Bank's use of 'leverage', see Mason and Asher, *op. cit.*, especially Chapter 13.
28. Interview in Washington with Teresa Hayter, September 1983.

7. The bank and ideology

1. *Development Co-operation*, The Labour Party 1982, p. 28.
2. *Ibid.*, pp. 31–32.
3. Quoted in Hayter, *Aid as Imperialism, op. cit.*, p. 198.
4. US Treasury report on multilateral development banks, *op. cit.*, p. 162.
5. Mason and Asher, *op. cit.*, Chapter 16, 'The World Bank and the International Monetary Fund', p. 550. On their co-operation in Latin America in the 1960s, see also Hayter, *Aid as Imperialism, op. cit.*
6. Memorandum to the Executive Directors, 'Lending for "Structural Adjustment"', p. 4, Annex A to *Program Lending for Structural Adjustment*, Joint Ministerial Committee of the Boards of Governors of the Bank and the Fund, 2 April 1980.
7. Mason and Asher, *op. cit.*, p. 555.
8. Interview with Teresa Hayter, September 1983.
9. Quoted in Mason and Asher, *op. cit.*, p. 550.
10. Mason and Asher, *op. cit.*, p. 557.
11. See also Mason and Asher, *op. cit.*, p. 552.
12. Interviews with Teresa Hayter in Washington, September 1983.
13. Interviewed by Teresa Hayter, May 1981.
14. Killick, 1984, *op. cit.*, p. 211.
15. Interviews with Teresa Hayter, May 1981 and September 1983.
16. 'The Bank's Recent Experience with Program Lending', Annex C *op. cit.*
17. Interviews with Teresa Hayter, May 1981 and September 1983.
18. *Ibid.*
19. *Ibid.*
20. *Ibid.*
21. Quoted in Stephany Griffiths-Jones, 'The evolution of external finance, economic policy and development in Chile, 1973–78', *op. cit.* (see ch. 3, note 30).
22. Isabel Letelier and Michael Moffitt, *Human Rights, Economic Aid and Private Banks: the Case of Chile*, Institute for Policy Studies, Washington DC, 1978.
23. Interview with Teresa Hayter, May 1981.
24. *Ibid.*
25. *Chile: An Economy in Transition*, World Bank, January 1980, pp. iv–vi.
26. Interview with Teresa Hayter, September 1983.
27. *Ibid.*
28. Quentin Peel, 'Shagari's four lean years', *Financial Times*, 22 November 1983.

29. Interview with Teresa Hayter, September 1983. For another example of figure-swapping on devaluation, see Hayter, *Aid as Imperialism, op. cit.*, Colombia case-study, pp. 107–119.
30. Quentin Peel, 'Debt and democracy', *Financial Times*, 16 August 1983.
31. *Financial Times, ibid.*
32. Interview with Teresa Hayter, September 1983.
33. Robin Broad, doctoral thesis. See also Bello et al, *op. cit.*
34. Anatole Kaletsky, 'Top two lending agencies manoeuvre closer together', *Financial Times*, 4 May 1982, supplement on world banking.
35. Interview with Teresa Hayter, February 1982.
36. In an interview with Teresa Hayter, January 1983.
37. For a full account, see Mason and Asher, *op. cit.*, p. 285, and Chapter 13.
38. *Peru: Development and Policy Issues of the Manufacturing Sector*, World Bank/United Nations Industrial Development Organisation, January 1981.
39. Interviews with Teresa Hayter, February 1982.
40. Comment by a Bank official to Teresa Hayter, September 1983.
41. Mason and Asher, *op. cit.*, p. 668.
42. The World Bank, *World Development Report 1983*, Box 7.4, p. 69.
43. Mason and Asher, *op. cit.*, p. 245.
44. See Mason and Asher *op. cit.*, p. 245, footnote 23.
45. *Ibid.*, p. 246.
46. *Ibid.*, pp. 276–277.
47. Interview with Colombian official by Teresa Hayter, 1982.
48. Interview in New Delhi by Teresa Hayter, January 1983.
49. Interview with Teresa Hayter, May 1981.
50. Bela Balassa, 'The "New Protectionism" and the international economy', World Bank Reprint Series: Number Seventy, reprinted from *Journal of World Trade Law*, Vol. 12, No. 5 (1978).
51. 'Trade and protectionism', Background Paper, World Bank, September 29 1983. See also the World Bank's *1981 World Development Report* and *1983 World Development Report*, Chapter 6.
52. Interview with Teresa Hayter, February 1982.
53. 'China textile sales talks deadlocked in Brussels', *Financial Times*, 29 November 1983.
54. Interview with Javier Iguiñez by Teresa Hayter, February 1982.
55. *Peru: Development and Policy Issues of the Manufacturing Sector, op. cit.*, pp. 71 and 85–86.
56. Interview with Teresa Hayter, February 1982.
57. World Bank, 'Political and administrative bases for economic policy in the Philippines', Memo from William Asher, Washington

DC, November 6 1980, p. 3, quoted in *Development Debacle, op. cit.*, p. 137.

58. Quoted in *Development Debacle, op. cit.*, p. 137.

59. See, for example, Hayter, *Aid as Imperialism, op. cit.*, p. 160, fn. 8.

60. World Bank, 'Report and Recommendations of the President of the IBRD to the Executive Directors on a Proposed Structural Adjustment Loan to the Republic of the Philippines', Report No. P-2872-PH, Washington DC, August 21 1980, p. 31, quoted in *Development Debacle, op. cit.*, p. 170.

61. World Bank, 'Random thoughts on rural development', Memo from David Steel to Michael Gould, Washington DC, September 1 1977, quoted in *Development Debacle*, op. cit., p. 148.

62. Brandt Commission, *North-South, op. cit.*, p. 67.

63. *Report on the World Bank Research Program*, grey cover, March 1983, p. 14.

64. *Ibid.*

65. See Lappe et al., Table 1, p. 73.

66. Paper presented to a Seminar at Cornell University, April 1984.

67. *World Bank Development Report 1983*, pp. 62–63.

68. Interview with Teresa Hayter in Washington, September 1983.

69. *Report on the World Bank Research Program, op. cit.*, p. 10.

70. Interview with Teresa Hayter in Washington, September 1983.

71. *Financial Times*, 10 January 1984.

72. Mason and Asher, *op. cit.*, p. 699.

73. *World Development Report, op. cit.*, p. 41.

74. *Ibid.*, pp. 43–44.

75. The quotations are from Chapter 5 of the *1983 World Development Report*, pp. 50–53.

76. *Ibid.*, p. 56.

77. *Ibid.*, p. 74.

78. *Ibid.*, p. 90.

79. Interview with Teresa Hayter in Washington, May 1981.

80. *Peru: Long-term Development Issues*, World Bank, April 1979.

81. Mason and Asher, *op. cit.*, p. 296.

82. *1983 World Development Report, op. cit.*, p. 296.

83. United States Participation in the Multilateral Development Banks, *op. cit.*, p. 44.

84. See also Gavin Williams, 'The World Bank and the Peasant Problem' in Judith Heyer, Pepe Roberts and Gavin Williams (eds), *Rural Development in Tropical Africa*, Macmillan 1981.

85. 'Report to the committee on appropriations, US House of Representatives', quoted in Mansour, *op. cit.*, p. 137.

86. John Elliott, 'World Bank tells India to improve efficiency', *Financial Times*, 10 May 1984.

87. Interview with Teresa Hayter, October 1981.
88. Interview with Teresa Hayter in New Delhi, January 1983.
89. Escott Reid, *Strengthening the World Bank*, Adlai Stevenson Institute of International Affairs, Chicago 1973, p. 195, quoted in Mansour, *op. cit.*, p. 189.
90. Mason and Asher, *op. cit.*, pp. 478–9.

8. The Bank and agriculture

1. Gavin Williams, 'The World Bank and the peasant problem', in Heyer, Roberts and Williams (eds), *Rural Development in Tropical Africa*, Macmillan 1981, p. 44. See also Cheryl Payer, *op. cit.*, Chapter 8; Ernest Feder, 'The new World Bank programme for the self-liquidation of the Third World peasantry', *Journal of Peasant Studies*, 3, 3, 1976.
2. Cheryl Payer, *op. cit.*, p. 236. See also Gavin Williams, *op. cit.*, pp. 22ff. (See note 84, p. 468 & above).
3. There is a massive literature on this subject. See, in particular, Frances Moore Lappe and Joseph Collins, *Food First*, Boston: Houghton Mifflin Company, 1977.
4. See Paul Clough and Gavin Williams, 'Decoding Berg: the World Bank in rural Northern Nigeria', in M. Watts (ed), *The State, Oil and Agriculture in Nigeria*, Berkeley: Institute of International Studies, forthcoming. See also Williams, 'The World Bank and the peasant problem', *op. cit.*, pp. 23–4. For the Bank's account of its 'trickle down' theory, see *Accelerated Development in Sub-Saharan Africa*, World Bank 1981.
5. *Peru: Public Investment Program 1981–85, Consultative Group Presentation*, World Bank, 27 April 1981, p. 6.
6. *Peru: Major Development Policy Issues and Recommendations*, World Bank, June 1981, p. 50.
7. *An Economic Review of the Agricultural Sector of Peru*, World Bank, 1980.
8. *Ibid.*
9. Personal communication to Teresa Hayter, 1979.
10. Quoted in T. de Wit, 'Notes on levels of fertiliser subsidies', Guided Change Team, Ahmado Bello, mimeo.
11. World Bank, *Land Reform Sector Policy Paper*, 1975, p. 41.
12. *Ibid.*, p. 41.
13. *Ibid.*, p. 11.
14. *Ibid.*, p. 46.
15. *Ibid.*, p. 14.
16. *Ibid.*, p. 14.

17. See Cheryl Payer, *op. cit*., pp. 238–9. See also Mason and Asher, *op. cit*., pp. 713–14.

18. World Bank, *IDA in Retrospect*, 1982, pp. 44 & 46.

19. World Bank, *Fifth Annual Review of Project Performance Audit Results*, Operations Evaluation Department, 27 August 1979, Table 2, p. 27.

20. World Bank, *Accelerated Development in Sub-Saharan Africa: An Agenda for Action*, 1981.

21. Interview with Teresa Hayter, May 1981.

22. Payer, *op. cit.*, pp. 217ff. See also Ernest Feder, *op. cit.*, and Gavin Williams, 'The World Bank and the peasant problem', *op. cit.*, pp. 33ff.

23. See Clough and Williams, *op. cit.*, forthcoming.

24. World Bank, *Accelerated Development, op. cit.*, p. 12.

25. *Ibid.*, p. 35.

26. IBRD, *The Basis of a Development Program for Colombia. Report of a Mission*, Baltimore: Johns Hopkins Press 1950, p. 63.

27. Operations Evaluations Department (OED) of the World Bank (WB), *Project Performance Audit Report (PPAR): Guatemala – Livestock Development Project (Loan 722–GU)*. Washington DC: 1980, p. 3.

28. OED of the WB, *Operations Evaluation Report: Agricultural Credit Programs Vol. II. Analytical Report*, Washington DC: 1976, pp. 97–98.

29. OED of the WB, 1975. *PPAR: Ecuador First and Second Livestock Development Projects (Loan 501–EC and Credit 173–EC)*, Washington DC: 1975, p. 9.

30. OED of the WB, *PPAR: Dominican Republic – Livestock Development Project (Credit 245–DO)*, Washington DC: 1978.

31. OED of the WB, *PPAR: Honduras – First Livestock Development Project (Credit 179–HO)*, Washington DC: 1978, p. 5.

32. OED of the WB, *PPAR: Colombia – Second Livestock Development Project (Loan 651–CO)*, Washington DC: 1976, p. 4.

33. *Honduras PPAR, op. cit.*, p. 4.

34. OED of the WB, *PPAR: Paraguay – Third Livestock Credit Project. (Credit 156–PA/Loan 620–PA)*, Washington DC: 1978, p. 11.

35. OED of the WB, *PPAR: Bolivia – Livestock Projects. (Credits 107–BO and 171–BO)*, Washington DC: 1974, p. ii.

36. *PPAR Dominican Republic, op. cit.*

37. *PPAR Ecuador, op. cit.*, p. 6.

38. *PPAR Paraguay, op. cit.*, 'Highlights' page.

39. *PPAR Dominican Republic, op. cit.*, p. 5.

40. OED of the WB, *Bank Operations in Colombia – An Evaluation*, Washington DC: 1972, p. 134.

41. *PPAR Honduras, op. cit.*, p. 6.
42. *Bank Operations in Colombia, op. cit.*
43. *Ibid.*, p. 134.
44. OED of the WB, *PPAR: Brazil – First and Interim Second Livestock Development Projects (Loans 516–BR and 868–BR)*, Washington DC: 1979, p. 8.
45. *PPAR Dominican Republic, op. cit.*, p. 6.
46. *PPAR Honduras, op. cit.*, p. 6.
47. OED of the WB, *Operations Evaluation Report: Agricultural Credit Programs*, Washington DC: 1976, p. 102.
48. *PPAR Guatemala, op. cit.*, p. 9.
49. *Operations Evaluation Report: Agricultural Credit Projects, op. cit.*, pp. 101–102.
50. *PPAR Guatemala, op. cit.*, p. 2.
51. *PPAR Dominican Republic, op. cit.*, p. 5.
52. *Ibid.*, pp. 5 & 7.
53. *PPAR Colombia, op. cit.*, p. 3.
54. *PPAR Honduras, op. cit.*, pp. 8–9.
55. *Agricultural Credit Programs*. p. 98.
56. *Agricultural Credit Programs*. p. 98.
57. *Bank Operations in Colombia*. p. 135.
58. *PPAR Colombia, op. cit.*, pp. 5–6.
59. *PPAR Ecuador, op. cit.*, pp. 10–11.
60. *PPAR Honduras, op. cit.*, pp. 8–9.
61. *Agricultural Credit Programs* pp. 66–67.
62. *PPAR Honduras, op. cit.*, p. 10.
63. *Ibid.*, p. 9.
64. *Ibid.*, p. 9.
65. *Bank Operations in Colombia, op. cit.*, p. 31.
66. *PPAR Dominican Republic, op. cit.*, p. 22.
67. *PPAR Ecuador, op. cit.*, p. 11.
68. D. Shane, 1980, *Hoofprints on the Forest: An Inquiry into the Beef Cattle Industry in the Tropical Forest Areas of Latin America.* Office of Environmental Affairs, US Department of State, Washington DC, p. 90.
69. IBRD. 1972. *Appraisal of Interim Second Livestock Development Project, Brazil.* p. 2.
70. *PPAR Ecuador, op. cit.*, p. 26.
71. World Bank, *Land Reform Sector Policy Paper,* Washington DC: 1976, p. 46.
72. Keith Griffin, *Land Concentration and Rural Poverty*, 2nd Edn. London: Macmillan Press, 1981, p. 226.
73. Ernest Feder, *The Rape of the Peasantry*, Garden City, New York: Doubleday, 1971, p. 244.

74. World Bank, *Economic Position and Prospects of Colombia. Vol. II.* Washington DC: 1981, p. 149.

75. Feder, *op. cit.*, p. 185.

76. Feder, *op. cit.*, p. 188.

77. Solon Barraclough, 'Agrarian Reform in Latin America: Actual Situation and Problems' in *Land Reform, Land Settlement and Co-operatives No. 2: 1–21.* Rome: FAO, 1969.

78. Feder, *op. cit.*, p. 208.

79. Feder, *op. cit.*, p. 244.

80. Feder, *op. cit.*, p. 248.

81. World Bank, *Development Problems and Prospects of Ecuador: Special Report Vol. 1.* Washington DC: 1979, pp. 46–47.

82. From summarised version of The Sixth Report on Progress in Land Reform as submitted to 58th Session of the Economic and Social Council of the UN, in *Land Reform, Land Settlement and Co-operatives. No. 1/2.* Rome: FAO p. 13.

83. Feder, *op. cit.*, pp. 289–290.

84. World Bank, *Land Reform Sector Policy Paper*, Washington DC: 1975, p. 44.

85. IBRD, *Bank Operations in Colombia: An Evaluation*, Washington DC: 1972, p. 128.

86. Griffin, *op. cit.*, p. 134.

87. World Bank, *Economic Position and Prospects of Colombia. Vol. 1*, Washington DC: 1981, p. 9.

88. IBRD 1950, *op. cit.*, p. 384.

89. *Ibid.*, p. 14.

90. E.A. Duff, 1968, *Agrarian Reform in Colombia*, New York: Frederick A. Praeger, 1968, p. 57.

91. IBRD 1972, *op. cit.*, p. 131.

92. *Ibid.*, p. 131.

93. *Ibid.*, p. 146.

94. World Bank 1981, *op. cit.*, p. 47.

95. Operations Evaluation Department (OED) of The World Bank, *Colombia – Caqueta Land Colonization Project (Loan 739–CO)*, Washington DC: 1978, p. A5.

96. *Ibid.*, p. A5.

97. *Ibid.*, p. 16.

98. *Ibid.*, p. 9.

99. *Ibid.*, p. A8.

100. *Ibid.*, p. 10.

101. *Ibid.*, p. 9.

102. *Ibid.*, 'Highlights' page.

103. *Ibid.*, p. 20.

104. *Ibid.*, p. 20.

105. *Ibid.*, pp. 20–21.
106. *Ibid.*, p. A14.
107. *World Bank Supervision Summary of Caqueta Projects*, September 27, 1978.
108. Sutli Ortiz, *Land Settlement Project – El Retorno – Socio-Economic Factors. Working Paper*, Washington DC: World Bank 1979, p. 11.
109. Sutli Ortiz, *op. cit.*, p. 11.
110. Office Memorandum November 12 1979, pp. 1–2.
111. *Ibid.*, p. 5.

9. Rhetoric and reality

1. Quoted in Max Holland and Kai Bird, forthcoming life of McCloy, to be published by Simon and Schuster.
2. *Accelerated Development in Sub-Saharan Africa*, World Bank 1981, p. v.
3. Quoted in Mason and Asher, *op. cit.*, p. 367.
4. The *Boston Globe*, April 21 1981.
5. *United States participation in the Multilateral Development Banks in the 1980s*, Department of the Treasury, Washington DC 1982, pp. 155–156.
6. *Wall Street Journal*, 2 March 1981.
7. Anatole Kaletsky, 'Clausenomics: how the World Bank is changing', *Financial Times*, March 30 1982.
8. *The Seventh Replenishment of IDA: Background Note*, World Bank Information and Public Affairs Department, August 1983, p. 5.
9. Mason and Asher, *op. cit.*, pp. 586–91.
10. *World Bank Annual Report 1983*, p. 230, and interview with Teresa Hayter, May 1981.
11. Interview with Teresa Hayter, 1981.
12. Frances Moore Lappé, Joseph Collins, David Kinley, *Aid as Obstacle: Twenty Questions about our Foreign Aid and the Hungry*, Institute for Food and Development Policy, San Francisco 1980, p. 31.
13. *Third Annual Report* 1947–1948, p. 14, quoted in Mason and Asher, *op. cit.*, p. 171.
14. Mason and Asher, *op. cit.*, p. 171, fn. 37.
15. See Hayter, *Aid as Imperialism, op. cit.*, especially pp. 96ff.
16. Personal communication to William Pike, March 1984. The following material on Tanzania is mainly written by William Pike. See also Cheryl Payer, 'Tanzania and the World Bank', *Third World Quarterly*, October 1983, Vol. 5 No. 4, and Gavin Williams, 'Taking

the part of peasants', in P.C.W. Gutkind and I. Wallerstein (eds), *The Political Economy of Contemporary Africa*, Beverley Hills and London: Sage, 2nd revised edition, 1984.

17. Personal communication to William Pike by Professor R.H. Green, 6 January 1984.

18. Andrew Coulson, *Tanzania – A Political Economy,* Oxford: Clarendon Press, 1982, p. 26.

19. Zaki Ergas, 'Why did the Ujamaa Policy fail?' *Journal of Modern African Studies* 1980, p. 405.

20. R.H. Green, D.G. Rwegasira, B. Van Arkadie, *Economic Shocks and National Policy Making: Tanzania in the 1970s*, Institute of Social Studies: The Hague Research Report Series No. 8., 1980, p. 40.

21. Cheryl Payer, *Tanzania and the World Bank* Chr. Michelsen Institute paper, December 1982, p. 17.

22. *Ibid.*, p. 798.

23. W. Schneider-Barthold et al., *Farmers' Reactions to the Present Economic Situation with Respect to Production and Marketing.* A Case-study of five villages in the Kilimanjaro Region. German Development Institute, Berlin 1983.

24. Green, interview, *op. cit.*

25. Cheryl Payer, *op. cit.*, p. 807.

26. Interview with Teresa Hayter, May 1981. The material on Algeria is based also on interviews in Algeria with Teresa Hayter in October-November 1981. Quotations are usually translated from French. Most of what follows was published in the *Guardian*, 5 January 1982.

27. The material on Nicaragua is written by Catharine Watson and based, in addition to the written sources referred to, on interviews by her with the World Bank, US Treasury and Nicaraguan officials, mainly in 1983; it has been slightly expanded on the basis of a few interviews with Bank officials and others by Teresa Hayter in 1983–4.

28. World Bank, *Country Program Paper: Nicaragua*, Washington DC, 1982.

29. Department of the Treasury, 1982, *United States Participation in the Multilateral Development Banks in the 1980s*, Washington DC.

30. World Bank 1981, *Nicaragua: The Challenge of Reconstruction*, Washington DC, World Bank, p (iv).

31. Morrell, Jim, and Biddle, William Jesse, *Central America: the Financial War*, Washington DC, 1983. The Center for International Policy, p. 10.

32. World Bank 1982, *Country Program Paper: Nicaragua, op. cit.*, p. 2.

33. *Ibid.*, p. 2.

34. *Ibid.*, p. 5.

35. *Ibid.*, p. 10.
36. *Ibid.*, p. 12.
37. *Ibid.*, p. 13.
38. *Ibid.*, p. 13.
39. *Ibid.*, p. 14.
40. *Ibid.*, p. 14.
41. World Bank, 1983, *Monthly Operations Summary*, Washington DC. Various pages depending on month.
42. *Washington Post*, 1 July 1983, 'US will oppose loans to Nicaragua'.
43. Conversation with Steve Hayes, Office of Multilateral Banks in the US Department of the Treasury, Washington DC, September 9 1983.
44. Interview with Teresa Hayter, September 1983.
45. Joseph Collins, *What Difference Could a Revolution Make: Food and Farming in the New Nicaragua*, San Francisco 1982, Institute for Food and Development Policy, p. 89–92.
46. *Ibid.*, p. 40.
47. Embassy of Grenada, Brussels, 'Proceedings of aid donors' meeting in Brussels at ACP House on 14 and 15 April 1981 – Airport Project, Grenada', speech by Bernard Coard.
48. Interview with Teresa Hayter in London, 1981.
49. Letter from Bernard Coard, a copy of which was given to Teresa Hayter by the Grenada High Commission in London.
50. Interview with Teresa Hayter, September 1983.
51. Interview with Teresa Hayter, September 1983.
52. Pfefferman is one of the Bank officials who refused to be interviewed by Teresa Hayter.
53. Interview with Teresa Hayter, September 1983.
54. Conversation with Teresa Hayter, September 1983.
55. See, for example, Barbara Stallings, *Peru and the US Banks: Privatisation of Financial Relations*, Wilson Working Paper No. 16.
56. Interview with Teresa Hayter, October 1983.
57. Quoted in M.J. Klare, *War without End*, Vintage Books 1972, and Bill Warren, 'Imperialism and Capitalist Industrialisation', *New Left Review, 1981*.
58. Quoted in *Development Debacle, op. cit.*, p. 77.
59. *Ibid.*, p. 77.
60. Interview with Teresa Hayter, November 1983.
61. World Bank, *Pakistan: Country Economic Report* 1979, p. i and p. 6.
62. *World Bank Economic Memorandum on Bolivia*, 1978, p. vi.
63. See Hayter, *Aid as Imperialism, op. cit.*, p. 197.
64. Interview by Teresa Hayter with one of the Brandt Report commissioners, 1982.
65. World Bank/UNIDO, *Peru: Development and Policy Issues of the Manufacturing Sector*, January 1981, draft, mimeo, pp. 78–79.

66. *Ibid.*, pp. 45–46.
67. Interview (not with Richard Webb) by Teresa Hayter, January 1982. See also C.R. Frank and R.C. Webb (eds), *Income Distribution and Growth in the Less-Developed Countries*, Brookings Institution, Washington DC 1977.
68. Interviews with Teresa Hayter in 1981 and 1983.
69. Hollis B. Chenery, Monket S. Ahluwalia, C.L.G. Bell, John H. Duloy and Richard Jolly, *Redistribution with Growth*, Oxford University Press 1974. For a theoretical critique of this work and many further references, see Gavin Williams, *op. cit.*, pp. 38–42.
70. See Payer, *op. cit.*, pp. 128–141.
71. *World Bank Annual Report 1982*, p. 125.
72. See Gavin Williams, 'The World Bank and the Peasant Problem', *op. cit.*, p. 21.
73. President's Address to the Board of Governors, World Bank, September 1975.
74. See *Development Debacle, op. cit.*, Chapter 4, and Payer, *The World Bank, op. cit.*, Chapter 11.
75. Mansour, *op. cit.*, pp. 119–120.

PART III – Conclusions and Proposals

10. Current forms of aid from the West

1. *North-South: A Programme for Survival, op. cit.*, especially pp. 64ff.
2. *Financial Times*, 1 October 1982, reporting on the Bank of England's Quarterly Bulletin, 30 September 1982.
3. *Financial Times* leader, 'Victims of the debt crisis', 24 January 1984.
4. *Financial Times*, 28 May 1984.
5. *Business Standard*, 9 April 1982.
6. Interview with Teresa Hayter, January 1983.

11. Alternatives

1. Bill Warren, *Imperialism: Pioneer of Capitalism*, London: New Left Books, 1980.
2. Arghiri Emmanuel, *Technologie Appropriée ou Technologie Sous-developpée?* Institut de Recherche et d'Information sur les Multinationales, Paris: 1981.
3. Rehman Sobhan, *The Crisis of External Dependence, op. cit.*
4. Conversations with Teresa Hayter, October 1981.
5. Interview with Teresa Hayter, 1967.
6. Interviews with Teresa Hayter, January 1983.
7. For a critique of the economic relations between these countries and

the Third World, see Andre Gunder Frank, *Crisis in the Third World*, Heinemann Education, 1980.

8. *Labour's Programme 1982*, The Labour Party 1982, p. 270ff.
9. *Ibid.*, p. 253.
10. *Ibid.*, pp. 273–74.
11. *Ibid.*, p. 273.
12. *Ibid.*, p. 273.

Appendix

1. R. Goodland, C. Watson, G. Ledec, *Environmental Management in Tropical Agriculture*, Boulder, Colorado: Westview Press, 1984.

Index